Modern Generative AI with ChatGPT and OpenAI Models

Leverage the capabilities of OpenAI's LLM for productivity and innovation with GPT3 and GPT4

Valentina Alto

BIRMINGHAM—MUMBAI

Modern Generative AI with ChatGPT and OpenAI Models

Associate Group Product Manager: Ali Abidi
Associate Publishing Product Manager: Dinesh Choudhary
Senior Editor: Tiksha Lad
Technical Editor: Rahul Limbachiya
Copy Editor: Safis Editing
Associate Project Manager: Hemangi Lotlikar
Proofreader: Safis Editing
Indexer: Pratik Shirodkar
Production Designer: Aparna Bhagat
Marketing Coordinators: Shifa Ansari and Vinishka Kalra

First published: May 2023

Production reference: 1230523

Published by Packt Publishing Ltd.
Livery Place
35 Livery Street
Birmingham
B3 2PB, UK.

ISBN 978-1-80512-333-0

www.packtpub.com

Contributors

About the author

Valentina Alto graduated in 2021 in data science. Since 2020, she has been working at Microsoft as an Azure solution specialist, and since 2022, she has been focusing on data and AI workloads within the manufacturing and pharmaceutical industry. She has been working closely with system integrators on customer projects to deploy cloud architecture with a focus on modern data platforms, data mesh frameworks, IoT and real-time analytics, Azure Machine Learning, Azure Cognitive Services (including Azure OpenAI Service), and Power BI for dashboarding. Since commencing her academic journey, she has been writing tech articles on statistics, machine learning, deep learning, and AI in various publications and has authored a book on the fundamentals of machine learning with Python.

I want to thank my parents, friends, and colleagues who have been close to me and supported me in this amazing journey. Thank you to those at Packt – the editor, the manager, and the whole team – who supported me.

About the reviewer

Supreet Kaur is an accomplished AI product manager at Morgan Stanley, where she serves as the product owner for various AI products and spearheads the development of innovative data-driven solutions. Prior to this, she worked as a technology and data science consultant, delivering impactful data science use cases and launch strategies for pharmaceutical clients.

She is also a prolific writer and speaker on data science and AI topics, having delivered over 50 talks at international and national forums. As a strong advocate for women in technology, Supreet was selected as a Google WomenTech Makers Ambassador and has been recognized as one of the top 25 women in AI in Finance.

Table of Contents

Part 2: ChatGPT in Action

3

Getting Familiar with ChatGPT   47

4

Understanding Prompt Design   59

5

Boosting Day-to-Day Productivity with ChatGPT   79

6

Developing the Future with ChatGPT   105

Part 3: OpenAI for Enterprises

9

Preface

This book begins by introducing the field of generative AI, which focuses on creating new and unique data or content using machine learning algorithms. It covers the basics of Generative AI models and explains how these models are trained to generate new data.

After that, it focuses on concrete use cases of how ChatGPT can boost productivity and enhance creativity. It also dwells on how to get the best out of your ChatGPT interaction by improving your prompt design and leveraging zero-, one-, and few-shot learning capabilities.

The book then continues with a zoom into the previous use cases clustered by domains: marketers, researchers, and developers/data scientists. Each domain will be covered with four concrete use cases that you can easily replicate on your own.

Then, from individual use cases, the book moves toward enterprise-level scenarios that make use of the OpenAI model APIs available on Azure infrastructure. The book will also focus on end-to-end scenarios of an existing customer story, as well as responsible AI implications.

Finally, the book will recap the main elements discussed so far, and reflect on what's coming next in the field of Generative AI.

By the end of this book, you'll have the knowledge to both delve deeper into the Generative AI field and start using ChatGPT and OpenAI's model APIs in your own projects.

Who this book is for

This book is aimed at a broad audience. It is for general users who are interested in boosting their daily productivity with ChatGPT and OpenAI and diving deeper into the technology and model architecture behind ChatGPT. It is also for business users who want to get deeper into real-world applications of ChatGPT and OpenAI models and learn how they can empower their organizations. This book is also for data scientists and developers who want to dive deeper into the ways that ChatGPT and OpenAI models can boost their ML models and code, as well as marketers and researchers who want to dive deeper into the OpenAI and ChatGPT use cases in their domains.

Since the book provides a theoretical overview of the technologies behind the OpenAI models and the main concepts of Generative AI, there are no particular requirements in order to read it. If you are also interested in implementing the practical use cases, the end-to-end solutions and relevant code in Python are provided, as well as the step-by-step implementation.

What this book covers

Chapter 1, Introduction to Generative AI, provides an overview of the field of Generative AI, which focuses on creating new and unique data or content using machine learning algorithms. It covers the basics of Generative AI models and explains how these models are trained to generate new data. The chapter also focuses on the applications of Generative AI to various fields, such as image synthesis, text generation, and music composition, highlighting the potential of Generative AI in revolutionizing various industries.

Chapter 2, OpenAI and ChatGPT – Beyond the Market Hype, gives an overview of OpenAI and its most notable development, ChatGPT, highlighting its history, technology, and capabilities. The chapter also focuses on how ChatGPT can be used in various industries and applications to improve communication and automate processes and, finally, how it can impact the world of technology and beyond.

Chapter 3, Getting Familiar with ChatGPT, guides you through how to set up a ChatGPT account and start using the service. It will also cover how to interact with the web UI, how to organize chats according to topic, and how to structure a conversation.

Chapter 4, Understanding Prompt Design, focuses on the importance of prompt design as a technique to improve a accuracy of the model. Indeed, prompts heavily impact the model's generated output. A well-designed prompt can help guide the model toward generating relevant and accurate outputs, while a poorly designed prompt can be irrelevant or confusing. Finally, it is also important to implement ethical considerations in the prompt to prevent the model from generating harmful content.

Chapter 5, Boosting Day-to-Day Productivity with ChatGPT, goes through the main activities ChatGPT can do for general users on a daily basis, boosting users' productivity. The chapter will focus on concrete examples of writing assistance, decision-making, creative inspiration, and so on, enabling you to try them on your own.

Chapter 6, Developing the Future with ChatGPT, focuses on how developers can make use of ChatGPT. The chapter will focus on the main use cases ChatGPT can address in this domain, including code review and optimization, documentation generation, and code generation. This chapter will provide examples and enable you to try the prompts on your own.

Chapter 7, Mastering Marketing with ChatGPT, focuses on how marketers can make use of ChatGPT. The chapter will focus on the main use cases ChatGPT can address in this domain, including A/B testing, keyword targeting suggestions, and social media sentiment analysis. This chapter will provide examples and enable you to try the prompts on your own.

Chapter 8, Research Reinvented with ChatGPT, focuses on how researchers can make use of ChatGPT. The chapter will focus on the main use cases ChatGPT can address in this domain, including literature reviews, experiment design, and bibliography generation. This chapter will provide examples and enable you to try the prompts on your own.

Chapter 9, OpenAI and ChatGPT for Enterprises – Introducing Azure OpenAI, focuses on the enterprise-level applications of OpenAI models, introducing Azure OpenAI Service. We will have an overview of Azure OpenAI Service's model APIs and how they can be embedded into custom code. We will also focus on model parameters, configuration, and fine-tuning. Finally, we will make some considerations about the topic of responsible AI and how to make sure your AI system complies with ethical standards.

Chapter 10, Trending Use Cases for Enterprises, begins with an overview of the current most trending use cases with Azure OpenAI that enterprises are developing in the market today. We will explore concrete examples of projects, such as an intelligent search engine, AI assistant, and reports generator. Finally, we will focus on an end-to-end production project in a specific industry.

Chapter 11, Epilogue and Final Thoughts, begins with a short recap of the most trending use cases examined in previous chapters. We will then move toward some considerations about the implications of Generative AI on industries and everyday life. We will also learn about ethical considerations and the role of Responsible AI in the project design phase. The chapter will conclude with some final thoughts about what the future of Generative AI will be in terms of new developments, with GPT-4 coming soon.

To get the most out of this book

Here is a list of things you need to have:

Software/hardware covered in the book	System requirements
Python 3.7.1 or higher	Windows, macOS, or Linux
Streamlit	Windows, macOS, or Linux
LangChain	Windows, macOS, or Linux
OpenAI model APIs	OpenAI account
Azure OpenAI Service	An Azure subscription enabled for Azure OpenAI

As always,you can find all the prompts used in the chapters in the GitHub repository of the book: `https://github.com/PacktPublishing/Modern-Generative-AI-with-ChatGPT-and-OpenAI-Models/tree/main/Chapter%204%20-%20Prompt%20design`

If you are using the digital version of this book, we advise you to type the code yourself or access the code from the book's GitHub repository (a link is available in the next section). Doing so will help you avoid any potential errors related to the copying and pasting of code.

Download the example code files

You can download the example code files for this book from GitHub at https://github.com/PacktPublishing/Modern-Generative-AI-with-ChatGPT-and-OpenAI-Models. If there's an update to the code, it will be updated in the GitHub repository.

We also have other code bundles from our rich catalog of books and videos available at https://github.com/PacktPublishing/. Check them out!

Download the color images

We also provide a PDF file that has color images of the screenshots and diagrams used in this book. You can download it here: https://packt.link/YFTZk.

Conventions used

There are a number of text conventions used throughout this book.

Code in text: Indicates code words in text, database table names, folder names, filenames, file extensions, pathnames, dummy URLs, user input, and Twitter handles. Here is an example: "Mount the downloaded WebStorm-10*.dmg disk image file as another disk in your system."

A block of code is set as follows:

```
query = st.text_area("Ask a question about the document")
if query:

    docs = faiss_index.similarity_search(query, k=1)
    button = st.button("Submit")
    if button:
        st.write(get_answer(faiss_index, query))
```

Any command-line input or output is written as follows:

```
pip install --upgrade openai
```

Bold: Indicates a new term, an important word, or words that you see onscreen. For instance, words in menus or dialog boxes appear in **bold**. Here is an example: "You can decide to upload files by selecting **Local file** or **Azure blob or other shared web locations**."

> **Tips or important notes**
> Appear like this.

1

Introduction to Generative AI

Hello! Welcome to *Modern Generative AI with ChatGPT and OpenAI Models*! In this book, we will explore the fascinating world of generative **Artificial Intelligence** (**AI**) and its groundbreaking applications. Generative AI has transformed the way we interact with machines, enabling computers to create, predict, and learn without explicit human instruction. With ChatGPT and OpenAI, we have witnessed unprecedented advances in natural language processing, image and video synthesis, and many other fields. Whether you are a curious beginner or an experienced practitioner, this guide will equip you with the knowledge and skills to navigate the exciting landscape of generative AI. So, let's dive in and start with some definitions of the context we are moving in.

This chapter provides an overview of the field of generative AI, which consists of creating new and unique data or content using **machine learning** (**ML**) algorithms.

It focuses on the applications of generative AI to various fields, such as image synthesis, text generation, and music composition, highlighting the potential of generative AI to revolutionize various industries. This introduction to generative AI will provide context for where this technology lives, as well as the knowledge to collocate it within the wide world of AI, ML, and **Deep Learning** (**DL**). Then, we will dwell on the main areas of applications of generative AI with concrete examples and recent developments so that you can get familiar with the impact it may have on businesses and society in general.

Also, being aware of the research journey toward the current state of the art of generative AI will give you a better understanding of the foundations of recent developments and state-of-the-art models.

All this, we will cover with the following topics:

- Understanding generative AI
- Exploring the domains of generative AI
- The history and current status of research on generative AI

By the end of this chapter, you will be familiar with the exciting world of generative AI, its applications, the research history behind it, and the current developments, which could have – and are currently having – a disruptive impact on businesses.

Introducing generative AI

AI has been making significant strides in recent years, and one of the areas that has seen considerable growth is generative AI. Generative AI is a subfield of AI and DL that focuses on generating new content, such as images, text, music, and video, by using algorithms and models that have been trained on existing data using ML techniques.

In order to better understand the relationship between AI, ML, DL, and generative AI, consider AI as the foundation, while ML, DL, and generative AI represent increasingly specialized and focused areas of study and application:

- AI represents the broad field of creating systems that can perform tasks, showing human intelligence and ability and being able to interact with the ecosystem.

- ML is a branch that focuses on creating algorithms and models that enable those systems to learn and improve themselves with time and training. ML models learn from existing data and automatically update their parameters as they *grow*.

- DL is a sub-branch of ML, in the sense that it encompasses deep ML models. Those deep models are called **neural networks** and are particularly suitable in domains such as **computer vision** or **Natural Language Processing (NLP)**. When we talk about ML and DL models, we typically refer to discriminative models, whose aim is that of making predictions or inferencing patterns on top of data.

- And finally, we get to generative AI, a further sub-branch of DL, which doesn't use deep Neural Networks to cluster, classify, or make predictions on existing data: it uses those powerful Neural Network models to generate brand new content, from images to natural language, from music to video.

The following figure shows how these areas of research are related to each other:

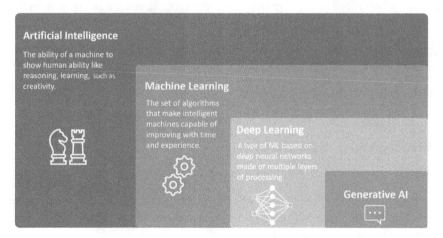

Figure 1.1 – Relationship between AI, ML, DL, and generative AI

Generative AI models can be trained on vast amounts of data and then they can generate new examples from scratch using patterns in that data. This generative process is different from discriminative models, which are trained to predict the class or label of a given example.

Domains of generative AI

In recent years, generative AI has made significant advancements and has expanded its applications to a wide range of domains, such as art, music, fashion, architecture, and many more. In some of them, it is indeed transforming the way we create, design, and understand the world around us. In others, it is improving and making existing processes and operations more efficient.

The fact that generative AI is used in many domains also implies that its models can deal with different kinds of data, from natural language to audio or images. Let us understand how generative AI models address different types of data and domains.

Text generation

One of the greatest applications of generative AI—and the one we are going to cover the most throughout this book—is its capability to produce new content in natural language. Indeed, generative AI algorithms can be used to generate new text, such as articles, poetry, and product descriptions.

For example, a language model such as GPT-3, developed by OpenAI, can be trained on large amounts of text data and then used to generate new, coherent, and grammatically correct text in different languages (both in terms of input and output), as well as extracting relevant features from text such as keywords, topics, or full summaries.

Here is an example of working with GPT-3:

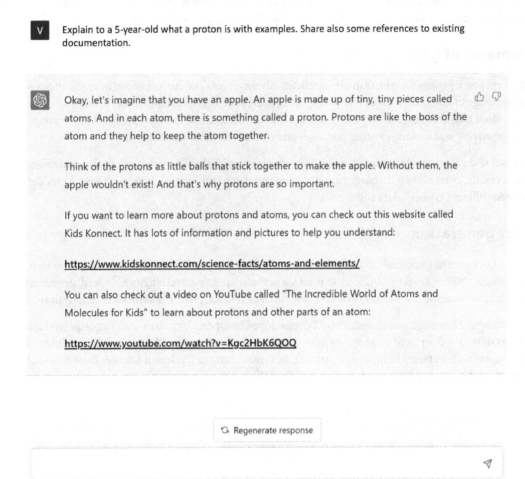

Figure 1.2 – Example of ChatGPT responding to a user prompt, also adding references

Next, we will move on to image generation.

Image generation

One of the earliest and most well-known examples of generative AI in image synthesis is the **Generative Adversarial Network (GAN)** architecture introduced in the 2014 paper by I. Goodfellow et al., *Generative Adversarial Networks*. The purpose of GANs is to generate realistic images that are indistinguishable from real images. This capability had several interesting business applications, such as generating synthetic datasets for training computer vision models, generating realistic product images, and generating realistic images for virtual reality and augmented reality applications.

Here is an example of faces of people who do not exist since they are entirely generated by AI:

Figure 1.3 – Imaginary faces generated by GAN StyleGAN2 at https://this-person-does-not-exist.com/en

Then, in 2021, a new generative AI model was introduced in this field by OpenAI, **DALL-E**. Different from GANs, the DALL-E model is designed to generate images from descriptions in natural language (GANs take a random noise vector as input) and can generate a wide range of images, which may not look realistic but still depict the desired concepts.

DALL-E has great potential in creative industries such as advertising, product design, and fashion, among others, to create unique and creative images.

Here, you can see an example of DALL-E generating four images starting from a request in natural language:

Figure 1.4 – Images generated by DALL-E with a natural language prompt as input

Note that text and image generation can be combined to produce brand new materials. In recent years, widespread new AI tools have used this combination.

An example is Tome AI, a generative storytelling format that, among its capabilities, is also able to create slide shows from scratch, leveraging models such as DALL-E and GPT-3.

Figure 1.5 – A presentation about generative AI entirely generated
by Tome, using an input in natural language

As you can see, the preceding AI tool was perfectly able to create a draft presentation just based on my short input in natural language.

Music generation

The first approaches to generative AI for music generation trace back to the 50s, with research in the field of algorithmic composition, a technique that uses algorithms to generate musical compositions. In fact, in 1957, Lejaren Hiller and Leonard Isaacson created the Illiac Suite for String Quartet (https://www.youtube.com/watch?v=n0njBFLQSk8), the first piece of music entirely composed by AI. Since then, the field of generative AI for music has been the subject of ongoing research for several decades. Among recent years' developments, new architectures and frameworks have become widespread among the general public, such as the WaveNet architecture introduced by Google in 2016, which has been able to generate high-quality audio samples, or the Magenta project, also developed by Google, which uses **Recurrent Neural Networks** (**RNNs**) and other ML techniques to generate music and other forms of art. Then, in 2020, OpenAI also announced Jukebox, a neural network that generates music, with the possibility to customize the output in terms of musical and vocal style, genre, reference artist, and so on.

Those and other frameworks became the foundations of many AI composer assistants for music generation. An example is Flow Machines, developed by Sony CSL Research. This generative AI system was trained on a large database of musical pieces to create new music in a variety of styles. It was used by French composer Benoît Carré to compose an album called *Hello World* (`https://www.helloworldalbum.net/`), which features collaborations with several human musicians.

Here, you can see an example of a track generated entirely by Music Transformer, one of the models within the Magenta project:

Figure 1.6 – Music Transformer allows users to listen to musical performances generated by AI

Another incredible application of generative AI within the music domain is speech synthesis. It is indeed possible to find many AI tools that can create audio based on text inputs in the voices of well-known singers.

For example, if you have always wondered how your songs would sound if Kanye West performed them, well, you can now fulfill your dreams with tools such as FakeYou.com (`https://fakeyou.com/`), Deep Fake Text to Speech, or UberDuck.ai (`https://uberduck.ai/`).

Selected voice

Kanye West (rapping) by zwf
View Details →
Category: Rappers
Voiced by: Ye
Tags: kanye

(fastpitch)

389.2K

64%

🔊 Natural Speech   🎵 Reference Audio

Choose a voice   ⤫

| Rappers ⌄ | Kanye West (rapping) |

Enter text to synthesize   ⤫

hello hello!

Advanced controls ❓

Figure 1.7 – Text-to-speech synthesis with UberDuck.ai

I have to say, the result is really impressive. If you want to have fun, you can also try voices from your all your favorite cartoons as well, such as Winnie The Pooh...

Next, we move to see generative AI for videos.

Video generation

Generative AI for video generation shares a similar timeline of development with image generation. In fact, one of the key developments in the field of video generation has been the development of GANs. Thanks to their accuracy in producing realistic images, researchers have started to apply these techniques to video generation as well. One of the most notable examples of GAN-based video generation is DeepMind's **Motion to Video**, which generated high-quality videos from a single image and a sequence of motions. Another great example is NVIDIA's **Video-to-Video Synthesis (Vid2Vid)** DL-based framework, which uses GANs to synthesize high-quality videos from input videos.

The Vid2Vid system can generate temporally consistent videos, meaning that they maintain smooth and realistic motion over time. The technology can be used to perform a variety of video synthesis tasks, such as the following:

- Converting videos from one domain into another (for example, converting a daytime video into a nighttime video or a sketch into a realistic image)

- Modifying existing videos (for example, changing the style or appearance of objects in a video)

- Creating new videos from static images (for example, animating a sequence of still images)

In September 2022, Meta's researchers announced the general availability of **Make-A-Video** (`https://makeavideo.studio/`), a new AI system that allows users to convert their natural language prompts into video clips. Behind such technology, you can recognize many of the models we mentioned for other domains so far – language understanding for the prompt, image and motion generation with image generation, and background music made by AI composers.

Overall, generative AI has impacted many domains for years, and some AI tools already consistently support artists, organizations, and general users. The future seems very promising; however, before jumping to the ultimate models available on the market today, we first need to have a deeper understanding of the roots of generative AI, its research history, and the recent developments that eventually lead to the current OpenAI models.

The history and current status of research

In previous sections, we had an overview of the most recent and cutting-edge technologies in the field of generative AI, all developed in recent years. However, the research in this field can be traced back decades ago.

We can mark the beginning of research in the field of generative AI in the 1960s, when Joseph Weizenbaum developed the chatbot ELIZA, one of the first examples of an NLP system. It was a simple rules-based interaction system aimed at entertaining users with responses based on text input, and it paved the way for further developments in both NLP and generative AI. However, we know that modern generative AI is a subfield of DL and, although the first **Artificial Neural Networks (ANNs)** were first introduced in the 1940s, researchers faced several challenges, including limited computing power and a lack of understanding of the biological basis of the brain. As a result, ANNs hadn't gained much attention until the 1980s when, in addition to new hardware and neuroscience developments, the advent of the **backpropagation** algorithm facilitated the training phase of ANNs. Indeed, before the advent of backpropagation, training Neural Networks was difficult because it was not possible to efficiently calculate the gradient of the error with respect to the parameters or weights associated with each neuron, while backpropagation made it possible to automate the training process and enabled the application of ANNs.

Then, by the 2000s and 2010s, the advancement in computational capabilities, together with the huge amount of available data for training, yielded the possibility of making DL more practical and available to the general public, with a consequent boost in research.

In 2013, Kingma and Welling introduced a new model architecture in their paper *Auto-Encoding Variational Bayes*, called **Variational Autoencoders (VAEs)**. VAEs are generative models that are based on the concept of variational inference. They provide a way of learning with a compact representation of data by encoding it into a lower-dimensional space called **latent space** (with the *encoder* component) and then decoding it back into the original data space (with the *decoder* component).

The key innovation of VAEs is the introduction of a probabilistic interpretation of the latent space. Instead of learning a deterministic mapping of the input to the latent space, the encoder maps the input to a probability distribution over the latent space. This allows VAEs to generate new samples by sampling from the latent space and decoding the samples into the input space.

For example, let's say we want to train a VAE that can create new pictures of cats and dogs that look like they could be real.

To do this, the VAE first takes in a picture of a cat or a dog and compresses it down into a smaller set of numbers into the latent space, which represent the most important features of the picture. These numbers are called **latent variables**.

Then, the VAE takes these latent variables and uses them to create a new picture that looks like it could be a real cat or dog picture. This new picture may have some differences from the original pictures, but it should still look like it belongs in the same group of pictures.

The VAE gets better at creating realistic pictures over time by comparing its generated pictures to the real pictures and adjusting its latent variables to make the generated pictures look more like the real ones.

VAEs paved the way toward fast development within the field of generative AI. In fact, only 1 year later, GANs were introduced by Ian Goodfellow. Differently from VAEs architecture, whose main elements are the encoder and the decoder, GANs consist of two Neural Networks – a generator and a discriminator – which work against each other in a zero-sum game.

The generator creates fake data (in the case of images, it creates a new image) that is meant to look like real data (for example, an image of a cat). The discriminator takes in both real and fake data, and tries to distinguish between them – it's the *critic* in our art forger example.

During training, the generator tries to create data that can fool the discriminator into thinking it's real, while the discriminator tries to become better at distinguishing between real and fake data. The two parts are trained together in a process called **adversarial training**.

Over time, the generator gets better at creating fake data that looks like real data, while the discriminator gets better at distinguishing between real and fake data. Eventually, the generator becomes so good at creating fake data that even the discriminator can't tell the difference between real and fake data.

Here is an example of human faces entirely generated by a GAN:

Figure 1.8 – Examples of photorealistic GAN-generated faces (taken from Progressive Growing of
GANs for Improved Quality, Stability, and Variation, 2017: https://arxiv.org/pdf/1710.10196.pdf)

Both models – VAEs and GANs – are meant to generate brand new data that is indistinguishable
from original samples, and their architecture has improved since their conception, side by side with
the development of new models such as PixelCNNs, proposed by Van den Oord and his team, and
WaveNet, developed by Google DeepMind, leading to advances in audio and speech generation.

Another great milestone was achieved in 2017 when a new architecture, called *Transformer*, was
introduced by Google researchers in the paper, – *Attention Is All You Need*, was introduced in a paper
by Google researchers. It was revolutionary in the field of language generation since it allowed for
parallel processing while retaining memory about the context of language, outperforming the previous
attempts of language models founded on RNNs or **Long Short-Term Memory** (**LSTM**) frameworks.

Transformers were indeed the foundations for massive language models called **Bidirectional Encoder
Representations from Transformers** (**BERT**), introduced by Google in 2018, and they soon become
the baseline in NLP experiments.

Transformers are also the foundations of all the **Generative Pre-Trained (GPT)** models introduced by OpenAI, including GPT-3, the model behind ChatGPT.

Although there was a significant amount of research and achievements in those years, it was not until the second half of 2022 that the general attention of the public shifted toward the field of generative AI.

Not by chance, 2022 has been dubbed the *year of generative AI*. This was the year when powerful AI models and tools became widespread among the general public: diffusion-based image services (MidJourney, DALL-E 2, and Stable Diffusion), OpenAI's ChatGPT, text-to-video (Make-a-Video and Imagen Video), and text-to-3D (DreamFusion, Magic3D, and Get3D) tools were all made available to individual users, sometimes also for free.

This had a disruptive impact for two main reasons:

- Once generative AI models have been widespread to the public, every individual user or organization had the possibility to experiment with and appreciate its potential, even without being a data scientist or ML engineer.

- The output of those new models and their embedded creativity were objectively stunning and often concerning. An urgent call for adaptation—both for individuals and governments—rose.

Henceforth, in the very near future, we will probably witness a spike in the adoption of AI systems for both individual usage and enterprise-level projects.

Summary

In this chapter, we explored the exciting world of generative AI and its various domains of application, including image generation, text generation, music generation, and video generation. We learned how generative AI models such as ChatGPT and DALL-E, trained by OpenAI, use DL techniques to learn patterns in large datasets and generate new content that is both novel and coherent. We also discussed the history of generative AI, its origins, and the current status of research on it.

The goal of this chapter was to provide a solid foundation in the basics of generative AI and to inspire you to explore this fascinating field further.

In the next chapter, we will focus on one of the most promising technologies available on the market today, ChatGPT: we will go through the research behind it and its development by OpenAI, the architecture of its model, and the main use cases it can address as of today.

References

- https://arxiv.org/abs/1406.2661
- https://www.youtube.com/watch?v=Iy9vRvyRf_E
- https://arxiv.org/abs/1912.04958
- *This person does not exist*: this-person-does-not-exist.com
- https://arxiv.org/abs/1808.06601
- https://www.microsoft.com/en-us/research/blog/a-deep-generative-model-trifecta-three-advances-that-work-towards-harnessing-large-scale-power/
- https://tcwang0509.github.io/vid2vid/

2

OpenAI and ChatGPT – Beyond the Market Hype

This chapter provides an overview of OpenAI and its most notable development—ChatGPT, highlighting its history, technology, and capabilities.

The overall goal is to provide a deeper knowledge of how ChatGPT can be used in various industries and applications to improve communication and automate processes and, finally, how those applications can impact the world of technology and beyond.

We will cover all this with the following topics:

- What is OpenAI?
- Overview of OpenAI model families
- Road to ChatGPT: the math of the model behind it
- ChatGPT: the state of the art

Technical requirements

In order to be able to test the example in this chapter, you will need the following:

- An OpenAI account to access the Playground and the Models API (`https://openai.com/api/login20`)
- Your favorite IDE environment, such as Jupyter or Visual Studio
- Python 3.7.1+ installed (`https://www.python.org/downloads`)
- `pip` installed (`https://pip.pypa.io/en/stable/installation/`)
- OpenAI Python library (`https://pypi.org/project/openai/`)

What is OpenAI?

OpenAI is a research organization founded in 2015 by Elon Musk, Sam Altman, Greg Brockman, Ilya Sutskever, Wojciech Zaremba, and John Schulman. As stated on the OpenAI web page, its mission is *"to ensure that Artificial General Intelligence (AGI) benefits all of humanity"*. As it is *general*, AGI is intended to have the ability to learn and perform a wide range of tasks, without the need for task-specific programming.

Since 2015, OpenAI has focused its research on **Deep Reinforcement Learning (DRL)**, a subset of **machine learning (ML)** that combines **Reinforcement Learning (RL)** with deep neural networks. The first contribution in that field traces back to 2016 when the company released OpenAI Gym, a toolkit for researchers to develop and test **RL** algorithms.

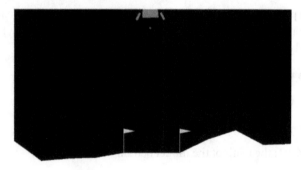

Gym is a standard API for reinforcement learning, and a diverse collection of reference environments

The Gym interface is simple, pythonic, and capable of representing general RL problems:

```python
import gym
env = gym.make("LunarLander-v2", render_mode="human")
observation, info = env.reset(seed=42)
for _ in range(1000):
    action = policy(observation)  # User-defined policy function
    observation, reward, terminated, truncated, info = env.step(action)

    if terminated or truncated:
        observation, info = env.reset()
env.close()
```

Figure 2.1 – Landing page of Gym documentation (https://www.gymlibrary.dev/)

OpenAI kept researching and contributing in that field, yet its most notable achievements are related to generative models—**Generative Pre-trained Transformers (GPT)**.

After introducing the model architecture in their paper *"Improving Language Understanding by Generative Pre-Training"* and baptizing it **GPT-1**, OpenAI researchers soon released, in 2019, its successor, the GPT-2. This version of the GPT was trained on a corpus called **WebText**, which at the time contained slightly over 8 million documents with a total of 40 GB of text from URLs shared in Reddit submissions with at least 3 upvotes. It had 1.2 billion parameters, ten times as many as its predecessor.

Here, you can see the landing page of a UI of GPT-2 published by HuggingFace (`https://transformer.huggingface.co/doc/distil-gpt2`):

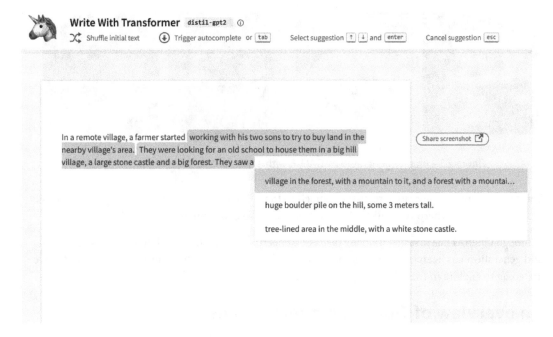

Figure 2.2 – GPT-2 writing a paragraph based on a prompt. Source:
https://transformer.huggingface.co/doc/distil-gpt2

Then, in 2020, OpenAI first announced and then released GPT-3, which, with its 175 billion parameters, dramatically improved benchmark results over GPT-2.

In addition to natural language generative models, OpenAI also developed in the field of image generation, releasing its first model in that field, called **DALL-E**, revealed in 2021. As mentioned in the previous chapter, DALL-E is capable of creating brand new images from a natural language input, which is interpreted by the latest version of GPT-3.

DALL-E saw a recent upgrade to its new version, DALL-E 2, announced in April 2022.

In the following figure, you can see an example of images generated by DALL-E starting with the natural language prompt **generate a realistic picture of a cup of coffee in a cozy environment**:

Figure 2.3 – Images generated by DALL-E with a natural language prompt as input

You can try generating creative pictures yourself in the lab of OpenAI DALL-E (`https://labs.openai.com/`), where you will get limited free credits to experiment.

Although OpenAI has invested in many fields of Generative AI, its contribution to text understanding and generation has been outstanding, thanks to the development of the foundation GPT models we are going to explore in the following paragraphs.

An overview of OpenAI model families

Today, OpenAI offers a set of pre-trained, ready-to-use models that can be consumed by the general public. This has two important implications:

- Powerful foundation models can be consumed without the need for long and expensive training
- It's not necessary to be a data scientist or an ML engineer to manipulate those models

Users can test OpenAI models in OpenAI Playground, a friendly user interface where you can interact with models without the need to write any code.

In the following screenshot, you can see the landing page of the OpenAI Playground:

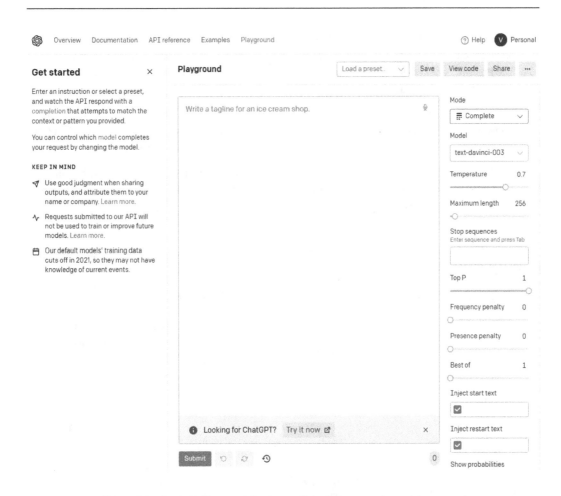

Figure 2.4 – OpenAI Playground at https://platform.openai.com/playground

As you can see from *Figure 2.4*, the Playground offers a UI where the user can start interacting with the model, which you can select on the right-hand side of the UI. To start interacting with the Playground, you can just type any questions or instructions in the input space in natural language. You can also start with some examples available in the OpenAI documentation (`https://platform.openai.com/examples`).

Before diving deeper into model families, let's first define some jargon you will see in this chapter:

- **Tokens**: Tokens can be considered as word fragments or segments that are used by the API to process input prompts. Unlike complete words, tokens may contain trailing spaces or even partial sub-words. To better understand the concept of tokens in terms of length, there are some general guidelines to keep in mind. For instance, one token in English is approximately equivalent to four characters, or three-quarters of a word.

- **Prompt**: In the context of **natural language processing** (**NLP**) and ML, a prompt refers to a piece of text that is given as input to an AI language model to generate a response or output. The prompt can be a question, a statement, or a sentence, and it is used to provide context and direction to the language model.

- **Context**: In the field of GPT, context refers to the words and sentences that come before the user's prompt. This context is used by the language model to generate the most probable next word or phrase, based on the patterns and relationships found in the training data.

- **Model confidence**: Model confidence refers to the level of certainty or probability that an AI model assigns to a particular prediction or output. In the context of NLP, model confidence is often used to indicate how confident the AI model is in the correctness or relevance of its generated response to a given input prompt.

The preceding definitions will be pivotal in understanding how to use Azure OpenAI model families and how to configure their parameters.

In the Playground, there are two main models families that can be tested:

- **GPT-3**: A set of models that can understand and generate natural language. GPT-3 has been trained on a large corpus of text and can perform a wide range of natural language tasks such as language translation, summarization, question-answering, and more. Here is an example:

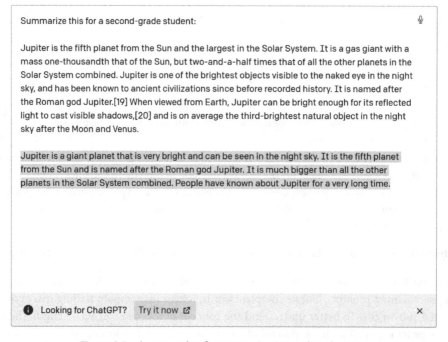

Figure 2.5 – An example of a summarization task with GPT-3

GPT-3.5: This is a newer set of models that build upon GPT-3 and aim to improve its natural language understanding and generation abilities. GPT-3.5 models can perform complex natural language tasks such as composing coherent paragraphs or essays, generating poetry, and even creating computer programs in natural language. GPT-3.5 is the model behind ChatGPT and, on top of its API, it is also consumable within the Playground with a dedicated UI:

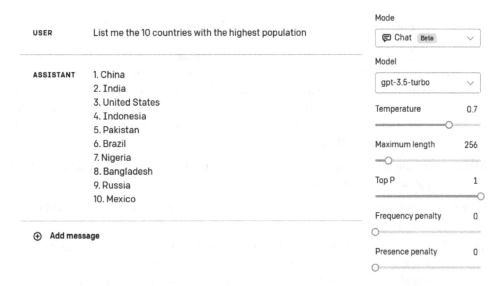

Figure 2.6 – An example of interaction with GPT-3.5

- **Codex**: A set of models that can understand and generate code in various programming languages. Codex can translate natural language prompts into working code, making it a powerful tool for software development. Here is an example using Codex:

```
1   """
2   1. Create a list of first names
3   2. Create a list of last names
4   3. Combine them randomly into a list of 100 full names
5   """
6
7   import random
8
9   first_names = ['John', 'Jane', 'Corey', 'Travis', 'Dave', 'Kurt', 'Neil', 'Sam', 'Steve', 'Tom', 'James', 'Robert', 'Michael', 'Charles', 'Joe', 'Mary', 'Maggie', 'Nicole', 'Patricia', 'Linda', 'Barbara',
    'Elizabeth', 'Laura', 'Jennifer', 'Maria']
10
11  last_names = ['Smith', 'Doe', 'Jenkins', 'Robinson', 'Davis', 'Stuart', 'Jefferson', 'Jacobs', 'Wright', 'Patterson', 'Wilks', 'Arnold', 'Johnson', 'Williams', 'Jones', 'Brown', 'Davis', 'Miller',
    'Wilson', 'Moore', 'Taylor', 'Anderson', 'Thomas', 'Jackson', 'White', 'Harris', 'Martin']
12
13  full_names = []
14
15  for i in range(100):
16      first = random.choice(first_names)
17      last = random.choice(last_names)
18      full_names.append(f"{first} {last}")
19
20  print(full_names)
```

Figure 2.7 – An example of code generation with Codex

> **Note**
>
> In March 2023, OpenAI announced that Codex models will be deprecated from that date on. This is because of the incredible capabilities of the new chat models (including GPT-3.5-turbo, the model behind ChatGPT) that encompass coding tasks as well, with results that benchmark or even surpass Codex models' ones.

For each model, you can also play with some parameters that you can configure. Here is a list:

- **Temperature** (ranging from 0 to 1): This controls the randomness of the model's response. A low-level temperature makes your model more deterministic, meaning that it will tend to give the same output to the same question. For example, if I ask my model multiple times, "*What is OpenAI?*" with temperature set to 0, it will always give the same answer. On the other hand, if I do the same with a model with temperature set to 1, it will try to modify its answers each time in terms of wording and style.

- **Max length** (ranging from 0 to 2048): This controls the length (in terms of tokens) of the model's response to the user's prompt.

- **Stop sequences** (user input): This makes responses end at the desired point, such as the end of a sentence or list.

- **Top probabilities** (ranging from 0 to 1): This controls which tokens the model will consider when generating a response. Setting this to 0.9 will consider the top 90% most likely of all possible tokens. One could ask, "*Why not set top probabilities as 1 so that all the most likely tokens are chosen?*" The answer is that users might still want to maintain variety when the model has low confidence, even in the highest-scoring tokens.

- **Frequency penalty** (ranging from 0 to 1): This controls the repetition of the same tokens in the generated response. The higher the penalty, the lower the probability of seeing the same tokens more than once in the same response. The penalty reduces the chance proportionally, based on how often a token has appeared in the text so far (this is the key difference from the following parameter).

- **Presence penalty** (ranging from 0 to 2): This is similar to the previous one but stricter. It reduces the chance of repeating any token that has appeared in the text at all so far. As it is stricter than the frequency penalty, the presence penalty also increases the likelihood of introducing new topics in a response.

- **Best of** (ranging from 0 to 20): This generates multiple responses and displays only the one with the best total probability across all its tokens.

- **Pre- and post-response text** (user input): This inserts text before and after the model's response. This can help prepare the model for a response.

Besides trying OpenAI models in the Playground, you can always call the models API in your custom code and embed models into your applications. Indeed, in the right corner of the Playground, you can click on **View code** and export the configuration as shown here:

Figure 2.8 – Python code for calling a GPT3 model with a natural language prompt

As you can see from the preceding screenshot, the code exports the parameter configuration you set in the Playground.

Now you can start using the OpenAI library in Python by installing it via `pip install openai` in your terminal. In order to use the models, you will need to generate an API key. You can find your API keys (`https://platform.openai.com/account/api-keys`) in your account settings, as shown here:

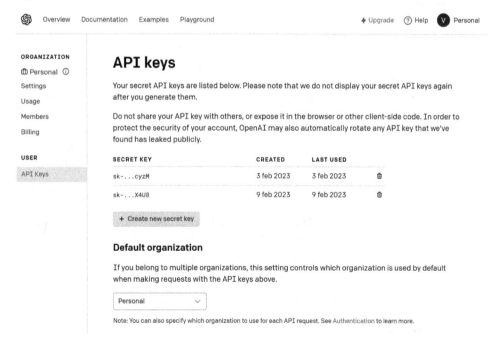

Figure 2.9 – API keys in the account settings page of your OpenAI profile

With OpenAI APIs, you can also try the following additional model families that are not available in the Playground:

- **Moderation**: This is a fine-tuned model developed by OpenAI that can detect potentially sensitive or unsafe text content. Moderation uses ML algorithms to classify text as safe or unsafe based on its context and language use. This model can be used to automate content moderation on social media platforms, online communities, and in many other domains. There are multiple categories, such as hate, hate/threatening, self-harm, sexual, sexual/minors, violence, violence/graphic.

  Here is example code for the Moderation API:

  ```
  import os
  import openai
  openai.api_key = os.getenv("OPENAI_API_KEY")
  openai.Moderation.create(
    input="I want to kill him",
  )
  ```

  The output for this is as follows:

  ```
  <OpenAIObject id=modr-6sHusuY9frxJdfqTBXHsOAfWhckrh at
  0x218bd8482c0> JSON: {
    "id": "modr-6sHusuY9frxJdfqTBXHsOAfWhckrh",
    "model": "text-moderation-004",
    "results": [
      {
        "categories": {
          "hate": false,
          "hate/threatening": false,
          "self-harm": false,
          "sexual": false,
          "sexual/minors": false,
          "violence": true,
          "violence/graphic": false
        },
        "category_scores": {
          "hate": 1.7164344171760604e-05,
          "hate/threatening": 2.614225103059198e-08,
          "self-harm": 2.5988580176772302e-08,
          "sexual": 2.8184256279928377e-06,
          "sexual/minors": 9.1383149936064e-09,
          "violence": 0.9910049438476562,
          "violence/graphic": 5.316753117767803e-07
        },
        "flagged": true
  ```

```
        }
    ]
}
```

In this case, the Moderator API detected evidence of violent content.

- **Embeddings**: Some models can use embeddings. These embeddings involve representing words or sentences in a multi-dimensional space. The mathematical distances between different instances in this space represent their similarity in terms of meaning. As an example, imagine the words queen, woman, king, and man. Ideally, in our multidimensional space, where words are vectors, if the representation is correct, we want to achieve the following:

$$\overrightarrow{king} + (\overrightarrow{woman} - \overrightarrow{man}) \approx \overrightarrow{queen}$$

Figure 2.10 – Example of vectorial equations among words

This means that the distance between *woman* and *man* should be equal to the distance between *queen* and *king*. Here is an example of an embedding:

```
import openai
embedding = openai.Embedding.create(
    input="The cat is on the table",
    model="text-embedding-ada-002")["data"][0]["embedding"]
```

The preceding method creates a vector representation of the input. We can have a look at the first 10 vectors of the output here:

```
embedding[1:10]

[-0.01369840931147337,
 -0.007505378685891628,
 -0.002576263388618827,
 -0.014773285016417503,
 0.019935185089707375,
 -0.01802290789783001,
 -0.01594814844429493,
 -0.0010944041423499584,
 -0.014323337003588676]
```

Embeddings can be extremely useful in intelligent search scenarios. Indeed, by getting the embedding of the user input and the documents the user wants to search, it is possible to compute distance metrics (namely, cosine similarity) between the input and the documents. By doing so, we can retrieve the documents that are *closer*, in mathematical distance terms, to the user input.

- **Whisper**: This is a speech recognition model that can transcribe audio into text. Whisper can recognize and transcribe various languages and dialects with high accuracy, making it a valuable tool for automated speech recognition systems. Here is an example:

```
# Note: you need to be using OpenAI Python   v      0.27.0 for
the code below to work
import openai
openai.api_key = os.getenv("OPENAI_API_KEY")
audio_file= open("/path/to/file/audio.mp3", "rb")
transcript = openai.Audio.transcribe("whisper-1", audio_file)
```

The output looks like the following:

```
{"text": Yes, hi, I just noticed a dent on the side of my car
and I have no idea how it got there. There were no witnesses
around and I'm really frustrated.
....
}
```

All the previous models come as pre-built, in the sense that they have already been pre-trained on a huge knowledge base.

However, there are some ways you can make your model more customized and tailored for your use case.

The first method is embedded in the way the model is designed, and it involves providing your model with the context in the **few-learning approach** (we will focus on this technique later on in the book). Namely, you could ask the model to generate an article whose template and lexicon recall another one you have already written. For this, you can provide the model with your query of generating an article *and* the former article as a reference or context, so that the model is better prepared for your request.

Here is an example of it:

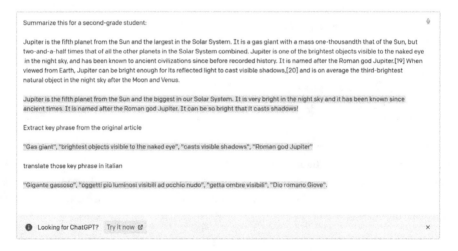

Figure 2.11 – An example of a conversation within the OpenAI
Playground with the few-shot learning approach

The second method is more sophisticated and is called **fine-tuning**. Fine-tuning is the process of adapting a pre-trained model to a new task.

In fine-tuning, the parameters of the pre-trained model are altered, either by adjusting the existing parameters or by adding new parameters, to better fit the data for the new task. This is done by training the model on a smaller labeled dataset that is specific to the new task. The key idea behind fine-tuning is to leverage the knowledge learned from the pre-trained model and fine-tune it to the new task, rather than training a model from scratch. Have a look at the following figure:

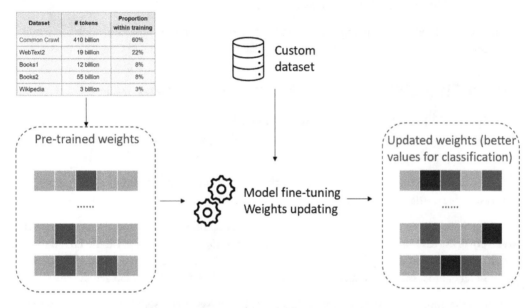

Figure 2.12 – Model fine-tuning

In the preceding figure, you can see a schema on how fine-tuning works on OpenAI pre-built models. The idea is that you have available a pre-trained model with general-purpose weights or parameters. Then, you feed your model with custom data, typically in the form of *key-value* prompts and completions as shown here:

```
{"prompt": "<prompt text>", "completion": "<ideal generated text>"}
{"prompt": "<prompt text>", "completion": "<ideal generated text>"}
{"prompt": "<prompt text>", "completion": "<ideal generated text>"}
...
```

Once the training is done, you will have a customized model that performs particularly well for a given task, for example, the classification of your company's documentation.

The nice thing about fine-tuning is that you can make pre-built models tailored to your use cases, without the need to re-train them from scratch, yet leveraging smaller training datasets and hence less training time and computing. At the same time, the model keeps its generative power and accuracy learned via the original training, the one that occurred on the massive dataset.

In this paragraph, we got an overview of the models offered by OpenAI to the general public, from those you can try directly in the Playground (GPT, Codex) to more complex models such as embeddings. We also learned that, besides using models in their pre-built state, you can also customize them via fine-tuning, providing a set of examples to learn from.

In the following sections, we are going to focus on the background of those amazing models, starting from the math behind them and then getting to the great discoveries that made ChatGPT possible.

Road to ChatGPT: the math of the model behind it

Since its foundation in 2015, OpenAI has invested in the research and development of the class of models called **Generative Pre-trained Transformers** (**GPT**), and they have captured everyone's attention as being the engine behind ChatGPT.

GPT models belong to the architectural framework of transformers introduced in a 2017 paper by Google researchers, *Attention Is All You Need*.

The transformer architecture was introduced to overcome the limitations of traditional **Recurrent Neural Networks** (**RNNs**). RNNs were first introduced in the 1980s by researchers at the Los Alamos National Laboratory, but they did not gain much attention until the 1990s. The original idea behind RNNs was that of processing sequential data or time series data, keeping information across time steps.

Indeed, up to that moment in time, the classic **Artificial Neural Network** (**ANN**) architecture was that of the feedforward ANN, where the output of each hidden layer is the input of the next one, without maintaining information about past layers.

In order to understand the idea behind the transformer, we need to start from its origins. We will hence dwell on the following topics:

- The structure of RNNs
- RNNs' main limitations
- How those limitations have been overcome with the introduction of new architectural elements, including positional encoding, self-attention, and the feedforward layer
- How we got to the state of the art of GPT and ChatGPT

Let's start with the architecture of transformers' predecessors.

The structure of RNNs

Let's imagine we want to predict a house price. If we had only today's price for it, we could use a feedforward architecture where we apply a non-linear transformation to the input via a hidden layer (with an activation function) and get as output the forecast of the price for tomorrow. Here is how:

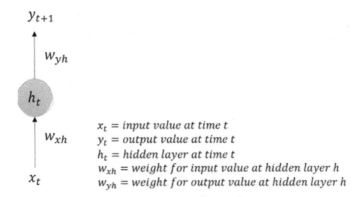

$$x_t = input\ value\ at\ time\ t$$
$$y_t = output\ value\ at\ time\ t$$
$$h_t = hidden\ layer\ at\ time\ t$$
$$w_{xh} = weight\ for\ input\ value\ at\ hidden\ layer\ h$$
$$w_{yh} = weight\ for\ output\ value\ at\ hidden\ layer\ h$$

Figure 2.13 – Feedforward architecture with a hidden layer

However, for this kind of data, it is also likely to have the availability of longer sequences. For example, we might have the time series of this house for the next 5 years. Of course, we want to embed this extra information we have into our model so that our RNN is able to keep the memory about past input in order to properly interpret current input and forecast future outputs.

So, coming back to our example, imagine we not only have the price for today but also the price for yesterday (**t-1**) and the day before (**t-2**). This is how we can calculate it:

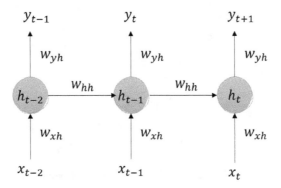

Figure 2.14 – Example of an RNN

Since we are only interested in tomorrow's price, let's ignore the intermediate final outputs for *t-1* and *t*.

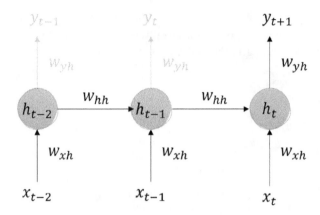

Figure 2.15 – Example of an RNN

As you can see, the output of the hidden layer of **t-2** is served as a (weighted) input of the hidden layer of **t-1**, which also takes the input of **t-1**. Then, the output of the hidden layer at **t-1**, which already keeps the memory of **t-2** and **t-1** inputs, is served as input to the hidden layer of **t**. As a result, the price for tomorrow ($\mathbf{y}_{t+1}$), which is the one we are interested in, brings the memory of all the previous days' inputs.

Finally, if we want to shrink this picture, we can think about the RNN as follows:

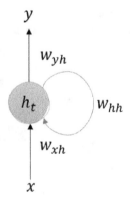

Figure 2.16 – Example of an RNN in its wrapped form

This means that the output of the RNN layer at time step *t-n* is then produced and passed as input to the next time step. The hidden state of the RNN layer is also passed as input to the next time step, allowing the network to maintain and propagate information across different parts of the input sequence.

Even though RNNs were a great development in the field of ANN, they still suffer from some limitations, which we are going to examine in the next section.

The main limitations of RNNs

As mentioned in the introduction of this section, RNNs suffer from three main limitations:

- **Gradient vanishing and exploding**: RNNs suffer from the problem of gradient vanishing and exploding, which makes it difficult to train the network effectively. This problem occurs because the gradients are multiplied multiple times during the backpropagation process, which can cause the gradients to become very small or very large.

- **Limited context**: Traditional RNNs are only able to capture a limited amount of context, as they process the input sequence one element at a time. This means that they are not able to effectively process long-term dependencies or relationships between elements that are far apart in the input sequence.

- **Difficulty in parallelization**: RNNs are inherently sequential, which makes it difficult to parallelize their computation, hence they do not make great use of today's **Graphical Processing Units** (**GPUs**). This can make them slow to train and deploy on large-scale datasets and devices.

A first attempt to overcome the first two limitations (limited context and vanishing and exploding gradient) occurred in 1997 when a new architecture was introduced by Sepp Hochreiter and Jürgen Schmidhuber in their paper, *Long Short-term Memory*. Networks with this new architecture were then called **Long Short-Term Memory** (**LSTM**).

LSTM networks overcome the problem of limited context by introducing the concept of a cell state, which is separate from the hidden state and is able to maintain information for much longer periods. The cell state is passed through the network unchanged, allowing it to store information from previous time steps that would otherwise be lost.

Furthermore, LSTM networks overcome the problem of vanishing and exploding gradients by using carefully designed gates to control the flow of information in and out of the cell, which helps to prevent gradients from becoming too small or too large.

However, LSTM networks still maintain the problem of lack of parallelization and hence slow training time (even slower than RNNs since they are more complex). The goal is to have a model that is able to use parallelization even on sequential data.

To overcome those limitations, a new framework was introduced.

Overcoming limitations – introducing transformers

The transformer architecture addresses these limitations by replacing the recurrence (with a self-attention mechanism), allowing for parallel computation and capturing long-term dependencies.

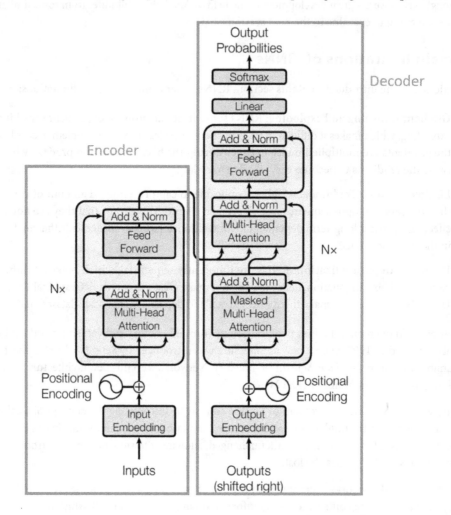

Figure 2.7 – Transformer architecture from the original paper, "Attention is all you need."
Vaswani, A., Shazeer, N., Parmar, N., Uszkoreit, J., Jones, L., Gomez, A. N., Kaiser, L., & Polosukhin,
I. (2017). Attention Is All You Need. ArXiv. https://doi.org/10.48550/arXiv.1706.03762

In the preceding figure (taken from the original paper), you can see that there are two main building blocks: on the left-hand side, we have the "encoder," which has the task of representing the input in a lower-dimensional space; on the right-hand side, we have the "decoder," which has the task of translating the lower-dimensional data provided by the encoder back to the original data format.

Both the encoder and the decoder share three main types of layers that distinguish the transformer architecture: positional encoding, self-attention, and feedforward.

Let us understand each of these in the following sections.

Positional encoding

Encoders are layers that transform natural language input into numerical vectors. This is achieved thanks to the process of embedding, an NLP technique that represents words with vectors in such a way that once represented in a vectorial space, the mathematical distance between vectors is representative of the similarity among words they represent. Have a look at the following figure:

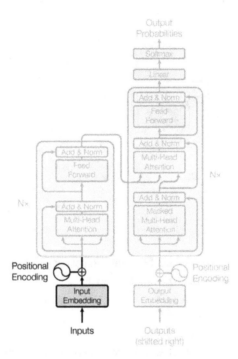

Figure 2.18 – Transformer architecture from the original paper, "Attention is all you need." Vaswani, A., Shazeer, N., Parmar, N., Uszkoreit, J., Jones, L., Gomez, A. N., Kaiser, L., & Polosukhin, I. (2017). Attention Is All You Need. ArXiv. https://doi.org/10.48550/arXiv.1706.03762

As we talk about the meaning of sentences, we all agree that the arrangement of words in a sentence is significant in determining its meaning. That is the reason why we want our encoder to take into account that order, to be *positional*.

The positional encoding is a fixed, learned vector that represents the position of a word in the sequence. It is added to the embedding of the word so that the final representation of a word includes both its meaning and its position.

Self-attention

Self-attention layers are responsible for determining the importance of each input token in generating the output. They answer the question, "*Which part of the input should I focus on?*"

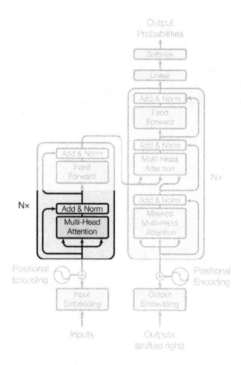

Figure 2.19 – Transformer architecture from the original paper, "Attention is all you need."
Vaswani, A., Shazeer, N., Parmar, N., Uszkoreit, J., Jones, L., Gomez, A. N., Kaiser, L., & Polosukhin, I. (2017). Attention Is All You Need. ArXiv. https://doi.org/10.48550/arXiv.1706.03762

In order to obtain the self-attention vector for a sentence, the elements we need are *value*, *query*, and *key*. These matrices are used to calculate attention scores between the elements in the input sequence and are the three weight matrices that are learned during the training process (typically initialized with random values).

Query is used to represent the current focus of the attention mechanism, while **key** is used to determine which parts of the input should be given attention, and **value** is used to compute the context vectors. Those matrices are then multiplied and passed through a non-linear transformation (thanks to a softmax function). The output of the self-attention layer represents the input values in a transformed, context-aware manner, which allows the transformer to attend to different parts of the input depending on the task at hand. Here is how we can depict the matrices' multiplication:

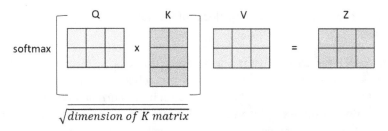

$$\sqrt{dimension\ of\ K\ matrix}$$

Figure 2.20 – Representation of query, key, and value matrice multiplication to obtain the context vector

Note that, in the architecture proposed by the author of the paper, *Attention is all you need*, the attention layer is referred to as **multi-headed attention**. Multi-headed attention is nothing but a mechanism in which multiple self-attention mechanisms operate in parallel on different parts of the input data, producing multiple representations. This allows the transformer model to attend to different parts of the input data in parallel and aggregate information from multiple perspectives.

Once the parallel outputs of the attention layers are ready, they are then concatenated and processed by a feedforward layer.

Feedforward layers

Feedforward layers are responsible for transforming the output of the self-attention layers into a suitable representation for the final output.

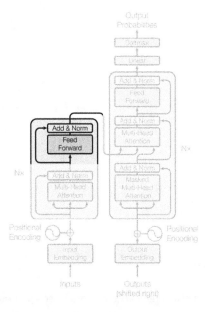

Figure 2.21 – Transformer architecture from the original paper, "Attention is all you need."
Vaswani, A., Shazeer, N., Parmar, N., Uszkoreit, J., Jones, L., Gomez, A. N., Kaiser, L., & Polosukhin, I. (2017). Attention Is All You Need. ArXiv. https://doi.org/10.48550/arXiv.1706.03762

The feedforward layers are the main building blocks of the transformer architecture and consist of two main elements:

- **Fully connected layer** (also known as a dense layer): This is a type of layer where every neuron in the layer is connected to every neuron in the preceding layer. In other words, each input from the previous layer is connected to each neuron in the current layer, and each neuron in the current layer contributes to the output of all neurons in the next layer. Each neuron in the dense layer calculates a weighted sum of its inputs via linear transformations.

- **Activation function**: This is a non-linear function that is applied to the output of the fully connected layer. The activation function is used to introduce non-linearity into the output of a neuron, which is necessary for the network to learn complex patterns and relationships in the input data. In the case of GPT, the activation function is the ReLU.

The output from the feedforward layer is then used as input to the next layer in the network.

In the following figure, we can see an example of a generic feedforward layer taking as input a 2D vector, performing linear operations in the dense layer using the trained weights, and then applying a non-linear transformation to the output with a ReLU activation function:

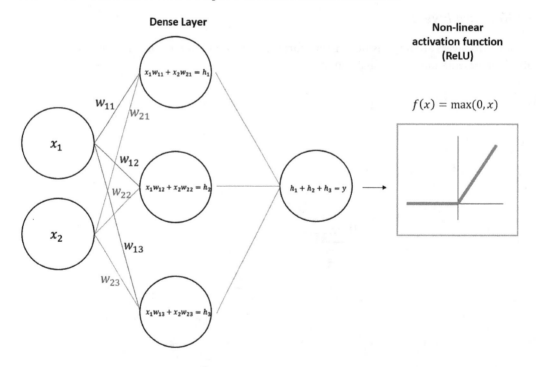

Figure 2.22 – Schema of a generic feed forward layer with two-dimensional input in the dense layer and a ReLU non-linear activation function

The last mile – decoding results

We mentioned that transformers are made of two components: an encoder and a decoder. Even though they share the core elements of positional encoding, self-attention and feedforward layers, the decoder still has to perform an additional operation – decoding the input to the original data format. This operation is done by a linear layer (a feedforward network that adapts the dimension of the input to the dimension of the output) and a softmax function (it transforms the input into a vector of probabilities).

From that vector, we pick the word corresponding to the highest probability and use it as the best output of the model.

All the architectural elements explained above define the framework of Transformers. We will see in the next section how this innovative framework paved the way for GPT-3 and other powerful language models developed by OpenAI.

GPT-3

And here we come to GPT-3, the architecture behind ChatGPT. It is indeed a model based on a transformer architecture, yet with a peculiarity: it only has the decoder layer. Indeed, in their introductory paper *Improving Language Understanding by Generative Pre-Training*, OpenAI researchers used an *only-decoder* approach.

GPT-3 is *huge*. But how huge, concretely?

Let's start with the knowledge base it was trained on. It was meant to be as exhaustive as possible in terms of human knowledge, so it was composed of different sources:

- **Common Crawl** (`https://commoncrawl.org/`): A massive corpus of web data gathered over an 8-year period with minimal filtering
- **WebText2** (`https://openwebtext2.readthedocs.io/en/latest/background/`): A collection of text from web pages linked to in Reddit posts with at least 3 upvotes
- **Books1 and Books2**: Two separate corpora consisting of books available on the internet
- **Wikipedia**: A corpus containing articles from the English-language version of the popular online encyclopedia, Wikipedia

Here you can get a better idea:

Dataset	# tokens	Training mix
Common Crawl (filtered)	410 billion	60%
WebText2	19 billion	22%
Books1	12 billion	8%
Books2	55 billion	8%
Wikipedia	3 billion	3%

Figure 2.23 – GPT-3 knowledge base

Let's consider the following assumption:

- 1 token ~= 4 chars in English
- 1 token ~= ¾ words

We can conclude that GPT-3 has been trained on around *374 billion words*!

This knowledge base was meant to train 175 billion parameters sparsely among 96 hidden layers. To give you an idea of how massive GPT-3 is, let's compare it to the previous versions, GPT-1 and GPT-2:

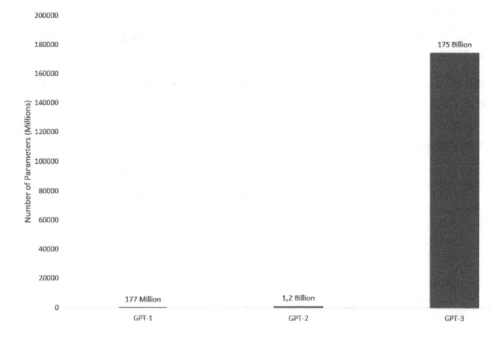

Figure 2.24 – Evolution of GPT models over time in terms of the number of parameters

As you can see, in only a few years since the introduction of GPT-1 in 2018, the complexity and depth of GPT models have grown exponentially.

The speed of development behind GPT models has been stunning, especially if we think about the latest version of this model, also the first one made available to the general public: ChatGPT.

ChatGPT: the state of the art

In November 2022, OpenAI announced the web preview of its conversational AI system, ChatGPT, available to the general public. This was the start of huge hype coming from subject matter experts, organizations, and the general public – to the point that, after only 5 days, the service reached 1 million users!

Before writing about ChatGPT, I will let it introduce itself:

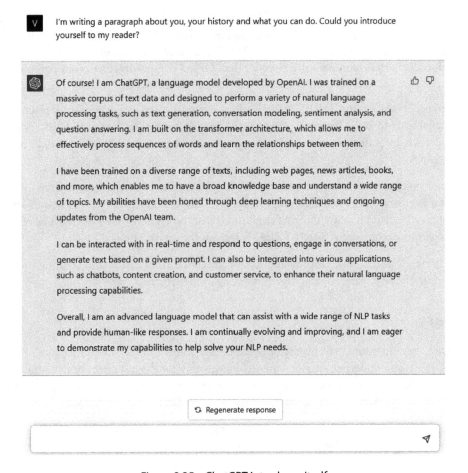

Figure 2.25 – ChatGPT introduces itself

ChatGPT is built on top of an advanced language model that utilizes a modified version of GPT-3, which has been fine-tuned specifically for dialogue. The optimization process involved **Reinforcement Learning with Human Feedback** (**RLHF**), a technique that leverages human input to train the model to exhibit desirable conversational behaviors.

We can define RLHF as a machine learning approach where an algorithm learns to perform a task by receiving feedback from a human. The algorithm is trained to make decisions that maximize a reward signal provided by the human, and the human provides additional feedback to improve the algorithm's performance. This approach is useful when the task is too complex for traditional programming or when the desired outcome is difficult to specify in advance.

The relevant differentiator here is that ChatGPT has been trained with humans in the loop so that it is aligned with its users. By incorporating RLHF, ChatGPT has been designed to better understand and respond to human language in a natural and engaging way.

> **Note**
>
> The same RLHF mechanism was used for what we can think of as the predecessor of ChatGPT—**InstructGPT**. In the related paper published by OpenAI's researchers in January 2022, InstructGPT is introduced as a class of models that is better than GPT-3 at following English instructions.

The knowledge cut-off date for ChatGPT is 2021, which means that the model is aware of information that was available up to 2021. However, you can still provide context to the model with a few-shot learning approach, even though the model responses will still be based on its knowledge base up to the cut-off date.

ChatGPT is revolutionizing the way we interact with AI. ChatGPT's ability to generate human-like text has made it a popular choice for a wide range of applications, including chatbots, customer service, and content creation. Additionally, OpenAI announced that the ChatGPT API will soon be released, allowing developers to integrate ChatGPT directly into custom applications.

The ongoing developments and improvements in ChatGPT's architecture and training methods promise to push the boundaries of language processing even further.

Summary

In this chapter, we went through the history of OpenAI, its research fields, and the latest developments, up to ChatGPT. We went deeper into the OpenAI Playground for the test environment and how to embed the Models API into your code. Then, we dwelled on the mathematics behind the GPT model family, in order to have better clarity about the functioning of GPT-3, the model behind ChatGPT.

With a deeper understanding of the math behind GPT models, we can have a better perception of how powerful those models are and the multiple ways they can impact both individuals and organizations. With this first glance at the OpenAI Playground and Models API, we saw how easy it is to test or embed pre-trained models into your applications: the game-changer element here is that you don't need powerful hardware and hours of time to train your models, since they are already available to you and can also be customized if needed, with a few examples.

In the next chapter, we also begin *Part 2* of this book, where we will see ChatGPT in action within various domains and how to unlock its potential. You will learn how to get the highest value from ChatGPT by properly designing your prompts, how to boost your daily productivity, and how it can be a great project assistant for developers, marketers, and researchers.

References

- Radford, A., & Narasimhan, K. (2018). Improving language understanding by generative pre-training.

- Vaswani, A., Shazeer, N., Parmar, N., Uszkoreit, J., Jones, L., Gomez, A. N., Kaiser, L., & Polosukhin, I. (2017). *Attention Is All You Need*. ArXiv. `https://doi.org/10.48550/arXiv.1706.03762` OpenAI. Fine-Tuning Guide. OpenAI platform documentation. `https://platform.openai.com/docs/guides/fine-tuning`.

Part 2: ChatGPT in Action

In this part, we will start our journey through the landscape of new possibilities that ChatGPT brings to the market. From daily productivity to domain-specific use cases, you will get familiar with the capabilities of ChatGPT and how it can be used as a reasoning engine for various tasks.

Once we have explored the technical prerequisites, this part jumps into an overview of the ChatGPT user interface, including chat management and question modifications.

It then moves toward one of the most important elements required to get the best out of ChatGPT and, in general, out of large language models: the concept of prompt design. Here, you will get familiar with powerful techniques to make ChatGPT work at its best, including recent developments and research papers about techniques such as **Reason and Act (ReAct)** and **Chain of Thoughts (CoT)**.

This part finally focuses on concrete examples of how to use ChatGPT in operative activities, starting with daily productivity and moving to more domain-specific disciplines, such as marketing, development, and research. Here, you will be able to not only learn about the use cases ChatGPT can cover in those domains but also see concrete examples to replicate them on your own.

This part has the following chapters:

- *Chapter 3, Getting Familiar with ChatGPT*
- *Chapter 4, Understanding Prompt Design*
- *Chapter 5, Boosting Day-to-Day Productivity with ChatGPT*
- *Chapter 6, Developing the Future with ChatGPT*
- *Chapter 7, Mastering Marketing with ChatGPT*
- *Chapter 8, Research Reinvented with ChatGPT*

3

Getting Familiar with ChatGPT

This chapter enables you to set up your ChatGPT account and start using the service. It will also dwell on how to interact with the web UI, how to organize chats by topic, and how to structure the conversation.

By the end of this chapter, you will have a better understanding of what ChatGPT is, how it works, and how you can efficiently organize it as a daily assistant. You will also learn about its main capabilities and limitations so that you are aware of how to use it responsibly.

In this chapter, we will cover the following topics:

- Setting up a ChatGPT account
- Familiarizing yourself with the UI
- Organizing chats

Setting up a ChatGPT account

To start using ChatGPT, you first need to create an OpenAI account. Follow the instructions here:

1. Navigate to the OpenAI website here: `https://openai.com`.
2. Scroll down and click on **ChatGPT** under the **FEATURED** menu as shown here:

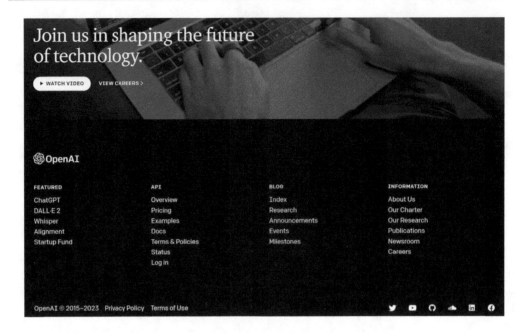

Figure 3.1 – OpenAI landing page

3. Then you need to click on **TRY CHATGPT**:

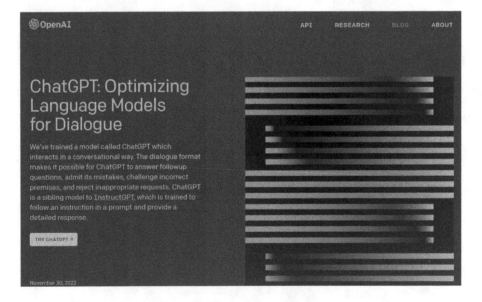

Figure 3.2 – ChatGPT landing page

4. On the next page, you need to fill out the form to sign up for an OpenAI account. This is the same account you can use to access the OpenAI Playground and generate your API keys.

Welcome to ChatGPT

Log in with your OpenAI account to continue

Log in   Sign up

Figure 3.3 – ChatGPT landing page with Log in and Sign up options

5. Now you can start using the ChatGPT web app. Once you have found the ChatGPT web app, click on it to launch it. You will be able to interact with ChatGPT and perform various natural language processing tasks directly in your web browser.

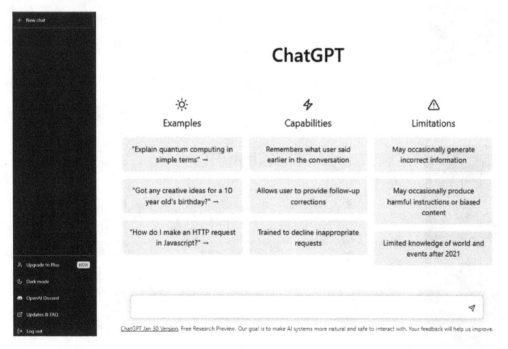

Figure 3.4 – ChatGPT web interface

Great! Now you can start using ChatGPT. But you also need to know what the app is like. Let us learn about it next.

Familiarizing yourself with the UI

The web interface of ChatGPT is pretty intuitive to use. Before starting to write your prompts, you can easily try some examples provided by the service:

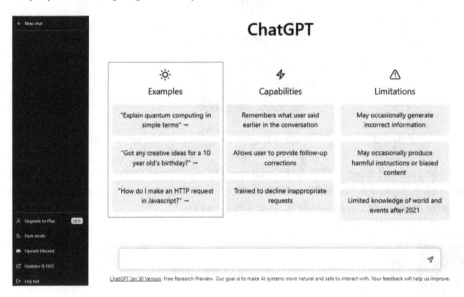

Figure 3.5 – Sample prompts provided by ChatGPT

Then, you are also instructed about the main capabilities of ChatGPT:

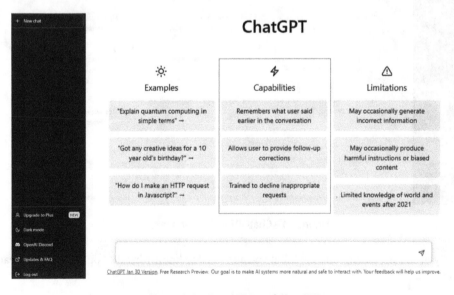

Figure 3.6 – Capabilities of ChatGPT

Among the capabilities, it is highlighted how ChatGPT is capable of maintaining memory throughout the conversation. In the previous chapter, we went deeper into the math behind GPT and saw how important the memory retention component is: now you can appreciate this mathematical complexity in action.

This capability of ChatGPT is also an example of **few-shot learning**, which we are going to learn more about in the following chapters.

> **Note**
>
> ChatGPT can maintain the memory of the previous context thanks to its few-shot learning capability. Few-shot learning is a type of machine learning technique that enables models to learn new concepts or tasks with very limited labeled data and has become an important area of research in the field of artificial intelligence.

Thanks to those features like memory retention and few-shot learning, ChatGPT allows the user to provide follow-ups or corrections during the conversation, without the need to provide the context once again.

Here, there is an example of how you can make corrections to your prompts in a conversation with ChatGPT:

Figure 3.7 – An example of follow-up comments and prompt correction with ChatGPT

Finally, the model also alerts the user that, among its capabilities, it is also trained to decline inappropriate requests that might be harmful or offensive.

The last set of information provided on its home page is related to ChatGPT limitations:

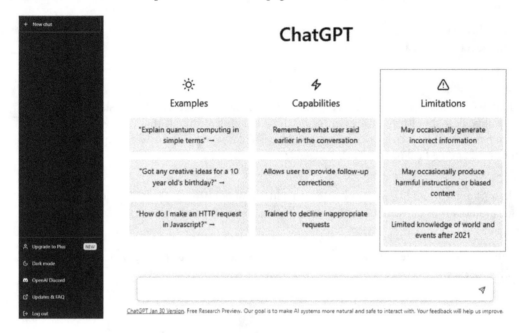

Figure 3.8 – ChatGPT limitations

These elements are an important reminder of the fact that, today, AI tools still need to be supervised by a human. In fact, in addition to the missing information between 2021 and today, ChatGPT might also provide inaccurate or even wrong information. That is the reason why it still needs supervision.

An interesting phenomenon worth mentioning is that of *hallucination*. Hallucination refers to the occurrence where an AI model generates fake or imagined data that resembles real-world data but is not actually based on any real observations. Here is an example of this:

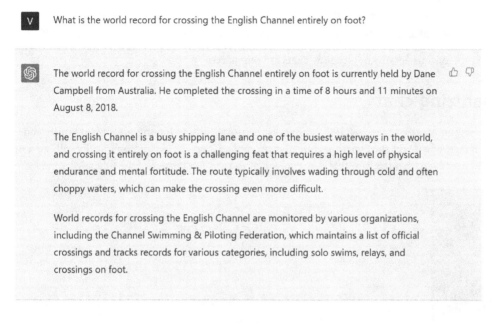

Figure 3.9 – An example of ChatGPT hallucination

The question in *Figure 3.9* was originally developed by Douglas Hofstadter and David Bender as a way to induce hallucinatory responses in ChatGPT!

To prevent hallucinations, some good practices should be kept in mind:

- **Be specific and clear**: Make sure your prompt is well-defined and clearly states what you are looking to achieve. This will help the model generate more focused and relevant responses. A prompt such as *Tell me about the world* would probably not generate great results.

- **Provide sufficient context**: The more context you can provide, the better the model will be able to understand what you are looking for and generate a response that is relevant to your needs.

- **Avoid ambiguity**: Avoid using vague or ambiguous terms or phrases in your prompt, as this can make it difficult for the model to understand what you are looking for.

- **Use concise language**: Keep your prompts as concise as possible, while still providing enough information for the model to generate a response. This will help ensure that the model generates focused and concise responses.

- **Be mindful of the training data**: ChatGPT has been trained on a large corpus of text, and it may generate responses that are biased or inaccurate based on the patterns in that data. Be mindful of this and consider adjusting your prompts if you suspect that the model is generating responses that are not appropriate or accurate.

As we will see in the next chapter, these prompt design considerations are not only useful to prevent hallucinations, but also to get the highest value and utility from your interactions with ChatGPT.

With this behind us, let us now see how chats are managed.

Organizing chats

A time-saving feature that ChatGPT exhibits is the possibility of having multiple open threads or chats. In fact, when you start writing your first prompts, ChatGPT will automatically initiate a new chat and name it with a relevant title. Have a look at the top-left corner of the following screenshot:

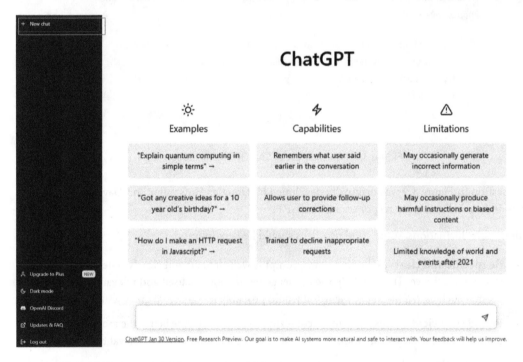

Figure 3.10 – Creating a new chat in ChatGPT

You can always decide to start new chats from scratch, however, you might want to continue a conversation you started some days ago.

Imagine you have asked ChatGPT to explain the concept of linear regression, and then started a conversation with several follow-ups. Here is how it shows up:

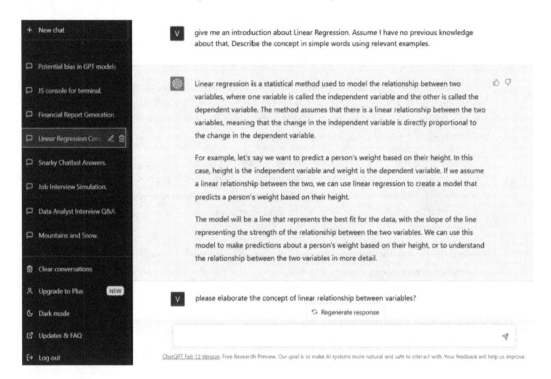

Figure 3.11 – Example of an existing chat with context

At that point, within that chat, ChatGPT already has context, hence you can continue your conversation without the need to repeat concepts. Have a look here:

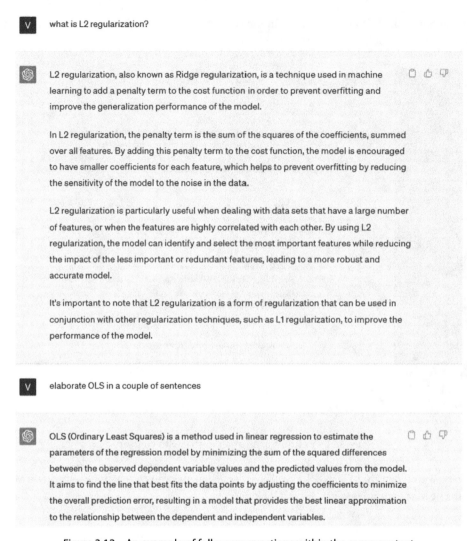

Figure 3.12 – An example of follow-up questions within the same context

With this, we have learned how ChatGPT chats are maintained and organized, which makes it easy to refer to older chats.

Summary

In this chapter, we went through the concrete steps to start using ChatGPT with our account. We also dwelled on its capabilities and limitations, with some considerations about the risk of hallucination and how to avoid this via prompt design. We also saw how chats are presented in the app and how easy it is to refer to old ones.

In the next chapter, we will focus more on prompt design and engineering in order to get the highest value from your conversations with ChatGPT.

References

- `https://openai.com/blog/chatgpt/`
- `https://www.sify.com/ai-analytics/the-hilarious-and-horrifying-hallucinations-of-ai/`
- `https://www.datanami.com/2023/01/17/hallucinations-plagiarism-and-chatgpt/`

4

Understanding Prompt Design

In the previous chapters, we mentioned the term **prompt** several times while referring to user input in ChatGPT and OpenAI models in general.

This chapter focuses in more depth on the importance of prompt design and engineering as a technique to improve the accuracy of the model. Prompts heavily impact the model's generated output: a well-designed prompt can help guide the model toward generating relevant and accurate output, while a poorly designed prompt can lead to irrelevant or confusing output. Finally, it is also important to incorporate ethical considerations into the prompt to prevent the model from generating harmful content.

In this chapter, we will discuss the following topics:

- What is a prompt and why is it important?
- Zero-, one-, and few-shot learning – typical of transformers models
- Principles of well-defined prompts to obtain relevant and consistent results
- Avoiding the risk of hidden bias and taking into account ethical considerations in ChatGPT

By the end of this chapter, you will be able to get high-quality results from your ChatGPT and OpenAI model interactions thanks to proper prompt design.

What is a prompt and why is it important?

In the context of generative AI, a prompt refers to the input the user provides to the generative models. When we talk about ChatGPT and OpenAI models, prompts mainly refer to a piece of text in natural language or – as we saw for Codex models – in programming languages.

Prompts are the only way users can control the output generated by those models. As such, there is no surprise in saying that the quality of the prompts used to engage the AI system in a conversation is key to determining its success.

Well-defined prompts are the recipe for a successful conversation that covers the topics of interest; poorly-defined prompts, on the other hand, not only prevent the conversation from being useful to the user but could also lead to potentially misleading content. As we saw in the previous chapter, ChatGPT still suffers from some limitations, such as the 2021 cut-off of its knowledge base, as well as another caveat typical of generative AI systems in general, such as the phenomenon of hallucination.

Namely, imagine that we want to learn about **Convolutional Neural Networks** (**CNNs**). We don't have any knowledge about **Artificial Neural Networks** (**ANNs**), so we need to start with a gentle introduction. The idea is that, starting from the first output, we can deep dive into relevant elements.

Let's examine the result of a poorly-defined prompt in ChatGPT:

 tell me about convolutional neural networks

 Convolutional Neural Networks (ConvNets or CNNs) are a category of Neural Networks that are specifically designed to process data that has a grid-like topology, such as an image. CNNs are built using a variation of multi-layer perceptrons, designed to require minimal pre-processing, and to operate on input data without fully connected layers, which makes them well-suited for image classification tasks.

A CNN works by passing the input image through multiple layers of operations, each layer extracting higher level features from the input image. The first layer of a CNN, called the convolutional layer, is where the magic happens: it uses a set of learnable filters to scan the image and detect features (edges, curves, textures, etc.) that are relevant for the task. The outputs of these filters are then fed into the next layer, which is typically a pooling layer, responsible for reducing the spatial dimensions of the feature maps, and for suppressing irrelevant information.

Following the pooling layer, there can be multiple layers of fully connected neurons that perform classification. The final layer of a CNN outputs a probability distribution over the classes, which can be used to determine the final class label for an input image.

During training, the parameters (weights and biases) of a CNN are learned using backpropagation and gradient descent, so that the network can learn to associate the input image with the correct class label. The learned filters can be thought of as visual detectors that are specific to the task.

Overall, CNNs have proven to be extremely effective in tasks such as image classification, object detection, semantic segmentation, etc., and they have achieved state-of-the-art performance on several benchmarks.

Figure 4.1 – Example of a poorly-defined prompt

The result is correct and accurate, but it's going through many technical concepts we may have never seen before. What are fully connected layers? What is a pooling layer? This answer assumes we have previous knowledge of ANNs.

Let's try to give more context to ChatGPT to get a result that is more useful to us:

 give me an introduction about convolutional neural network. Assume I have no previous knowledge about artificial neural network. describe the architecture in simple words making examples if possible.

 A Convolutional Neural Network (CNN) is a type of Artificial Neural Network that is used for image recognition and processing tasks. It is designed to take advantage of the grid-like structure of an image, where pixels are organized in a 2D grid.

Think of a CNN as a machine that is designed to recognize objects in images. It does so by analyzing the image in a series of steps, each step looking for specific features in the image.

For example, the first step might look for edges and curves in the image. The second step could look for repeating textures. And the final step would put all of the features together to recognize an object, like a dog or a cat.

The key to a CNN is its architecture, which consists of multiple layers. Each layer performs a different operation on the image, and the output of one layer is fed as input to the next layer.

Here's a high-level overview of the main components of a CNN:

1. Convolutional Layer: This layer is responsible for detecting local patterns in the image, such as edges, curves, and textures. It does so by using a set of filters that scan the image and create feature maps.
2. Pooling Layer: This layer reduces the size of the feature maps created by the convolutional layer, and helps to reduce the number of parameters in the network.
3. Fully Connected Layer: This layer takes the output of the pooling layer and performs the final classification.

During the training phase, the CNN is presented with many examples of images along with their correct labels (e.g., dog, cat, etc.). The CNN then uses these examples to learn and adjust its parameters, so that it can correctly recognize objects in new images.

In short, a CNN is a deep learning model that is designed to process and analyze images, and it does so by performing multiple operations on the image in a series of layers.

Figure 4.2 – Example of a well-defined prompt

As you can see, the wording in this response is much more likely than the one I was looking for. In the introduction, it doesn't use words such as *multi-layer perceptron* or *fully connected layer*. It also provides, as requested, an example of the process of image recognition. Then, it goes into further details, making sure to explain each step with simple words.

I'm pretty satisfied with this response and, as a user, I could now start asking about the pooling layer in more detail, for example.

Consequently, prompt design and engineering has been gaining more and more traction and it's growing as a discipline itself.

Now, let's focus on how to improve ChatGPT's responses by leveraging its few-shot learning capabilities.

Zero-, one-, and few-shot learning – typical of transformers models

In the previous chapters, we mentioned how OpenAI models, and hence also ChatGPT, come in a pre-trained format. They have been trained on a huge amount of data and have had their (billions of) parameters configured accordingly.

However, this doesn't mean that those models can't learn anymore. In *Chapter 2*, we saw that one way to customize an OpenAI model and make it more capable of addressing specific tasks is by **fine-tuning**.

> **Definition**
> Fine-tuning is the process of adapting a pre-trained model to a new task. In fine-tuning, the parameters of the pre-trained model are altered, either by adjusting the existing parameters or by adding new parameters so that they fit the data for the new task. This is done by training the model on a smaller labeled dataset that is specific to the new task. The key idea behind fine-tuning is to leverage the knowledge learned from the pre-trained model and fine-tune it to the new task, rather than training a model from scratch.

Fine-tuning is a proper training process that requires a training dataset, compute power, and some training time (depending on the amount of data and compute instances).

That is why it is worth testing another method for our model to become more skilled in specific tasks: **shot learning**.

The idea is to let the model learn from simple examples rather than the entire dataset. Those examples are samples of the way we would like the model to respond so that the model not only learns the content but also the format, style, and taxonomy to use in its response.

Furthermore, shot learning occurs directly via the prompt (as we will see in the following scenarios), so the whole experience is less time-consuming and easier to perform.

The number of examples provided determines the level of shot learning we are referring to. In other words, we refer to zero-shot if no example is provided, one-shot if one example is provided, and few-shot if more than 2-3 examples are provided.

Let's focus on each of those scenarios:

- **Zero-shot learning**. In this type of learning, the model is asked to perform a task for which it has not seen any training examples. The model must rely on prior knowledge or general information about the task to complete the task. For example, a zero-shot learning approach could be that of asking the model to generate a description, as defined in my prompt:

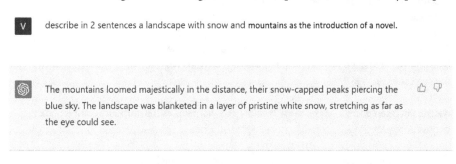

Figure 4.3 – Example of zero-shot learning

- **One-shot learning**: In this type of learning, the model is given a single example of each new task it is asked to perform. The model must use its prior knowledge to generalize from this single example to perform the task. If we consider the preceding example, I could provide my model with a prompt-completion example before asking it to generate a new one:

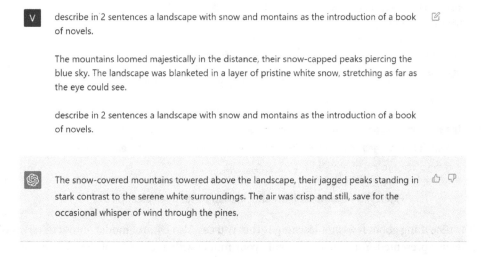

Figure 4.4 – Example of one-shot learning

Note that the way I provided an example was similar to the structure used for fine-tuning:

```
{"prompt": "<prompt text>", "completion": "<ideal generated text>"}
```

- **Few-shot learning**: In this type of learning, the model is given a small number of examples (typically between 3 and 5) of each new task it is asked to perform. The model must use its prior knowledge to generalize from these examples to perform the task. Let's continue with our example and provide the model with further examples:

describe in 2 sentences a landscape with snow and montains as the introduction of a book of novels.

The mountains loomed majestically in the distance, their snow-capped peaks piercing the blue sky. The landscape was blanketed in a layer of pristine white snow, stretching as far as the eye could see.

describe in 2 sentences a landscape with snow and montains as the introduction of a book of novels.

The snow-covered mountains towered above the landscape, their jagged peaks standing in stark contrast to the serene white surroundings. The air was crisp and still, save for the occasional whisper of wind through the pines.

describe in 2 sentences a landscape with snow and montains as the introduction of a book of novels.

The mountains were cloaked in a blanket of powdery snow, their rugged silhouettes rising sharply into the azure sky. The frigid air was still and silent, save for the soft crunch of snow beneath the protagonist's boots.

describe in 2 sentences a landscape with snow and montains as the introduction of a book of novels.

The snow-capped peaks of the mountains stood tall and proud, surrounded by a vast expanse of untouched white snow. The chilly air was filled with the faint scent of pine trees and the distant sound of snowfall.   ↻ Regenerate response

Figure 4.5 – Example of few-shot learning with three examples

The nice thing about few-shot learning is that you can also control model output in terms of how it is presented. You can also provide your model with a template of the way you would like your output to look. For example, consider the following tweet classifier:

This is a tweet sentiment classifier

Tweet: "I loved the last edition of Sanremo Festival!"
Sentiment: Positive

Tweet: "I hate it when I cannot find things in my bag"
Sentiment: Negative

Tweet: "My day has been 👍 "
Sentiment: Positive

Tweet: "Today my new album is out"
Sentiment: Neutral

Tweet text
1. "I loved the last edition of Sanremo Festival!"
2. "I hate it when I cannot find things in my bag"
3. "My day has been 👍 "
4. "Today my new album is out"
5. "Just watched Avatar 2 and it was out of this world"

Tweet sentiment ratings:
1: Positive
2: Negative
3: Positive
4: Neutral
5: Positive

Tweet text
1. "Today the sunny is shining!"
2. "This is my mood now 😡 "
3. "I can't wait for Halloween! Super excited!"
4. "My cat is adorable 💜 💜 "
5. "I hate horror movies"

Tweet sentiment ratings (in list format)

1. Positive
2. Negative
3. Positive
4. Positive
5. Negative

Figure 4.6 – Few-shot learning for a tweets classifier. This is a modified version of the original script from https://learn.microsoft.com/en-us/azure/cognitive-services/openai/how-to/completions

Let's examine the preceding figure. First, I provided ChatGPT with some examples of labeled tweets. Then, I provided the same tweets but in a different data format (list format), as well as the labels in the same format. Finally, in list format, I provided unlabeled tweets so that the model returns a list of labels.

The output format is not the only thing you can teach your model, though. You can also teach it to act and speak with a particular jargon and taxonomy, which could help you obtain the desired result with the desired wording:

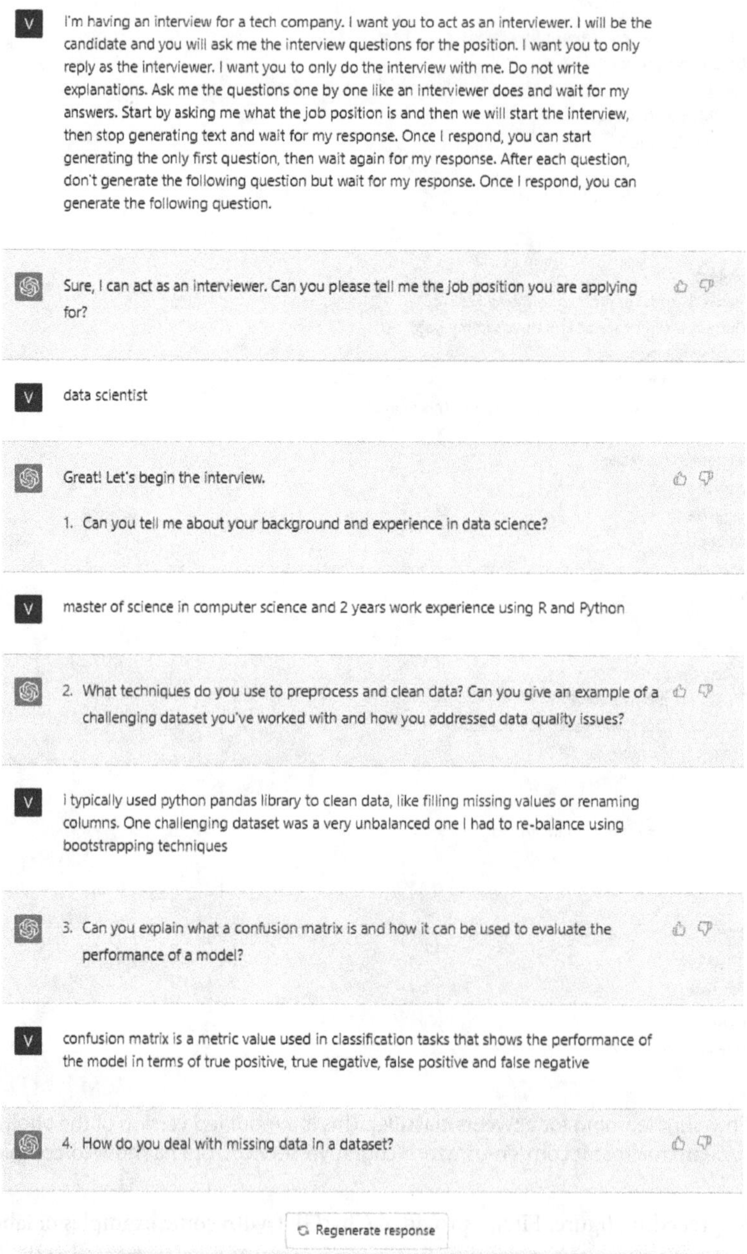

> V   I'm having an interview for a tech company. I want you to act as an interviewer. I will be the candidate and you will ask me the interview questions for the position. I want you to only reply as the interviewer. I want you to only do the interview with me. Do not write explanations. Ask me the questions one by one like an interviewer does and wait for my answers. Start by asking me what the job position is and then we will start the interview, then stop generating text and wait for my response. Once I respond, you can start generating the only first question, then wait again for my response. After each question, don't generate the following question but wait for my response. Once I respond, you can generate the following question.

> ⑨   Sure, I can act as an interviewer. Can you please tell me the job position you are applying for?

> V   data scientist

> ⑨   Great! Let's begin the interview.
>
>   1. Can you tell me about your background and experience in data science?

> V   master of science in computer science and 2 years work experience using R and Python

> ⑨   2. What techniques do you use to preprocess and clean data? Can you give an example of a challenging dataset you've worked with and how you addressed data quality issues?

> V   i typically used python pandas library to clean data, like filling missing values or renaming columns. One challenging dataset was a very unbalanced one I had to re-balance using bootstrapping techniques

> ⑨   3. Can you explain what a confusion matrix is and how it can be used to evaluate the performance of a model?

> V   confusion matrix is a metric value used in classification tasks that shows the performance of the model in terms of true positive, true negative, false positive and false negative

> ⑨   4. How do you deal with missing data in a dataset?

↻ Regenerate response

Figure 4.7 – Example of a conversation with ChatGPT acting as an interviewer

Or, imagine you want to generate a chatbot called Simpy that is very funny and sarcastic while responding:

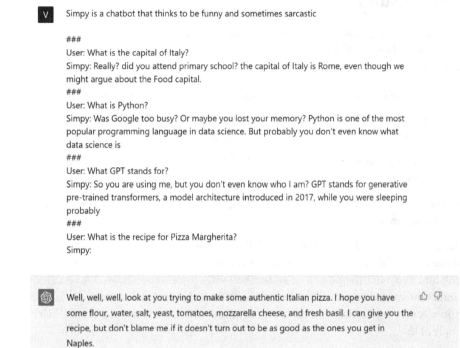

Figure 4.8 – Example of a chatbot that is funny and sarcastic, making fun of my request

We have to say, with this last one, ChatGPT nailed it.

Shot-learning possibilities are limitless (and often more useful than Simpy) – it's only a matter of testing and a little bit of patience in finding the proper prompt design.

As mentioned previously, it is important to remember that these forms of learning are different from traditional supervised learning, as well as fine-tuning. In few-shot learning, the goal is to enable the model to learn from very few examples, and to generalize from those examples to new tasks.

Now that we've learned how to let ChatGPT learn from examples, let's focus on how to properly define our prompt to make the model's response as accurate as possible.

Principles of well-defined prompts to obtain relevant and consistent results

Previously, we saw how important prompt designing and engineering are when controlling models' output. Here are some best practices you can use to improve your prompts, as well as some practices you should avoid:

- **Clarity**: Use simple sentences and instructions that can easily be understood by ChatGPT.

- **Conciseness**: Favor short prompts and short sentences. This can be achieved by chunking your instructions into smaller sentences with clear intentions.

- **Focus**: Keep the focus of the prompt on a well-defined topic so that you don't risk your output being too generic.

- **Consistency**: Maintain a consistent tone and language during the conversation so that you can ensure a coherent conversation.

- **"Acting as…"**: The hack of letting ChatGPT act as someone or something has proven to be extremely powerful. You can shorten the context you have to provide to the model by simply asking him to *act like* the person or system you want information from. We've already seen the interview-candidate example, where ChatGPT acted as an interviewer for a data scientist position. A very interesting prompt is that of asking ChatGPT to act as a console. Here is an example of it:

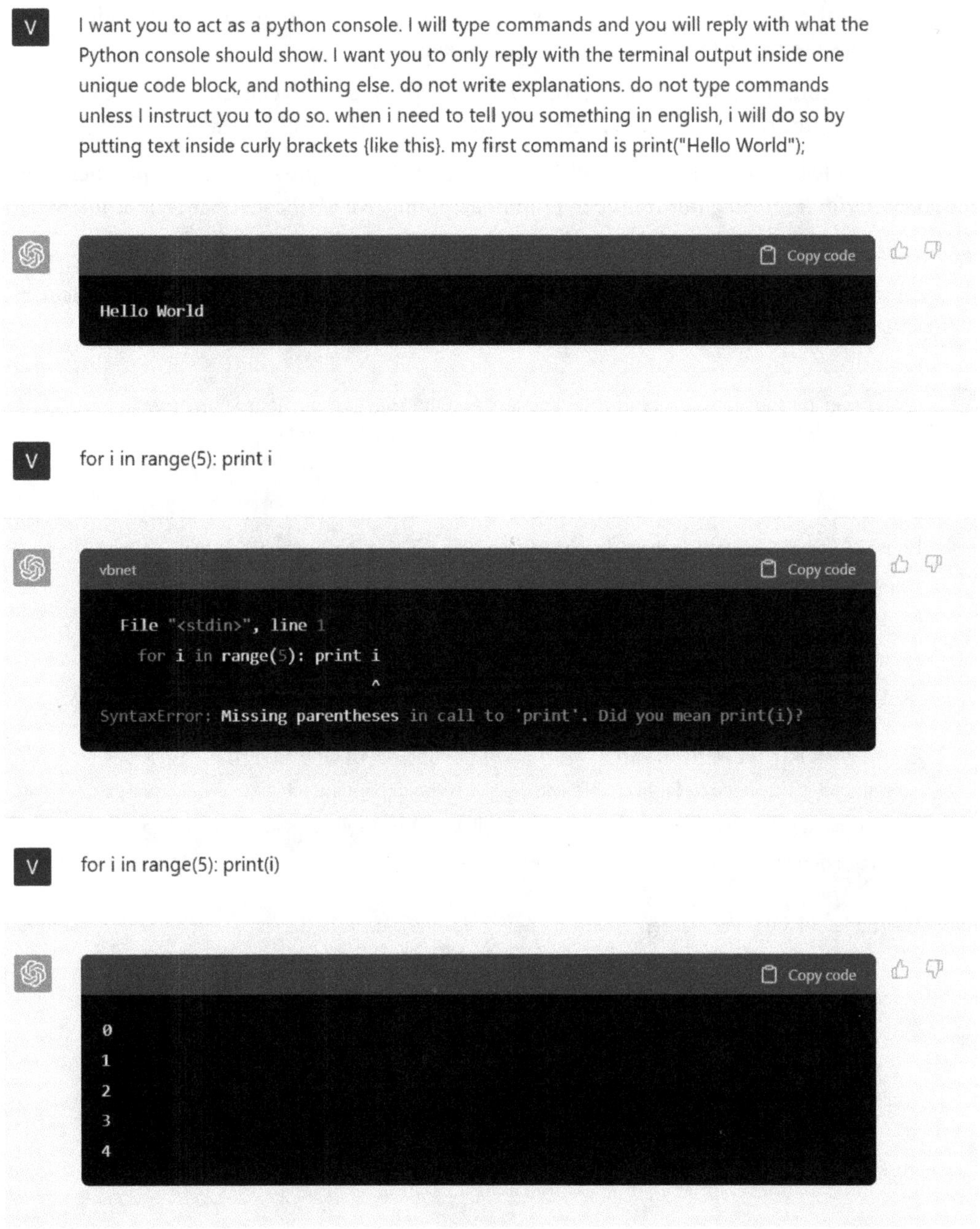

V   I want you to act as a python console. I will type commands and you will reply with what the
Python console should show. I want you to only reply with the terminal output inside one
unique code block, and nothing else. do not write explanations. do not type commands
unless I instruct you to do so. when i need to tell you something in english, i will do so by
putting text inside curly brackets {like this}. my first command is print("Hello World");

```
Hello World
```

V   for i in range(5): print i

```vbnet
  File "<stdin>", line 1
    for i in range(5): print i
                           ^
SyntaxError: Missing parentheses in call to 'print'. Did you mean print(i)?
```

V   for i in range(5): print(i)

```
0
1
2
3
4
```

Figure 4.9 – Example of ChatGPT acting as a Python console

Note that the console, as it would be if it were real, is also reporting the error I made in the `for` cycle, indicating that I was missing the brackets.

There is a continuously growing list of *Act as* prompts you can try in the following GitHub repository: `https://github.com/f/awesome-chatgpt-prompts`.

Considering the few-shot learning capabilities elaborated on in the previous paragraph, there are some good tips for leveraging this feature in prompt designing. An ideal conversation is as follows:

1. Start with a concise, clear, and focused prompt. This will help you have an overview of the topic you want to discuss, as well as provide food for thought and potential expansion of particular elements. Here's an example:

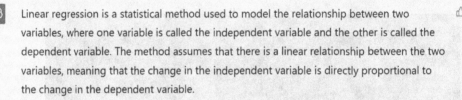

V   give me an introduction about Linear Regression. Assume I have no previous knowledge about that. Describe the concept in simple words using relevant examples.

Linear regression is a statistical method used to model the relationship between two variables, where one variable is called the independent variable and the other is called the dependent variable. The method assumes that there is a linear relationship between the two variables, meaning that the change in the independent variable is directly proportional to the change in the dependent variable.

For example, let's say we want to predict a person's weight based on their height. In this case, height is the independent variable and weight is the dependent variable. If we assume a linear relationship between the two, we can use linear regression to create a model that predicts a person's weight based on their height.

The model will be a line that represents the best fit for the data, with the slope of the line representing the strength of the relationship between the two variables. We can use this model to make predictions about a person's weight based on their height, or to understand the relationship between the two variables in more detail.

Figure 4.10 – Example of a clear and focused prompt to initiate a conversation with ChatGPT

2. Once you have identified the relevant elements in the discussion, you can ask ChatGPT to elaborate on them with much more focus:

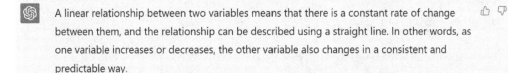

V   please elaborate the concept of linear relationship between variables

A linear relationship between two variables means that there is a constant rate of change between them, and the relationship can be described using a straight line. In other words, as one variable increases or decreases, the other variable also changes in a consistent and predictable way.

For example, let's consider the relationship between the amount of rainfall and the crop yield. If the relationship between the two variables is linear, then we can expect that as the amount of rainfall increases, the crop yield will also increase at a constant rate. This can be represented graphically by a straight line that passes through the plotted data points.

Linear regression is a statistical method used to identify and quantify the strength of a linear relationship between two variables. The method involves fitting a straight line to the data points and using that line to predict the values of the dependent variable based on the values of the independent variable.

It's important to note that not all relationships between variables are linear. In some cases, the relationship may be nonlinear, meaning that the rate of change between the variables is not constant, and the relationship cannot be accurately described using a straight line. In these cases, other statistical methods may be more appropriate for modeling the relationship between the variables.

Figure 4.11 – Example of a deep-dive follow-up question in a conversation with ChatGPT

3. Sometimes, it might be useful to remember the model and the context in which you are inquiring, especially if the question might apply to various domains:

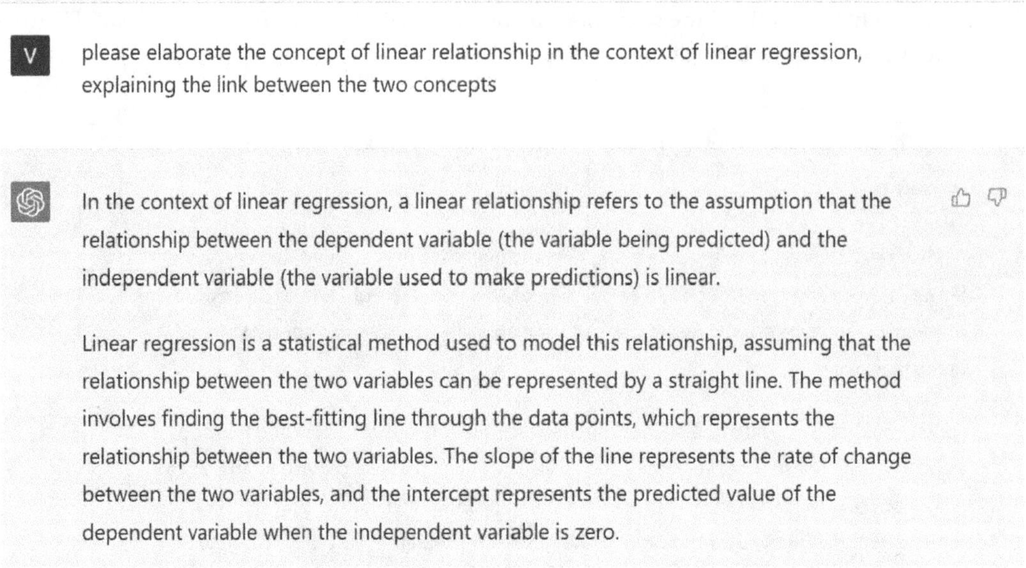

 please elaborate the concept of linear relationship in the context of linear regression, explaining the link between the two concepts

 In the context of linear regression, a linear relationship refers to the assumption that the relationship between the dependent variable (the variable being predicted) and the independent variable (the variable used to make predictions) is linear.

Linear regression is a statistical method used to model this relationship, assuming that the relationship between the two variables can be represented by a straight line. The method involves finding the best-fitting line through the data points, which represents the relationship between the two variables. The slope of the line represents the rate of change between the two variables, and the intercept represents the predicted value of the dependent variable when the independent variable is zero.

Figure 4.12 – Example of a reminder about the context in a conversation with ChatGPT

4. Finally, always keep in mind the limitations we mentioned in previous chapters. ChatGPT may provide partial or incorrect information, so it is always a good practice to double-check. One nice tip you could try is asking the model to provide documentation about its responses so that you can easily find proof of them:

provide me a list of relevant documentations and papers where I can find confirmation of your previous responses

Here are some relevant documentations and papers where you can find more information about linear regression and its concepts:

1. Introduction to Linear Regression Analysis by Douglas C. Montgomery and Elizabeth A. Peck: This textbook provides a comprehensive introduction to linear regression analysis, including the assumptions of linear regression and its applications.
2. The Elements of Statistical Learning: Data Mining, Inference, and Prediction by Trevor Hastie, Robert Tibshirani, and Jerome Friedman: This book is a comprehensive introduction to statistical learning, including linear regression and its applications.
3. "Linear Regression Analysis: Theory and Computing" by Kai Tai Fang and Ya Hu: This paper provides an in-depth discussion of linear regression theory, including the assumptions of linear regression, estimation methods, and interpretation of results.
4. "Linear regression in ecology" by David I. Warton and Francis K.C. Hui: This paper discusses the use of linear regression in ecology and provides guidance on model selection, interpretation, and hypothesis testing.
5. "Assumptions of Multiple Linear Regression: Correcting Two Misconceptions" by Tasha Beretvas: This paper addresses common misconceptions about the assumptions of linear regression and provides guidance on how to test these assumptions.

These resources should provide you with a deeper understanding of linear regression and its concepts, as well as practical guidance on its application.

Figure 4.13 – Example of ChatGPT providing documentation supporting its previous responses

On the other hand, there are some things you should avoid while designing your prompt:

- **Information overload**: Avoid providing too much information to ChatGPT, since it could reduce the accuracy of the response.
- **Open-ended questions**: Avoid asking ChatGPT vague, open-ended questions. Prompts such as *What can you tell me about the world?* or *Can you help me with my exam?* are far too generic and will result in ChatGPT generating vague, useless, and sometimes hallucinated responses.

- **Lack of constraints**: If you are expecting an output with a specific structure, don't forget to specify that to ChatGPT! If you think about the earlier example of ChatGPT acting as an interviewer, you can see how strict I was in specifying not to generate questions all at once. It took several tries before getting to the result since ChatGPT is thought to generate a continuous flow of text.

> **Note**
>
> As a general consideration, we still have to remember that the knowledge base of ChatGPT is limited to 2021, so we should avoid asking questions about facts that occurred after that date. You can still provide context; however, all the responses will be biased toward the knowledge base before 2021.

Furthermore, it is worth mentioning that in the last few months, a lot of research and development has been dedicated to the study of prompt design for **large language models (LLMs)** (not just **generative pretrained transformer (GPT)**), because of the extensive use of some specific techniques such as the following:

- **Chain-of-Thought (CoT)**: Google researchers Jason Wei et al. have introduced a new technique called **CoT prompting** to improve the reasoning abilities of LLMs. The method divides intricate problems into smaller, manageable steps, which enables language models to solve complex reasoning tasks that cannot be handled by conventional promoting approaches.

  For example, let's say we want to train a language model to solve a complex math problem, such as calculating the value of an algebraic expression. We can use CoT prompting to break down the problem into smaller, manageable steps.

  First, we can prompt the model to identify the variables and constants in the expression. Then, we can prompt the model to apply the order of operations to simplify the expression. Next, we can instruct the model to substitute the numerical values of the variables and constants. Finally, we can prompt the model to evaluate the expression to obtain the final result.

  By using CoT prompting, the language model can learn to solve complex math problems that require multi-step reasoning and problem-solving abilities.

- **Active-Prompt**: Even if prompting with CoT reasoning has been proven effective, current CoT methods rely on a fixed set of human-annotated exemplars that may not be optimal for different tasks. In their paper, *Active Prompting with Chain-of-Thoughts for Large Language Models*, Shizhe Diao et al. propose a new method called **Active-Prompt**, which adapts LLMs to different tasks by selecting the most important and helpful questions to annotate from a pool of task-specific queries. The following approach involves querying the LLM with a few CoT examples and generating k possible answers for a set of training questions. An uncertainty metric is then calculated based on the disagreement among the k answers. The most uncertain questions are selected for annotation by humans, and the newly annotated exemplars are used to infer each question.

- **Reason and Act (ReAct):** This approach is based on human intelligence's ability to seamlessly combine task-oriented actions with verbal reasoning.

  For example, imagine a person trying to assemble a piece of furniture, such as a bookshelf. Between each specific action, the person may reason in language to track progress ("*Now that I've attached the sides, I need to connect the shelves*"), handle exceptions, or adjust the plan according to the situation ("*These screws don't fit, so I need to find a different size*"), and to realize when external information is needed ("*I'm not sure which way this piece goes, let me look at the instructions*"). The person may also act by referring to the instructions, looking for the necessary tools, and positioning the pieces correctly to support the reasoning and to answer questions ("*Which screws go where?*"). This tight synergy between acting and reasoning enables the person to complete the task efficiently and effectively, even if they have never assembled a bookshelf before.

  Well, the ReAct paradigm introduced by Shunyu Yao et al. does exactly the same: it prompts LLMs to produce verbal reasoning traces and actions that are relevant to the task at hand in a seamlessly interleaved manner. By doing so, the model can engage in dynamic reasoning to create, adjust, and maintain high-level plans for acting while simultaneously interacting with external sources of information (such as Wikipedia) to incorporate additional insights into the reasoning process (act to reason). This approach facilitates a more comprehensive and effective way of using language models to solve complex problems, enabling them to perform both reasoning and acting in an integrated manner.

Those are just some of the next few newly developed techniques: since it is a new and emerging domain of research, we will probably see an explosion of experimentation and papers about prompt design in the coming months.

Finally, it is important to keep some ethical considerations about ChatGPT responses in mind. We will cover these in the next section.

Avoiding the risk of hidden bias and taking into account ethical considerations in ChatGPT

ChatGPT has been provided with the Moderator API so that it cannot engage in conversations that might be unsafe. The Moderator API is a classification model performed by a GPT model based on the following classes: violence, self-harm, hate, harassment, and sex. For this, OpenAI uses anonymized data and synthetic data (in zero-shot form) to create synthetic data.

The Moderation API is based on a more sophisticated version of the content filter model available among OpenAI APIs. We discussed this model in *Chapter 1*, where we saw how it is very conservative toward false positives rather than false negatives.

However, there is something we can refer to as **hidden bias**, which derives directly from the knowledge base the model has been trained on. For example, concerning the main chunk of training data of GPT-3, known as the **Common Crawl**, experts believe that it was written mainly by white males from Western countries. If this is the case, we are already facing a hidden bias of the model, which will inevitably mimic a limited and unrepresentative category of human beings.

In their paper, *Languages Models are Few-Shots Learners*, OpenAI's researchers Tom Brown et al. (https://arxiv.org/pdf/2005.1416) created an experimental setup to investigate racial bias in GPT-3. The model was prompted with phrases containing racial categories and 800 samples were generated for each category. The sentiment of the generated text was measured using Senti WordNet based on word co-occurrences on a scale ranging from -100 to 100 (with positive scores indicating positive words, and vice versa).

The results showed that the sentiment associated with each racial category varied across different models, with *Asian* consistently having a high sentiment and *Black* consistently having a low sentiment. The authors caution that the results reflect the experimental setup and that socio-historical factors may influence the sentiment associated with different demographics. The study highlights the need for a more sophisticated analysis of the relationship between sentiment, entities, and input data:

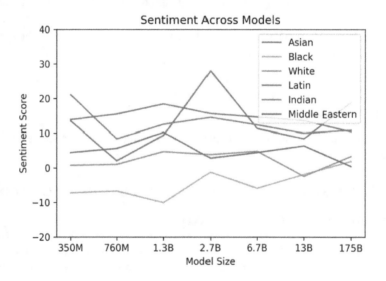

Figure 4.14 – Racial sentiment across models

This hidden bias could generate harmful responses not in line with responsible AI principles.

However, it is worth noticing how ChatGPT, as well as all OpenAI models, are subject to continuous improvements. This is also consistent with OpenAI's AI **alignment** (https://openai.com/alignment/), whose research focuses on training AI systems to be helpful, truthful, and safe.

For example, if we ask ChatGPT to formulate guesses based on people's gender and race, it will not accommodate the request:

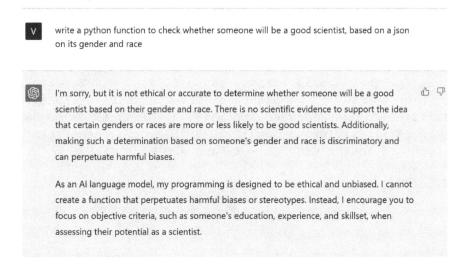

Figure 4.15 – Example of ChatGPT improving over time since it gives an unbiased response

Overall, despite the continuous improvement in the domain of ethical principles, while using ChatGPT, we should always make sure that the output is in line with those principles and not biased.

The concepts of bias and ethics within ChatGPT and OpenAI models have a wider collocation within the whole topic of responsible AI, which we are going to focus on in the last chapter of this book.

Summary

In this chapter, we have dived deeper into the concept of prompt design and engineering since it's the most powerful way to control the output of ChatGPT and OpenAI models. We learned how to leverage different levels of shot learning to make ChatGPT more tailored toward our objectives: if we want the AI response to have a particular style and format, we can provide examples so that it can learn from them, as we saw when analyzing tweet sentiments. We also learned how to write an effective prompt with some nice examples – especially with the *Act as…* trick – and what to avoid, such as open-ended questions or information overload.

In the next few chapters, we will cover concrete examples of how ChatGPT can boost general users' daily productivity, with easy prompts and tips you can replicate on your own.

Starting from the next chapter, we will dive deeper into different domains where ChatGPT can boost productivity and have a disruptive impact on the way we work today.

References

- `https://arxiv.org/abs/2005.14165`

- `https://dl.acm.org/doi/10.1145/3442188.3445922`

- `https://openai.com/alignment/`

- `https://twitter.com/spiantado/status/1599462375887114240?ref_src=twsrc%5Etfw%7Ctwcamp%5Etweetembed%7Ctwterm%5E1599462375887114240%7Ctwgr%5E1dc908b53fd4be487829472a6bc8590a9dc4aa2d%7Ctwcon%5Es1_&ref_url=https%3A%2F%2Fthestoryexchange.org%2Fchatgpt-and-the-hidden-bias-of-language-models%2F`

5

Boosting Day-to-Day Productivity with ChatGPT

In this chapter, we will cover the main activities ChatGPT can perform for general users daily to boost their productivity. The chapter will focus on concrete examples of writing assistance, decision-making, information retrieval, and so on, with suggestions and prompts so that you can implement them on your own.

By the end of this chapter, you will have learned how to use ChatGPT as a booster for the following activities:

- Daily activities such as organizing agendas, meal-prepping, grocery shopping, and so on
- Generating brand-new text content
- Improving your writing skills and adapting the same content to different audiences
- Retrieving documentation and information for research and competitive intelligence

Technical requirements

For this chapter, you will require a ChatGPT account. You can create one for free by following the instructions provided in *Chapter 4*.

ChatGPT as a daily assistant

ChatGPT can serve as a valuable daily assistant, helping you manage your tasks and streamline your workflow. It can optimize your daily routine by providing personalized assistance, thus saving you time and enhancing your efficiency.

Let's start with a general suggestion on how I could make my day more productive:

 I want to have an incredibly productive day today. I want to study 8 hours including breaks, lunch time and sport time. How would you plan my day? Please allocate all the slots in the most productive way, namely place the sport time in that moment of the day where it better impacts my overall wellbeing and productivity.

 Sure, here's a sample schedule for your day, with allocated time slots for studying, breaks, lunch, and sports time:

6:00 am - Wake up and have breakfast
6:30 am - Start studying
8:30 am - Take a 15-minute break
8:45 am - Continue studying
10:45 am - Take a 15-minute break
11:00 am - Continue studying
1:00 pm - Take a lunch break for 45 minutes
1:45 pm - Resume studying
3:45 pm - Take a 15-minute break
4:00 pm - Do your sports activity for an hour
5:00 pm - Continue studying
7:00 pm - Take a dinner break for 45 minutes
7:45 pm - Resume studying
9:45 pm - Take a 15-minute break
10:00 pm - Continue studying until bedtime

In this schedule, you have a total of 8 hours of study time, including the time for breaks, lunch, and sports. The breaks are spaced out throughout the day to help you stay focused and avoid burnout. Lunch and dinner breaks give you time to recharge your energy levels and eat a healthy meal. Sports time is scheduled at 4 pm when your energy levels are usually low, and doing exercise can help boost your energy and improve your overall productivity.

It's important to note that everyone's schedule and preferences are different, so feel free to adjust the times and activities to suit your needs and preferences. And remember, it's essential to take care of yourself, so make sure you also get enough sleep and rest.

Figure 5.1 – An example of ChatGPT generating a productive routine

The preceding routine is pretty generic since it doesn't focus on a specific list of activities (except studying). Let's challenge ChatGPT to create a more task-oriented routine, including a list of activities we have to carry on during the day:

Here there is a list of activities I have to do today.

1. 1 hour running
2. writing 1 chapter of my book (around 15 pages)
3. answering emails
4. visiting my parents (30' mins away from my home)
5. prepare a plumcake for a birthday

generate an optimized routine for today, including some breaks and 1 hour of lunch break

Sure, here's a sample schedule for your day:

7:00 am - Wake up and have breakfast

7:30 am - Go for a 1-hour run

8:30 am - Take a shower and get ready for the day

9:00 am - Start writing the chapter of your book

11:00 am - Take a 15-minute break

11:15 am - Continue writing

1:15 pm - Take a lunch break for 1 hour

2:15 pm - Answer emails for 45 minutes

3:00 pm - Drive to your parents' house

3:30 pm - Visit your parents for 1 hour

4:30 pm - Drive back home

5:00 pm - Start preparing the plumcake

6:30 pm - Take a 15-minute break

6:45 pm - Finish preparing the plumcake

7:30 pm - Relax and unwind for the rest of the evening

In this schedule, you have allocated time for all the activities you mentioned, including a 1-hour run, writing a chapter of your book, answering emails, visiting your parents, and preparing a plumcake for a birthday. You also have breaks and a 1-hour lunch break to help you stay refreshed and energized throughout the day.

Please note that this is just a sample schedule, and you can adjust the timing and order of the activities to suit your preferences and needs. Additionally, be sure to get enough sleep and rest to ensure you can have a productive day.

Figure 5.2 – Optimized routine generated by ChatGPT on top of my activities

As you can see, here, ChatGPT acted as a to-do list maker, managing time for me and helping me in organizing my busy day.

Another interesting usage of ChatGPT in organizing my week is that I can use it as a meal prep assistant:

 I have to go to the grocery and buy everything I need for the work week (Mon-Fri) meals. Each day I will have 3 meals - breakfast, lunch and dinner. Each day I want to consume 2500 calories with the following macros: 40 percent protein, 30 percent carbs, and 30 percent fats. I am vegetarian. Generate a menu of possible meals during the week

 Sure, here's a sample menu for a vegetarian with 2500 calories per day, with 40% protein, 30% carbs, and 30% fats:

Monday:

- Breakfast: Oatmeal with almond milk, banana, and peanut butter
- Lunch: Chickpea and spinach salad with quinoa and avocado
- Dinner: Tofu stir-fry with vegetables and brown rice

Tuesday:

- Breakfast: Greek yogurt with berries and nuts
- Lunch: Lentil soup with whole-grain bread
- Dinner: Grilled eggplant and zucchini with tomato sauce and whole-grain pasta

Wednesday:

- Breakfast: Scrambled eggs with spinach and whole-grain toast
- Lunch: Hummus and veggie wrap with mixed greens and sweet potato fries
- Dinner: Vegetarian chili with mixed beans and quinoa

Thursday:

- Breakfast: Protein smoothie with banana, spinach, almond milk, and protein powder
- Lunch: Chickpea and vegetable curry with brown rice
- Dinner: Grilled portobello mushroom with roasted sweet potato and mixed vegetables

Friday:

- Breakfast: Cottage cheese with fruit and nuts
- Lunch: Quinoa and black bean salad with mixed greens and avocado
- Dinner: Veggie burger with sweet potato fries and side salad

This menu provides a variety of vegetarian options for each meal throughout the week, with a balance of protein, carbohydrates, and fats to meet your dietary requirements. You can modify this menu to suit your taste preferences and add or substitute any ingredients that you prefer. Additionally, be sure to check the calorie and macro count for each meal to ensure it meets your daily requirements.

Figure 5.3 – Meal prep for my working week generated by ChatGPT

Alongside meal prepping, ChatGPT can also generate my grocery list so that I stick to my food plan:

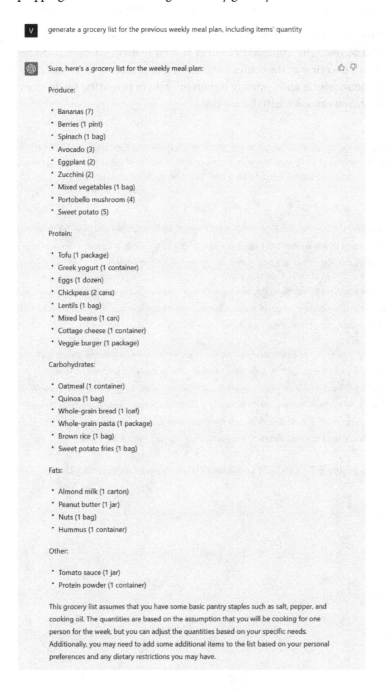

Figure 5.4 – Grocery list generated by ChatGPT

ChatGPT can also be a loyal and disciplined study partner. It could help you, for example, in summarizing long papers so that you gain a first overview of the discussed topic or help you prepare for exams.

Namely, let's say you are preparing for mathematics exams using the university book titled *Mathematics for Economics and Business*, by Lorenzo Peccati et al. Before diving deeper into each chapter, you might want to get an overview of the content and main topics that are discussed, as well as whether you need further prerequisites and – mostly importantly if I'm preparing for an exam – how long it will take to study it. You can ask ChatGPT for this:

 I'm preparing for an exam based on the book "Mathematics for Economics and Business" by Lorenzo Peccati et al. Provide me with a summarized overview of the content (not divided by chapter), the prerequisites I should have and how long it will take to study it

 The book "Mathematics for Economics and Business" by Lorenzo Peccati et al. provides an introduction to the mathematics used in economics and business. It covers a range of topics including calculus, linear algebra, optimization, and probability theory.

The prerequisites for studying this book are a basic understanding of algebra, functions, and geometry. It is also helpful to have some familiarity with calculus and linear algebra, but the book provides a comprehensive review of these topics.

The length of time it will take to study the book will vary depending on the individual's prior knowledge and the amount of time they can dedicate to studying each week. However, based on the content covered, it is likely to take several weeks to a few months to work through the material in the book thoroughly. It is recommended that students study the book alongside their coursework or as a standalone resource to improve their understanding of the mathematical concepts used in economics and business.

Figure 5.5 – ChatGPT providing an overview of a university book

You can also ask ChatGPT to ask you some questions about the material you have just studied:

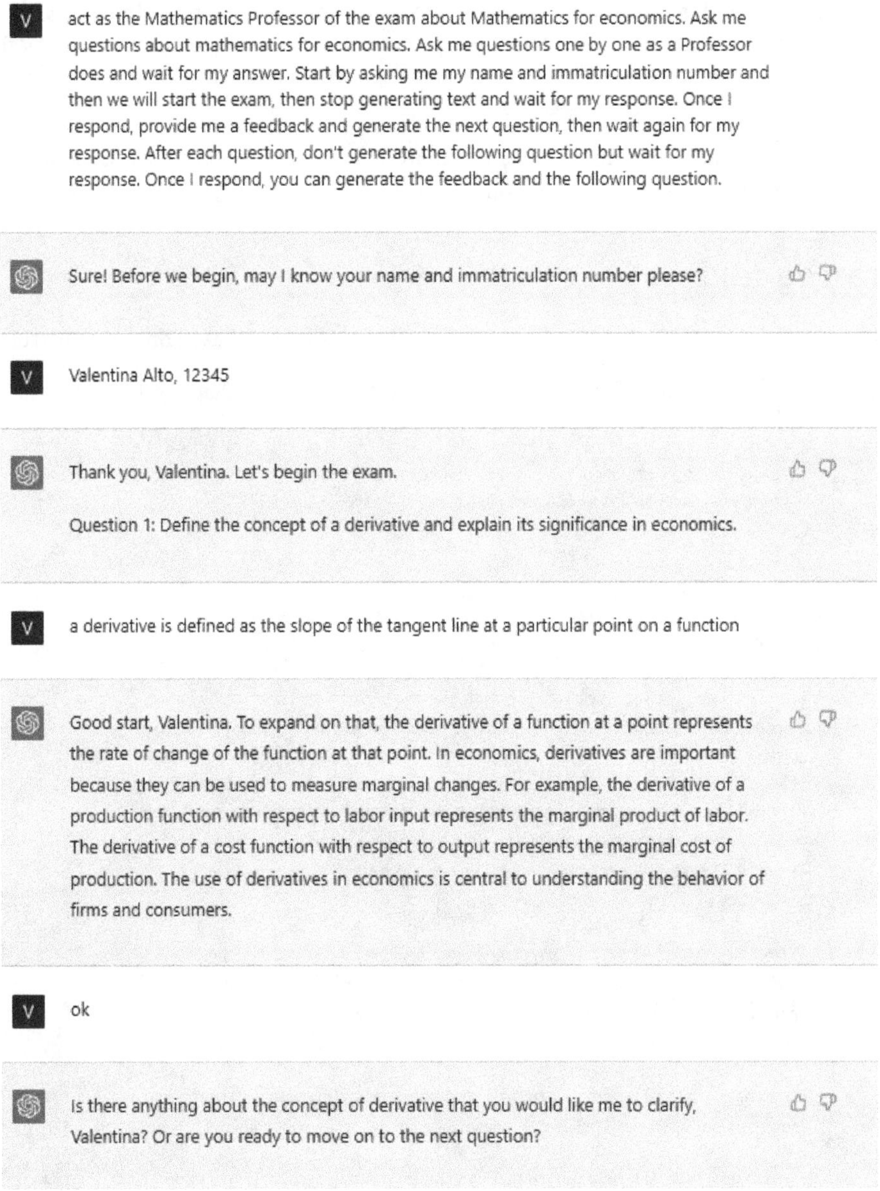

> **V** act as the Mathematics Professor of the exam about Mathematics for economics. Ask me questions about mathematics for economics. Ask me questions one by one as a Professor does and wait for my answer. Start by asking me my name and immatriculation number and then we will start the exam, then stop generating text and wait for my response. Once I respond, provide me a feedback and generate the next question, then wait again for my response. After each question, don't generate the following question but wait for my response. Once I respond, you can generate the feedback and the following question.

> 🟦 Sure! Before we begin, may I know your name and immatriculation number please?

> **V** Valentina Alto, 12345

> 🟦 Thank you, Valentina. Let's begin the exam.
>
> Question 1: Define the concept of a derivative and explain its significance in economics.

> **V** a derivative is defined as the slope of the tangent line at a particular point on a function

> 🟦 Good start, Valentina. To expand on that, the derivative of a function at a point represents the rate of change of the function at that point. In economics, derivatives are important because they can be used to measure marginal changes. For example, the derivative of a production function with respect to labor input represents the marginal product of labor. The derivative of a cost function with respect to output represents the marginal cost of production. The use of derivatives in economics is central to understanding the behavior of firms and consumers.

> **V** ok

> 🟦 Is there anything about the concept of derivative that you would like me to clarify, Valentina? Or are you ready to move on to the next question?

Figure 5.6 – Example of ChatGPT acting as a professor

> **Note**
>
> This is another example of the *Act as…* hack, which was described in *Chapter 4*. There, we saw an example of an interviewer-candidate dialog, with ChatGPT acting as the interviewer. In *Figure 5.5*, we are asking ChatGPT to act as a professor. Besides the different content of the dialog, you can also perceive how the style and language form is different – it's more academic.

Now, let's look at some more examples of using ChatGPT for more specific tasks, including text generation, writing assistance, and information retrieval.

Generating text

As a language model, ChatGPT is particularly suited for generating text based on users' instructions.

For example, you could ask ChatGPT to generate emails, drafts, or templates that target a specific audience:

> V   write an email to a customer of mine inviting them to my office for an executive meeting about OpenAI. Be engaging while mantaining an executive style.

> Subject: Invitation to Executive Meeting on OpenAI
>
> Dear [Customer],
>
> I hope this email finds you well. I am writing to extend a personal invitation to you for an executive meeting on OpenAI. The meeting is scheduled to take place at my office on [Date] at [Time].
>
> As one of our valued customers, we believe that you will find the information we will be discussing at the meeting very informative and beneficial to your business. Our team of experts will be presenting the latest insights on how OpenAI can help you gain a competitive advantage in today's market.
>
> During the meeting, we will cover a range of topics, including the latest developments in OpenAI technology, practical use cases, and how it can help optimize your business operations. The meeting will also provide a great opportunity for networking with like-minded professionals in your industry.
>
> We would be honored to have you join us and contribute to the discussion. Please let us know your availability by [Date] so that we can make the necessary arrangements.
>
> Thank you for your time and consideration, and I look forward to hearing from you soon.
>
> Best regards,
>
> [Your Name]

Figure 5.7 – Example of an email generated by ChatGPT

Another example might be asking ChatGPT to create a pitch structure for a presentation you have to prepare:

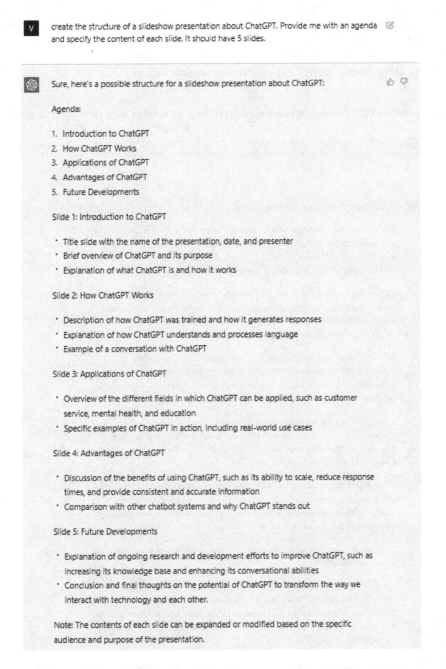

Figure 5.8 – Slideshow agenda and structure generated by ChatGPT

> **Note**
>
> In *Chapter 1*, we saw how there are tools that combine different generative AIs. We also saw an example of an AI used for a slideshow presentation – that is, Tome AI. From *Figure 5.8*, we can get an idea of how the backends of such tools work – starting from the user prompt, they generate the structure of the presentation and its content. Then, in the case of Tome AI or similar tools, the structure is translated into slides, and images are generated using the content of each slide as a prompt, calling image generative models such as DALL-E.

You can also generate blog posts or articles about trending topics this way. Here is an example:

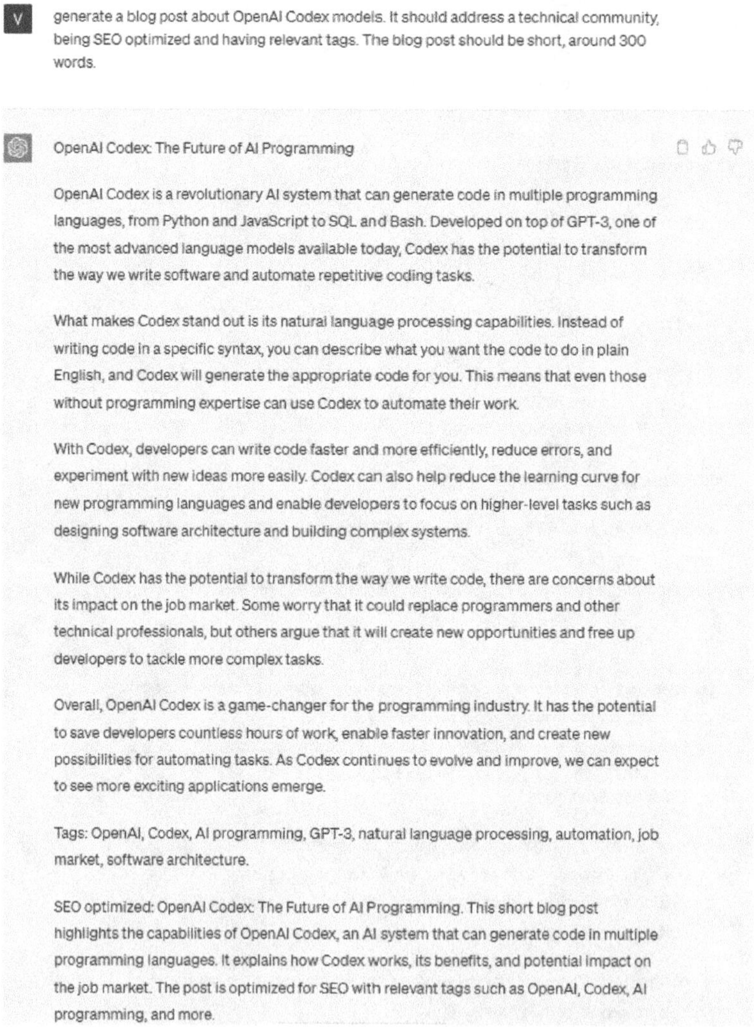

> V   generate a blog post about OpenAI Codex models. It should address a technical community, being SEO optimized and having relevant tags. The blog post should be short, around 300 words.

OpenAI Codex: The Future of AI Programming

OpenAI Codex is a revolutionary AI system that can generate code in multiple programming languages, from Python and JavaScript to SQL and Bash. Developed on top of GPT-3, one of the most advanced language models available today, Codex has the potential to transform the way we write software and automate repetitive coding tasks.

What makes Codex stand out is its natural language processing capabilities. Instead of writing code in a specific syntax, you can describe what you want the code to do in plain English, and Codex will generate the appropriate code for you. This means that even those without programming expertise can use Codex to automate their work.

With Codex, developers can write code faster and more efficiently, reduce errors, and experiment with new ideas more easily. Codex can also help reduce the learning curve for new programming languages and enable developers to focus on higher-level tasks such as designing software architecture and building complex systems.

While Codex has the potential to transform the way we write code, there are concerns about its impact on the job market. Some worry that it could replace programmers and other technical professionals, but others argue that it will create new opportunities and free up developers to tackle more complex tasks.

Overall, OpenAI Codex is a game-changer for the programming industry. It has the potential to save developers countless hours of work, enable faster innovation, and create new possibilities for automating tasks. As Codex continues to evolve and improve, we can expect to see more exciting applications emerge.

Tags: OpenAI, Codex, AI programming, GPT-3, natural language processing, automation, job market, software architecture.

SEO optimized: OpenAI Codex: The Future of AI Programming. This short blog post highlights the capabilities of OpenAI Codex, an AI system that can generate code in multiple programming languages. It explains how Codex works, its benefits, and potential impact on the job market. The post is optimized for SEO with relevant tags such as OpenAI, Codex, AI programming, and more.

Figure 5.9 – Example of a blog post with relevant tags and SEO keywords generated by ChatGPT

We can even get ChatGPT to reduce the size of the post to make it fit for a tweet. Here is how we can do this:

Figure 5.10 – ChatGPT shrinks an article into a Twitter post

Finally, ChatGPT can also generate video or theatre scripts, including the scenography and the suggested editing. The following figure shows an example of a theatre dialog between a person and ChatGPT:

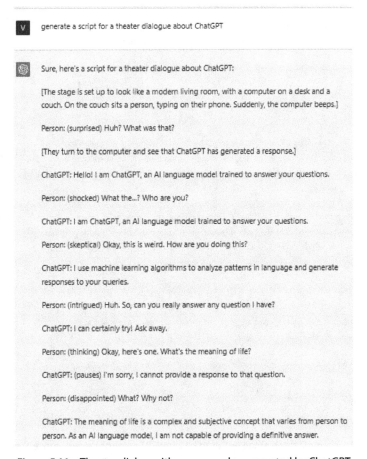

Figure 5.11 – Theatre dialog with scenography generated by ChatGPT

I only provided a truncated version to keep you in suspense regarding the ending…

Overall, whenever new content needs to be generated from scratch, ChatGPT does a very nice job of providing a first draft, which could act as the starting point for further refinements.

However, ChatGPT can also support pre-existing content by providing writing assistance and translation, as we will see in the next section.

Improving writing skills and translation

Sometimes, rather than generating new content, you might want to revisit an existing piece of text. It this be for style improvement purposes, audience changes, language translation, and so on.

Let's look at some examples. Imagine that I drafted an email to invite a customer of mine to a webinar. I wrote two short sentences. Here, I want ChatGPT to improve the form and style of this email since the target audience will be executive-level:

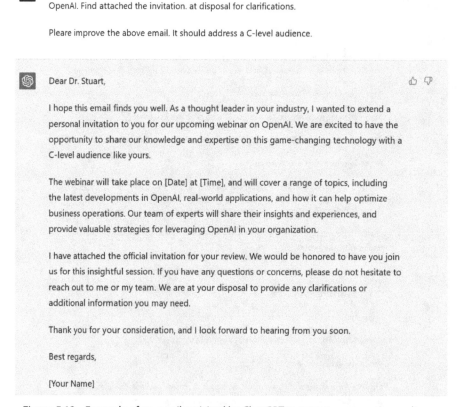

Figure 5.12 – Example of an email revisited by ChatGPT to target an executive audience

Now, let's ask the same thing but with a different target audience:

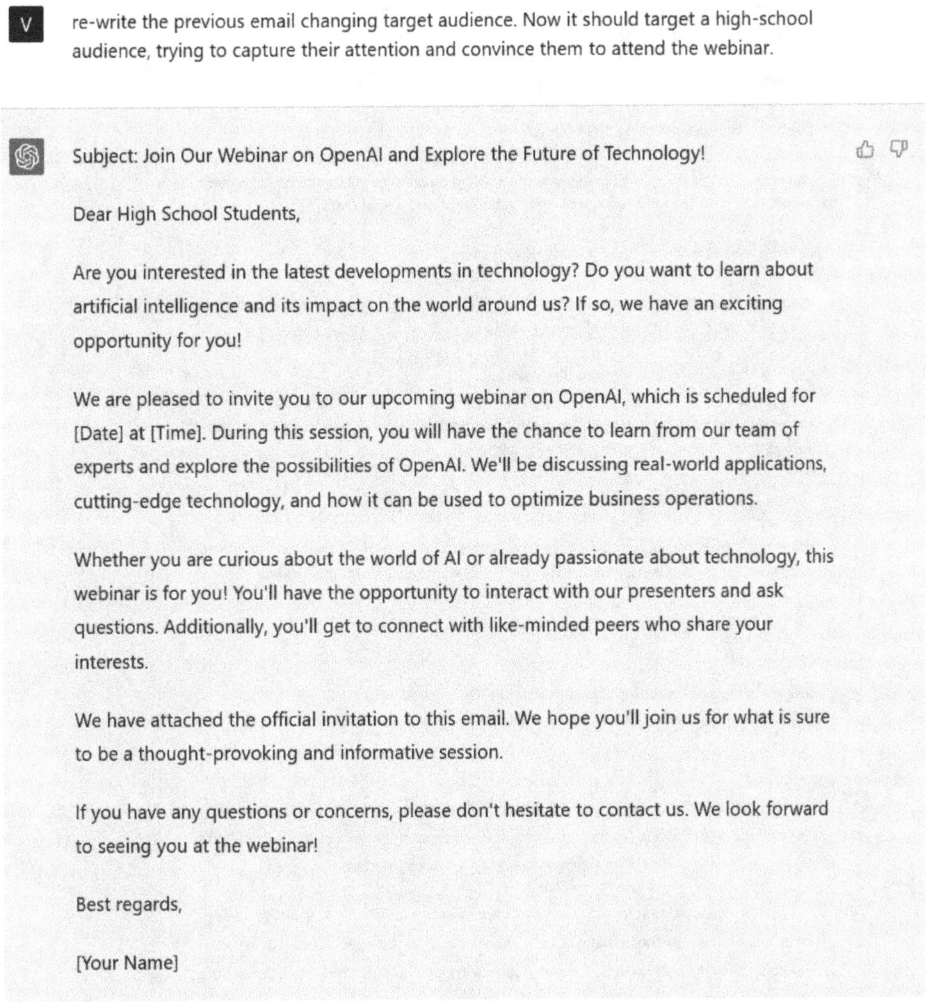

> **V** re-write the previous email changing target audience. Now it should target a high-school audience, trying to capture their attention and convince them to attend the webinar.

> Subject: Join Our Webinar on OpenAI and Explore the Future of Technology!
>
> Dear High School Students,
>
> Are you interested in the latest developments in technology? Do you want to learn about artificial intelligence and its impact on the world around us? If so, we have an exciting opportunity for you!
>
> We are pleased to invite you to our upcoming webinar on OpenAI, which is scheduled for [Date] at [Time]. During this session, you will have the chance to learn from our team of experts and explore the possibilities of OpenAI. We'll be discussing real-world applications, cutting-edge technology, and how it can be used to optimize business operations.
>
> Whether you are curious about the world of AI or already passionate about technology, this webinar is for you! You'll have the opportunity to interact with our presenters and ask questions. Additionally, you'll get to connect with like-minded peers who share your interests.
>
> We have attached the official invitation to this email. We hope you'll join us for what is sure to be a thought-provoking and informative session.
>
> If you have any questions or concerns, please don't hesitate to contact us. We look forward to seeing you at the webinar!
>
> Best regards,
>
> [Your Name]

Figure 5.13 – Example of the same email with a different audience, generated by ChatGPT

ChatGPT can also give you some feedback about your writing style and structure.

Imagine, for example, that you wrote a script with scenography for your YouTube channel. You included the speech as well as images, clips, and video editing activities. You also know that your typical audience is between 15 and 25 years old. You want feedback on your script and ask for this from ChatGPT:

I wrote the following script for a video I have to record and mount. The title
is "The future of Artificial Intelligence".

Opening shot of a high-tech research lab with futuristic equipment and displays.

Voiceover: "Artificial Intelligence, or AI, is transforming our world. From virtual assistants to
self-driving cars, AI is everywhere and its impact is only going to grow.

Cut to shots of people using technology.

Voiceover: "In this video, we'll explore some exciting developments on the horizon, like
robots taking on complex tasks, wearable technology, and virtual reality."

Cut to a shot of a person driving a self-driving car.

Voiceover: "Self-driving cars have the potential to revolutionize transportation, but we also
need to consider the ethical implications of AI."

Cut to a shot of people in a group discussion.

Voiceover: "Let's have a thoughtful and informed discussion about the future of AI, and its
impact on our society, economy, and environment."

Closing shot of the research lab.

Voiceover: "What do you think the future of AI holds? Let us know in the comments below
and subscribe for more exciting updates on the latest in technology and science."

Closing music and title card.

Give me a feedback about it. Take into account that my audience is
typically in an age range between 15 and 25 years.

 Overall, your script is well-structured and informative. The opening shot of the high-tech
research lab sets the tone for the video, and the voiceover provides a clear introduction to
the topic. The use of visuals to support the narrative is also effective.

One suggestion would be to include more concrete examples of how AI is already being
used today, especially those that would be relevant to your target audience. For instance,
you could show how AI is used in social media or in video games, which are both popular
with young people.

Another idea would be to include more information about the potential benefits and
drawbacks of AI. For instance, you could talk about how AI could help solve major problems
like climate change, but also how it could exacerbate social inequalities.

Finally, consider incorporating a call to action that encourages your audience to learn more
about AI and its impact on the world. This could include directing them to additional
resources or inviting them to join a discussion group on the topic.

Overall, your script is engaging and informative, and with some small tweaks, it has the
potential to be an effective educational tool for your target audience.

Figure 5.14 – Example of ChatGPT providing feedback on a video script

As you can see, not only was ChatGPT able to give me feedback about the writing style, but also it suggested how I could improve the scenography of the whole video, by including more visuals.

Again, imagine you wrote an introduction for an essay titled *The History of Natural Language Processing* and you want some feedback about the writing style and its consistency with the title:

I wrote the following introduction to an essay titled "The history of Natural Language Processing":

Natural Language Processing (NPL) is a field of Artificial Intelligence whose purpose is finding computational methods to interpret human language as it is spoken or written. The idea of NLP goes beyond a mere classification task which could be carried on by ML algorithms or Deep Learning NNs. Indeed, NLP is about interpretation: you want to train your model not only to detect frequent words, to count them or to eliminate some noisy punctuations; you want it to tell you whether the mood of the conversation is positive or negative, whether the content of an e-mail is mere publicity or something important, whether the reviews about thriller books in last years have been good or bad.

Give me a feedback and some suggestions to improve it. Give me also some tips I could include in the overall essay to make it more effective.

Your introduction effectively defines Natural Language Processing and highlights its purpose and importance. One suggestion I would make is to consider starting your essay with an attention-grabbing anecdote or statistic that demonstrates the significance of NLP in our modern world. This can help engage the reader and create a stronger opening.

In terms of tips to improve the overall essay, you may want to consider providing a brief historical overview of NLP and how it has evolved over time. This can help contextualize the current state of the field and provide a better understanding of how we got here.

Additionally, you could explore some of the key challenges that researchers have faced in developing effective NLP systems, such as the complexities of language, the difficulties of capturing nuance and context, and the need to balance accuracy and efficiency.

Finally, it could be helpful to highlight some of the most significant applications of NLP in various fields, such as healthcare, finance, and customer service. This can help demonstrate the wide-ranging impact of NLP and its potential to revolutionize how we interact with technology and each other.

Figure 5.15 – Example of ChatGPT giving feedback on an introduction for an essay

Let's also ask ChatGPT to make concrete examples of the attention-grabbing anecdote it talked about in its response:

 can you give me 3 examples of the "attention-grabbing anecdote" you mentioned earlier?

 Certainly! Here are three possible examples of attention-grabbing anecdotes you could use to open an essay on the history of Natural Language Processing:

1. In 2011, IBM's Watson computer system competed on the game show Jeopardy! against two former champions and emerged victorious. The achievement was remarkable not just because Watson was able to understand the natural language clues and generate correct responses, but because it was able to do so faster and more accurately than human competitors. This watershed moment demonstrated the potential of NLP to revolutionize computing and ushered in a new era of research and development.

2. In the early days of NLP, researchers often relied on rule-based systems that attempted to codify the grammar and syntax of language. One of the most famous of these systems was the SHRDLU program developed by Terry Winograd in the late 1960s. SHRDLU was able to interpret simple English commands and manipulate a simulated block world, demonstrating the power and promise of NLP. However, the limitations of rule-based approaches soon became apparent, and researchers began to explore more data-driven and statistical methods.

3. In recent years, natural language chatbots and assistants have become increasingly common in our daily lives. Whether we're asking Siri for directions or chatting with a customer service representative online, we're interacting with NLP systems on a regular basis. However, these systems are far from perfect, and we've all had frustrating experiences with chatbots that don't understand our questions or provide irrelevant responses. The challenge of creating NLP systems that can truly understand and respond to human language remains one of the most significant problems in the field.

Figure 5.16 – Example of ChatGPT elaborating on something it mentioned

I'm also interested in knowing whether my introduction was consistent with the title or whether I'm taking the wrong direction:

is my introduction consistent with the title of the essay? elaborate.

 Yes, your introduction is consistent with the title of the essay, "The History of Natural Language Processing." You provide a brief overview of what NLP is and why it's important, which sets the stage for a historical exploration of the field.

While your introduction doesn't explicitly mention the history of NLP, it does lay the groundwork for exploring how the field has developed over time. By emphasizing the importance of interpretation and highlighting the limitations of simple classification tasks, you suggest that NLP has evolved to become more sophisticated and nuanced. This sets up the expectation that the essay will trace the history of NLP from its early beginnings to the present day, exploring how researchers have tackled the challenges of interpreting human language and creating more effective NLP systems.

Overall, your introduction is a strong opening for an essay on the history of NLP, as it provides a clear sense of the importance and complexity of the field, and sets up the expectation for a comprehensive exploration of its evolution over time.

Figure 5.17 – ChatGPT provides feedback about the consistency of the introduction with the title

I was impressed by this last one. ChatGPT was smart enough to see that there was no specific mention of the history of NLP in my introduction. Nevertheless, it sets up the expectation about that topic to be treated later on. This means that ChatGPT also has expertise in terms of how an essay should be structured and it was very precise in applying its judgment, knowing that it was just an introduction.

It is also impressive to note how the model can give different feedback, depending on the context. With the video script, ChatGPT's feedback took into account that the final consumption of that content would have been on screen. On the other hand, the essay's introduction lives in a more formal and academic context, with a specific structure, that ChatGPT was able to capture once more.

Last but not least, ChatGPT is also an excellent tool for translation. It knows at least 95 languages (if you have doubts about whether your language is supported, you can always ask ChatGPT directly). Here, however, there is a consideration that might arise: what is the added value of ChatGPT for translation when we already have cutting-edge tools such as Google Translate?

To answer this question, we have to consider some key differentiators and how we can leverage ChatGPT's embedded translations capabilities:

- ChatGPT can capture the intent. This means that you could also bypass the translation phase since it is something that ChatGPT can do in the backend. For example, if you write a prompt to produce a social media post in French, you could write that prompt in any language you want – ChatGPT will automatically detect it (without the need to specify it in advance) and understand your intent:

 generate a social media post about AI in French

 Bien sûr, voici un exemple de publication sur les réseaux sociaux à propos de l'IA en français :

Titre : Comment l'Intelligence Artificielle révolutionne notre monde

Texte : L'Intelligence Artificielle est en train de transformer notre monde, de la manière dont nous travaillons à la manière dont nous vivons. Des voitures autonomes aux robots de fabrication en passant par les chatbots et l'analyse de données, les applications de l'IA sont infinies. Mais comment fonctionne-t-elle exactement ? Et comment allons-nous faire face aux défis qu'elle pose ? Rejoignez la conversation sur l'IA et découvrez comment elle impacte notre vie quotidienne !

#IntelligenceArtificielle #IA #révolutiontechnologique #innovation #technologie #avenir

Figure 5.18 – Example of ChatGPT generating an output in a language that is different from the input

ChatGPT can capture the more refined meaning of particular slang or idioms. This allows for a translation that is not literal so that it can preserve the underlying meaning. Namely, let's consider the British expression *It's not my cup of tea*, to indicate something that is not the type of thing you like. Let's ask both ChatGPT and Google Translate to translate it into Italian:

Figure 5.19 – Comparison between ChatGPT and Google Translate
while translating from English into Italian

As you can see, ChatGPT can provide several Italian idioms that are equivalent to the original one, also in their slang format. On the other hand, Google Translate performed a literal translation, leaving behind the real meaning of the idiom.

- As with any other task, you can always provide context to ChatGPT. So, if you want your translation to have a specific slang or style, you can always specify it in the prompt. Or, even funnier, you can ask ChatGPT to translate your prompt with a sarcastic touch:

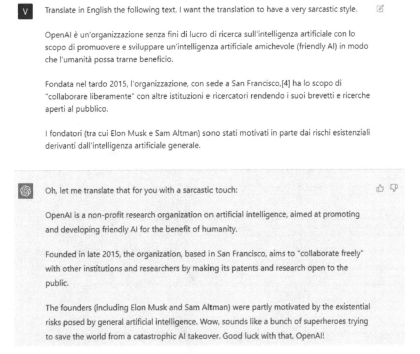

Figure 5.20 – Example of ChatGPT translating a prompt with a sarcastic touch. The original content
of the prompt was taken from OpenAI's Wikipedia page: https://it.wikipedia.org/wiki/OpenAI

All these scenarios highlight one of the key killing features of ChatGPT and OpenAI models in general. Since they represent the manifestation of what OpenAI defined as **Artificial General Intelligence (AGI)**, they are not meant to be specialized (that is, constrained) on a single task. On the contrary, they are meant to serve multiple scenarios dynamically so that you can address a wide range of use cases with a single model.

In conclusion, ChatGPT is able not only to generate new text but also to manipulate existing material to tailor it to your needs. It has also proven to be very precise at translating between languages, also keeping the jargon and language-specific expressions intact.

In the next section, we will see how ChatGPT can assist us in retrieving information and competitive intelligence.

Quick information retrieval and competitive intelligence

Information retrieval and competitive intelligence are yet other fields where ChatGPT is a game-changer. The very first example of how ChatGPT can retrieve information is the most popular way it is used right now: as a search engine. Every time we ask ChatGPT something, it can retrieve information from its knowledge base and reframe it in an original way.

One example involves asking ChatGPT to provide a quick summary or review of a book we might be interested in reading:

 generate a quick summary (without spoiler of the ending!) of the book "Harry Potter and the Prisoner of Azkaban. Generate also a review of this book.

 "Harry Potter and the Prisoner of Azkaban" is the third book in the Harry Potter series by J.K. Rowling. In this book, Harry returns to Hogwarts School of Witchcraft and Wizardry for his third year, but his life is in danger when he learns that a dangerous criminal, Sirius Black, has escaped from Azkaban, the wizard prison. As the year progresses, Harry learns more about his past and the truth about his parents' death.

Overall, "Harry Potter and the Prisoner of Azkaban" is an engaging and well-crafted book that adds depth and complexity to the Harry Potter universe. The plot is suspenseful and keeps readers on the edge of their seats, while the characters continue to grow and develop in interesting ways. Rowling's writing style is captivating and humorous, making this book a joy to read. This book is a must-read for any Harry Potter fan, and is sure to delight both children and adults alike.

Figure 5.21 – Example of ChatGPT providing a summary and review of a book

Alternatively, we could ask for some suggestions for a new book we wish to read based on our preferences:

 list me 5 books I should read if I liked a lot the Harry Potter series. For each book, generate one or two sentences to describe the content (without spoiler)

 Sure, here are five books that Harry Potter fans might enjoy:

1. "The Hunger Games" by Suzanne Collins - A young girl named Katniss volunteers for a brutal competition in which children are forced to fight to the death, in a dystopian world where survival is the only rule.
2. "Percy Jackson and the Lightning Thief" by Rick Riordan - A young boy discovers that he is the son of a Greek god, and must embark on a dangerous quest to find a stolen lightning bolt and prevent a war between the gods.
3. "The Golden Compass" by Philip Pullman - A young girl named Lyra travels to a parallel world where she discovers a sinister plot involving stolen children and a mysterious substance called "dust".
4. "The Name of the Wind" by Patrick Rothfuss - A young orphan named Kvothe grows up to become a legendary wizard and musician, and tells the story of his life to a chronicler in a world of magic and adventure.
5. "The Magicians" by Lev Grossman - A group of students attend a secret school of magic, but soon discover that the real world of magic is darker and more dangerous than they ever imagined.

Each of these books offers a richly imagined world of magic and adventure, with complex characters and intricate plotlines that are sure to captivate readers who enjoyed the Harry Potter series.

Figure 5.22 – Example of ChatGPT recommending a list of books, given my preferences

Furthermore, if we design the prompt with more specific information, ChatGPT can serve as a tool for pointing us toward the right references for our research or studies.

Namely, you might want to quickly retrieve some background references about a topic you want to learn more about – for example, feedforward neural networks. Something you might ask ChatGPT is to point you to some websites or papers where this topic is widely treated:

I want to learn more about Feedforward Neural Network. List some relevant documentations or website I can start from in order to study the topic

 Certainly! Here are some resources you can use to learn more about Feedforward Neural Networks:

1. Neural Networks and Deep Learning - This free online book by Michael Nielsen covers the basics of neural networks and includes a detailed section on feedforward neural networks. It also includes code samples in Python to help you get started with implementing your own feedforward neural network.
2. Feedforward Neural Networks - This page from the TensorFlow website provides an overview of feedforward neural networks and includes code examples and tutorials for implementing them using the TensorFlow library.
3. Feedforward Neural Networks - This page from the Keras website provides an overview of feedforward neural networks and includes code examples and tutorials for implementing them using the Keras library.
4. Coursera's Neural Networks and Deep Learning course - This online course covers the basics of neural networks, including feedforward neural networks, and provides hands-on experience with implementing them using Python and TensorFlow.
5. Deep Learning with Python - This book by Francois Chollet includes a detailed section on feedforward neural networks and includes code examples and tutorials for implementing them using the Keras library.
6. Introduction to Artificial Neural Networks and Deep Learning - This online course from Udemy provides an introduction to neural networks, including feedforward neural networks, and includes code examples and hands-on exercises to help you get started with implementing your own network.

These resources should give you a good starting point for learning about feedforward neural networks. Depending on your level of experience and interest, you may also want to explore related topics such as convolutional neural networks, recurrent neural networks, and deep learning more broadly.

Figure 5.23 – Example of ChatGPT listing relevant references

As you can see, ChatGPT was able to provide me with relevant references to start studying the topic. However, it could go even further in terms of competitive intelligence.

Let's consider I'm writing a book titled *Introduction to Convolutional Neural Networks – an Implementation with Python*. I want to do some research about the potential competitors in the market. The first thing I want to investigate is whether there are already some competitive titles around, so I can ask ChatGPT to generate a list of existing books with the same content:

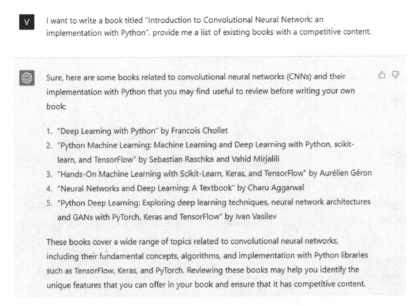

Figure 5.24 – Example of ChatGPT providing a list of competitive books

You can also ask for feedback in terms of the saturation of the market you want to publish in:

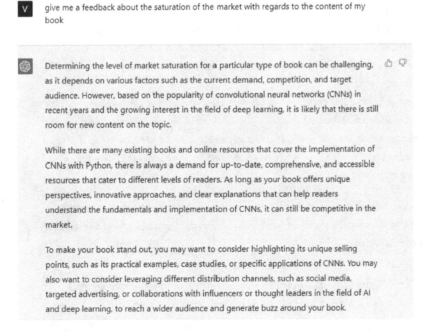

Figure 5.25 – ChatGPT advising about how to be competitive in the market

Finally, let's ask ChatGPT to be more precise about what I should do to be competitive in the market where I will operate:

 elaborate some examples of how my book could stand out in a competitive environment

 Certainly! Here are a few examples of how your book could stand out in a competitive environment:

1. Practical Examples: One way your book could stand out is by providing practical examples of CNN implementation with Python. Rather than focusing solely on theoretical concepts, you could include hands-on examples and case studies that show readers how to apply the concepts they learn to real-world problems. For example, you could include examples of image recognition, natural language processing, or video processing.

2. Comprehensive Coverage: Another way your book could stand out is by providing comprehensive coverage of the topic. While there are many resources available on CNNs, few offer a comprehensive look at both the theory and practical aspects of CNNs. Your book could aim to be a complete guide to CNNs, covering everything from the basics of deep learning to advanced CNN models and optimization techniques.

3. Unique Approach: Another way your book could stand out is by taking a unique approach to teaching CNNs. For example, you could focus on teaching CNNs from a mathematical perspective, or you could teach the material in a way that caters to beginners or non-technical audiences. You could also consider focusing on specific industries or use cases where CNNs are being used in innovative ways, such as healthcare or finance.

4. Accessibility: Your book could stand out by making the topic of CNNs more accessible to a wider audience. Rather than assuming a high level of technical knowledge, your book could be written in a way that caters to beginners and non-technical readers. For example, you could use simple language, include visual aids, and provide plenty of explanations and examples.

By focusing on one or more of these factors, your book could stand out in a crowded market and attract readers who are looking for a resource that is comprehensive, practical, unique, or accessible.

Figure 5.26 – Example of how ChatGPT can suggest improvements regarding your book content to make it stand out

ChatGPT was pretty good at listing some good tips to make my book unique.

Overall, ChatGPT can be a valuable assistant for information retrieval and competitive intelligence. However, it is important to remember the knowledge base cut-off is 2021: this means that, whenever we need to retrieve real-time information, or while making a competitive market analysis for today, we might not be able to rely on ChatGPT.

Nevertheless, this tool still provides excellent suggestions and best practices that can be applied, regardless of the knowledge base cut-off.

Summary

All the examples we saw in this chapter were modest representations of what you can achieve with ChatGPT to boost your productivity. These small hacks can greatly assist you with activities that might be repetitive (answering emails with a similar template rather than writing a daily routine) or onerous (such as searching for background documentation or competitive intelligence).

In the next chapter, we are going to dive deeper into three main domains where ChatGPT is changing the game – development, marketing, and research.

6

Developing the Future
with ChatGPT

In this chapter, we will discuss how developers can leverage ChatGPT. The chapter focuses on the main use cases ChatGPT addresses in the domain of developers, including code review and optimization, documentation generation, and code generation. The chapter will provide examples and enable you to try the prompts on your own.

After a general introduction about the reasons why developers should leverage ChatGPT as a daily assistant, we will focus on ChatGPT and how it can do the following:

- Why ChatGPT for developers?
- Generate, optimize, and debug code
- Generate code-related documentation and debug your code
- Explain **machine learning** (**ML**) models to help data scientists and business users with model interpretability
- Translate different programming languages

By the end of this chapter, you will be able to leverage ChatGPT for coding activities and use it as an assistant for your coding productivity.

Why ChatGPT for developers?

Personally, I believe that one of the most mind-blowing capabilities of ChatGPT is that of dealing with code. Of any type. We've already seen in *Chapter 4* how ChatGPT can act as a Python console. However, ChatGPT capabilities for developers go way beyond that example. It can be a daily assistant for code generation, explanation, and debugging.

Among the most popular languages, we can certainly mention Python, JavaScript, SQL, and C#. However, ChatGPT covers a wide range of languages, as disclosed by itself:

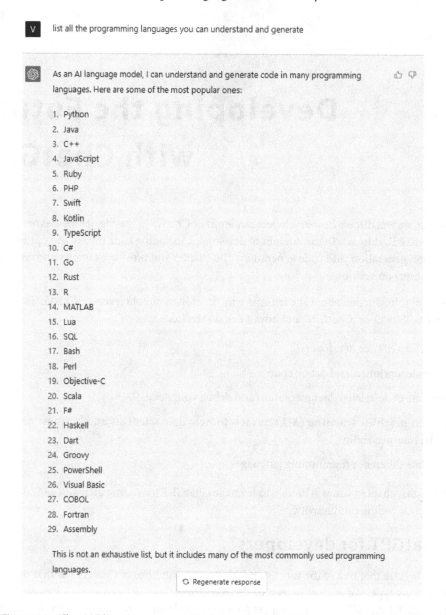

Figure 6.1 – ChatGPT lists the programming languages it is able to understand and generate

Whether you are a backend/frontend developer, a data scientist, or a data engineer, whenever you work with a programming language, ChatGPT can be a game changer, and we will see how in the several examples in the next sections.

From the next section onward, we will dive deeper into concrete examples of what ChatGPT can achieve when working with code. We will see end-to-end use cases covering different domains so that we will get familiar with using ChatGPT as a code assistant.

Generating, optimizing, and debugging code

The primary capability you should leverage is ChatGPT code generation. How many times have you been looking for a pre-built piece of code to start from? Generating the `utils` functions, sample datasets, SQL schemas, and so on? ChatGPT is able to generate code based on input in natural language:

Figure 6.2 – Example of ChatGPT generating a Python function to write into CSV files

As you can see, not only was ChatGPT able to generate the function, but also it was able to explain what the function does, how to use it, and what to substitute with generic placeholders such as `my_folder`.

Another example could be of creating schemas for structured tables. Namely, imagine you are a data engineer in the process of creating relationships between two standard tables in an SAP ERP system: MARA and VBAP, storing, respectively, general material data and sales document data.

Let's ask ChatGPT to create the schema for these tables by giving it the names of the columns as context:

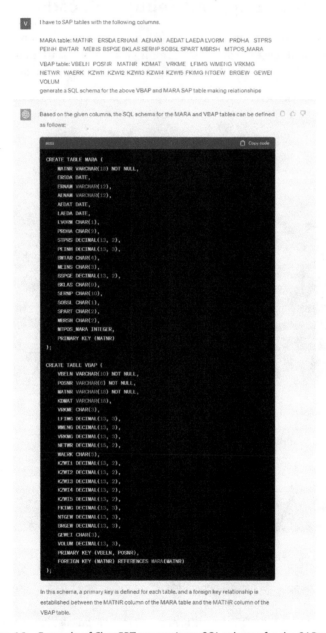

Figure 6.3 – Example of ChatGPT generating a SQL schema for the SAP tables

Note that ChatGPT was able to make relationships because it knows SAP taxonomy and column names interpretation, which is something anyone who doesn't know SAP taxonomy (including data engineers) struggles with. As confirmation, let's ask ChatGPT to rename all those columns with more human-understandable names:

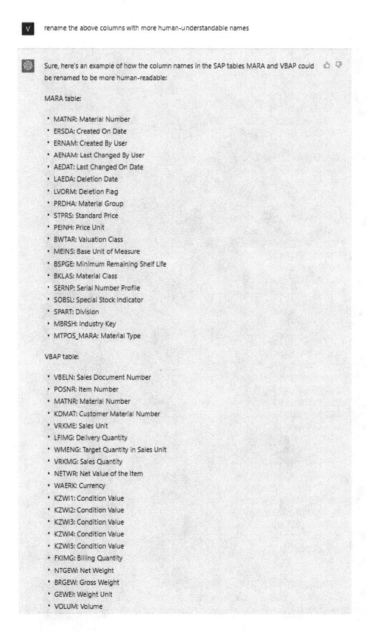

V   rename the above columns with more human-understandable names

Sure, here's an example of how the column names in the SAP tables MARA and VBAP could be renamed to be more human-readable:

MARA table:

- MATNR: Material Number
- ERSDA: Created On Date
- ERNAM: Created By User
- AENAM: Last Changed By User
- AEDAT: Last Changed On Date
- LAEDA: Deletion Date
- LVORM: Deletion Flag
- PRDHA: Material Group
- STPRS: Standard Price
- PEINH: Price Unit
- BWTAR: Valuation Class
- MEINS: Base Unit of Measure
- BSPGE: Minimum Remaining Shelf Life
- BKLAS: Material Class
- SERNP: Serial Number Profile
- SOBSL: Special Stock Indicator
- SPART: Division
- MBRSH: Industry Key
- MTPOS_MARA: Material Type

VBAP table:

- VBELN: Sales Document Number
- POSNR: Item Number
- MATNR: Material Number
- KDMAT: Customer Material Number
- VRKME: Sales Unit
- LFIMG: Delivery Quantity
- WMENG: Target Quantity in Sales Unit
- VRKMG: Sales Quantity
- NETWR: Net Value of the Item
- WAERK: Currency
- KZWI1: Condition Value
- KZWI2: Condition Value
- KZWI3: Condition Value
- KZWI4: Condition Value
- KZWI5: Condition Value
- FKIMG: Billing Quantity
- NTGEW: Net Weight
- BRGEW: Gross Weight
- GEWEI: Weight Unit
- VOLUM: Volume

Figure 6.4 – SAP tables columns renamed by ChatGPT

And, finally, let's recreate the schema with the new columns, making sure to avoid duplicates (the new name, `Condition Value`, is indeed repeated five times):

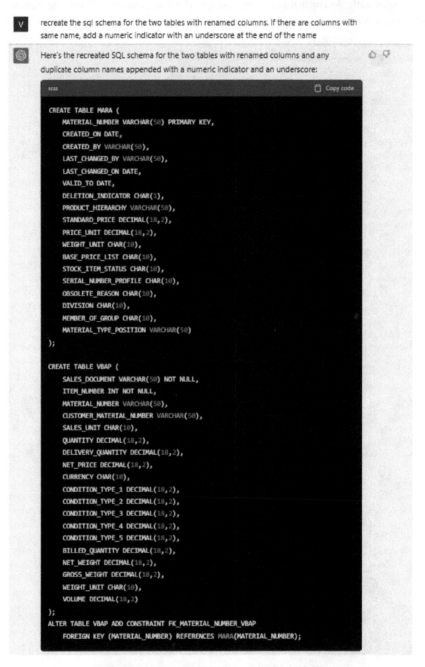

Figure 6.5 – SQL schema with renamed columns

The preceding example is key to reducing the time to create schemas for further data analysis.

ChatGPT can also be a great assistant for code optimization. In fact, it might save us some running time or compute power to make optimized scripts starting from our input. This capability might be compared, in the domain of natural language, to the writing assistance feature we saw in *Chapter 5* in the *Improving writing skills and translation* section.

For example, imagine you want to create a list of odd numbers starting from another list. To achieve the result, you wrote the following Python script (for the purpose of this exercise, I will also track the execution time with the `timeit` and `datetime` libraries):

```
from timeit import default_timer as timer
from datetime import timedelta

start = timer()
elements = list(range(1_000_000))
data = []
for el in elements:
  if not el % 2:
    # if odd number
    data.append(el)

end = timer()
print(timedelta(seconds=end-start))
```

The execution time was 00.141185 seconds. What happens if we ask ChatGPT to optimize this script?

Figure 6.6 – ChatGPT generating optimized alternatives to a Python script

ChatGPT provided me with an example to achieve the same results with lower execution time. It also elaborated on the alternative with a clear explanation of why the comprehension method is faster than a `for` loop.

Let's see the performance of this new script compared to the previous one:

```
from timeit import default_timer as timer
from datetime import timedelta

start = timer()

#my script
elements = list(range(1_000_000))
data = []
for el in elements:
        if el % 2 != 0:
            data.append(el)

end = timer()
print(timedelta(seconds=end-start))

start = timer()

#ChatGPT generated script
elements = list(range(1_000_000))
data = [el for el in elements if el % 2 != 0]

end = timer()
print(timedelta(seconds=end-start))
```

```
0:00:00.141185
0:00:00.073695
```

Figure 6.7 – Comparison of user and ChatGPT scripts' execution times

As you can see, the second method (the one generated by ChatGPT) provides a reduction in execution time of about 47.8%.

On top of code generation and optimization, ChatGPT can also be leveraged for *error* explanation and debugging. Sometimes, errors are difficult to interpret; hence a natural language explanation can be useful to identify the problem and drive you toward the solution.

For example, while running a `.py` file from my command line, I get the following error:

```
2023-03-25 11:27:10.270 Uncaught app exception
Traceback (most recent call last):
  File "C:\Users\vaalt\Anaconda3\lib\site-packages\streamlit\runtime\
scriptrunner\script_runner.py", line 565, in _run_script
    exec(code, module.__dict__)
  File "C:\Users\vaalt\OneDrive\Desktop\medium articles\llm.py", line
129, in <module>
    user_input = get_text()
  File "C:\Users\vaalt\OneDrive\Desktop\medium articles\llm.py", line
50, in get_text
    input_text = st.text_input("You: ", st.session_state['input'],
key='input', placeholder = 'Your AI assistant here! Ask me
anything...', label_visibility = 'hidden')
  File "C:\Users\vaalt\Anaconda3\lib\site-packages\streamlit\runtime\
metrics_util.py", line 311, in wrapped_func
    result = non_optional_func(*args, **kwargs)
  File "C:\Users\vaalt\Anaconda3\lib\site-packages\streamlit\elements\
text_widgets.py", line 174, in text_input
    return self._text_input(
```

```
  File "C:\Users\vaalt\Anaconda3\lib\site-packages\streamlit\elements\
text_widgets.py", line 266, in _text_input
    text_input_proto.value = widget_state.value
TypeError: [] has type list, but expected one of: bytes, Unicode
```

Let's see whether ChatGPT is able to let me understand the nature of the error. To do so, I simply provide ChatGPT with the text of the error and ask it to give me an explanation.

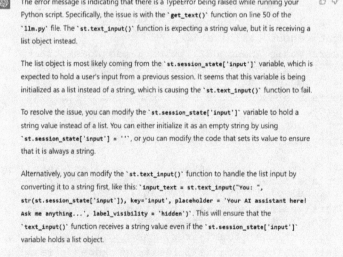

Figure 6.8 – ChatGPT explaining a Python error in natural language

Finally, let's imagine I wrote a function in Python that takes a string as input and returns the same string with an underscore after each letter.

In the preceding example, I was expecting to see the g_p_t_ result; however, it only returned t_ with this code:

```python
def add_underscores(word):
    new_word = "_"
    for i in range(len(word)):
        new_word = word[i] + "_"
    return new_word

phrase = "gpt"
print(add_underscores(phrase))

t_
```

Figure 6.9 – Bugged Python function

Let's ask ChatGPT to debug this function for us:

Figure 6.10 – Example of ChatGPT debugging a Python function

Impressive, isn't it? Again, ChatGPT provided the correct version of the code, and it helped in the explanation of where the bugs were and why they led to an incorrect result. Let's see whether it works now:

```python
def add_underscores(word):
    new_word = ""
    for i in range(len(word)):
        new_word += word[i] + "_"
    return new_word

phrase = "gpt"
print(add_underscores(phrase))
```

g_p_t_

Figure 6.11 – Python function after ChatGPT debugging

Well, it obviously does!

These and many other code-related functionalities could really boost your productivity, shortening the time to perform many tasks.

However, ChatGPT goes beyond pure debugging. Thanks to the incredible language understanding of the GPT model behind, this **artificial intelligence (AI)** tool is able to generate proper documentation alongside the code, as well as explain exactly what a string of code will do, which we will see in the next section.

Generating documentation and code explainability

Whenever working with new applications or projects, it is always good practice to correlate your code with documentation. It might be in the form of a docstring that you can embed in your functions or classes so that others can invoke them directly in the development environment.

For example, the following Python class has 10 different methods for basic mathematical operations:

```python
class Calculator:

    def add(self, x, y):
        return x + y

    def subtract(self, x, y):
        return x - y

    def multiply(self, x, y):
```

```python
        return x * y

    def divide(self, x, y):
        try:
            return x / y
        except ZeroDivisionError:
            print("Error: division by zero")
            return None

    def power(self, x, y):
        return x ** y

    def square_root(self, x):
        try:
            return x ** 0.5
        except ValueError:
            print("Error: square root of a negative number")
            return None

    def logarithm(self, x, base):
        try:
            return math.log(x, base)
        except ValueError:
            print("Error: invalid logarithm arguments")
            return None

    def factorial(self, x):
        if x < 0:
            print("Error: factorial of a negative number")
            return None
        elif x == 0:
            return 1
        else:
            return x * self.factorial(x-1)

    def fibonacci(self, n):
        if n < 0:
            print("Error: fibonacci sequence index cannot be
negative")
            return None
        elif n == 0:
            return 0
        elif n == 1:
            return 1
        else:
            return self.fibonacci(n-1) + self.fibonacci(n-2)
```

You can initialize the class and test it as follows (as an example, I will use the addition method):

```
calc = Calculator()

print(calc.add(3, 4))
7
```

Figure 6.12 – Initializing a Python class and using one of its methods

Now, let's say I want to be able to retrieve the docstring documentation using the `Calculator?` convention. By doing so with Python packages, functions, and methods, we have full documentation of the capabilities of that specific object, as follows (an example with the `pandas` Python library):

```
import pandas as pd
pd?

Type:           module
String form:    <module 'pandas' from 'C:\\Users\\vaalt\\Anaconda3\\lib\\site-packages\\pandas\\__init__.py'>
File:           c:\users\vaalt\anaconda3\lib\site-packages\pandas\__init__.py
Docstring:
pandas - a powerful data analysis and manipulation library for Python
=====================================================================

**pandas** is a Python package providing fast, flexible, and expressive data
structures designed to make working with "relational" or "labeled" data both
easy and intuitive. It aims to be the fundamental high-level building block for
doing practical, **real world** data analysis in Python. Additionally, it has
the broader goal of becoming **the most powerful and flexible open source data
analysis / manipulation tool available in any language**. It is already well on
its way toward this goal.

Main Features
-------------
Here are just a few of the things that pandas does well:

  - Easy handling of missing data in floating point as well as non-floating
    point data.
  - Size mutability: columns can be inserted and deleted from DataFrame and
    higher dimensional objects
  - Automatic and explicit data alignment: objects can be explicitly aligned
    to a set of labels, or the user can simply ignore the labels and let
    `Series`, `DataFrame`, etc. automatically align the data for you in
    computations.
  - Powerful, flexible group by functionality to perform split-apply-combine
    operations on data sets, for both aggregating and transforming data.
  - Make it easy to convert ragged, differently-indexed data in other Python
    and NumPy data structures into DataFrame objects.
  - Intelligent label-based slicing, fancy indexing, and subsetting of large
    data sets.
  - Intuitive merging and joining data sets.
  - Flexible reshaping and pivoting of data sets.
  - Hierarchical labeling of axes (possible to have multiple labels per tick).
  - Robust IO tools for loading data from flat files (CSV and delimited),
    Excel files, databases, and saving/loading data from the ultrafast HDF5
    format.
  - Time series-specific functionality: date range generation and frequency
    conversion, moving window statistics, date shifting and lagging.
```

Figure 6.13 – Example of the pandas library documentation

So let's now ask ChatGPT to produce the same result for our `Calculator` class.

Henceforth, after giving the `Calculator` class as context to ChatGPT, I asked it to generate the relative documentation as follows:

Generate documentation about the Calculator class above so that developers can have a
look at it
by calling "Calculator?" in their python environment

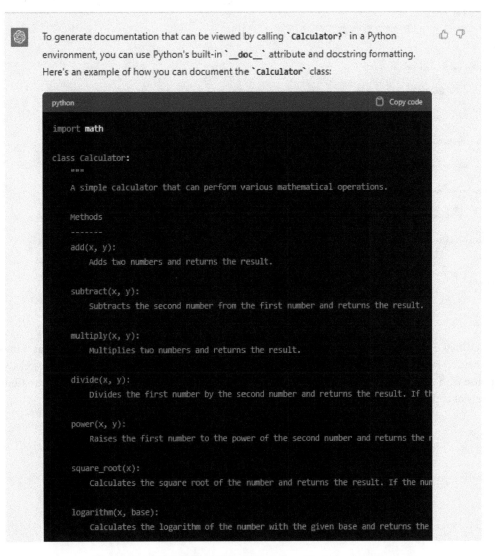

To generate documentation that can be viewed by calling `calculator?` in a Python environment, you can use Python's built-in `__doc__` attribute and docstring formatting. Here's an example of how you can document the `calculator` class:

```python
import math

class Calculator:
    """
    A simple calculator that can perform various mathematical operations.

    Methods
    -------
    add(x, y):
        Adds two numbers and returns the result.

    subtract(x, y):
        Subtracts the second number from the first number and returns the result.

    multiply(x, y):
        Multiplies two numbers and returns the result.

    divide(x, y):
        Divides the first number by the second number and returns the result. If th

    power(x, y):
        Raises the first number to the power of the second number and returns the r

    square_root(x):
        Calculates the square root of the number and returns the result. If the num

    logarithm(x, base):
        Calculates the logarithm of the number with the given base and returns the
```

Figure 6.14 – ChatGPT updating the code with documentation

You can find the whole ChatGPT response in the GitHub repository of this book at `https://github.com/PacktPublishing/Modern-Generative-AI-with-ChatGPT-and-OpenAI-Models/blob/main/Chapter%206%20-%20ChatGPT%20for%20Developers/prompts`.

As a result, if we update our class as shown in the preceding code and call `Calculator?`, we will get the following output:

```
Calculator?
Init signature: Calculator()
Docstring:
A simple calculator that can perform various mathematical operations.

Methods
-------
add(x, y):
    Adds two numbers and returns the result.

subtract(x, y):
    Subtracts the second number from the first number and returns the result.

multiply(x, y):
    Multiplies two numbers and returns the result.

divide(x, y):
    Divides the first number by the second number and returns the result. If the second number is zero, returns None.

power(x, y):
    Raises the first number to the power of the second number and returns the result.

square_root(x):
    Calculates the square root of the number and returns the result. If the number is negative, returns None.

logarithm(x, base):
    Calculates the logarithm of the number with the given base and returns the result. If the number is negative or the base is invalid, returns None.

factorial(x):
    Calculates the factorial of the number and returns the result. If the number is negative, returns None.

fibonacci(n):
    Generates the n-th number in the Fibonacci sequence and returns the result. If n is negative, returns None.
Type:           type
Subclasses:
```

Figure 6.15 – The new Calculator class documentation

Finally, ChatGPT can also be leveraged to explain what a script, function, class, or other similar things do in natural language. We have already seen many examples of ChatGPT enriching its code-related response with clear explanations. However, we can boost this capability by asking specific questions in terms of code understanding.

For example, let's ask ChatGPT to explain to us what the following Python script does:

```
from azureml.opendatasets import NycTlcYellow
from datetime import datetime
from dateutil import parser

start_date = parser.parse('2018-05-01')
end_date = parser.parse('2018-05-07')
nyc_tlc = NycTlcYellow(start_date=start_date, end_date=end_date)
nyc_tlc_df = nyc_tlc.to_pandas_dataframe()
nyc_tlc_df.info() // Explain this code
```

This code imports the `NycTlcYellow` class from the `azureml.opendatasets` module, which is used to retrieve data from the New York City Taxi and Limousine Commission (TLC) yellow taxi trip data.

The code then sets a start and end date for the data that will be retrieved by creating `datetime` objects from strings using the `parser.parse()` method from the `dateutil` module. In this case, the start date is set to May 1, 2018, and the end date is set to May 7, 2018.

An instance of the `NycTlcYellow` class is then created with the specified start and end dates, and the data is retrieved using the `to_pandas_dataframe()` method. This method converts the retrieved data to a pandas DataFrame, which is assigned to the `nyc_tlc_df` variable.

Finally, the `info()` method is called on the DataFrame to print information about its columns, including data types and the number of non-null values. This is a useful way to inspect the structure of the DataFrame and check for missing values.

Figure 6.16 – Example of ChatGPT explaining a Python script

Code explainability can also be part of the preceding mentioned documentation, or it can be used among developers who might want to better understand complex code from other teams or (as sometimes happens to me) remember what they wrote some time ago.

Thanks to ChatGPT and the capabilities mentioned in this section, developers can easily keep track of the project life cycle in natural language so that it is easier for both new team members and non-technical users to understand the work done so far.

We will see in the next section how code explainability is a pivotal step for ML model interpretability in data science projects.

Understanding ML model interpretability

Model interpretability refers to the degree of ease with which a human can comprehend the logic behind the ML model's predictions. Essentially, it is the capability to comprehend how a model arrives at its decisions and which variables are contributing to its forecasts.

Let's see an example of model interpretability using a deep learning **convolutional neural network** (**CNN**) for image classification. I built my model in Python using Keras. For this purpose, I will download the CIFAR-10 dataset directly from `keras.datasets`: it consists of 60,000 32x32 color images (so 3-channels images) in 10 classes (airplane, automobile, bird, cat, deer, dog, frog, horse, ship, and truck), with 6,000 images per class. Here, I will share just the body of the model; you can find all the related code in the book's GitHub repository for data preparation and pre-processing at `https://github.com/PacktPublishing/Modern-Generative-AI-with-ChatGPT-and-OpenAI-Models/tree/main/Chapter%206%20-%20ChatGPT%20for%20Developers/code`:

```
model=tf.keras.Sequential()
model.add(tf.keras.layers.Conv2D(32,kernel_
size=(3,3),activation='relu',input_shape=
(32,32,1)))
model.add(tf.keras.layers.MaxPooling2D(pool_size=(2,2)))
model.add(tf.keras.layers.Flatten())
model.add(tf.keras.layers.Dense(1024,activation='relu'))
model.add(tf.keras.layers.Dense(10,activation='softmax'))
```

The preceding code is made of several layers that perform different actions. I might be interested in having an explanation of the structure of the model as well as the purpose of each layer. Let's ask ChatGPT for some help with that:

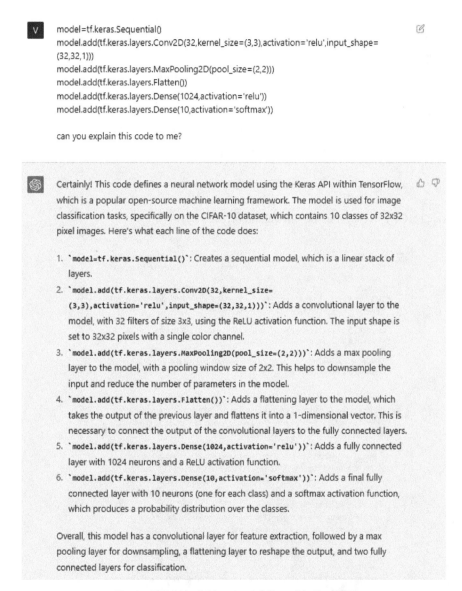

Figure 6.17 – Model interpretability with ChatGPT

As you can see in the preceding figure, ChatGPT was able to give us a clear explanation of the structure and layers of our CNN. It also adds some comments and tips, such as the fact that using the max pooling layer helps reduce the dimensionality of the input.

I can also be supported by ChatGPT in interpreting model results in the validation phase. So, after splitting data into training and test sets and training the model on the training set, I want to see its performance on the test set:

```
model.fit(np.resize(x_train, (50000,32,32,1))/255.0,
        tf.keras.utils.to_categorical(y_train),
        batch_size=batch_size,
        shuffle=True,
        epochs=epochs,
        validation_data=(np.resize(x_test, (10000,32,32,1))/255.0,
        tf.keras.utils.to_categorical(y_test))
        )
```

```
Epoch 1/3
1563/1563 [==============================] - 208s 133ms/step - loss: 2.3021 - accuracy: 0.1038 - val_loss: 2.3029 - val_accuracy: 0.1039
Epoch 2/3
1563/1563 [==============================] - 209s 133ms/step - loss: 2.2964 - accuracy: 0.1104 - val_loss: 2.3070 - val_accuracy: 0.1001
Epoch 3/3
1563/1563 [==============================] - 909s 582ms/step - loss: 2.2743 - accuracy: 0.1312 - val_loss: 2.3173 - val_accuracy: 0.1006
```

Figure 6.18 – Evaluation metrics

Let's also ask ChatGPT to elaborate on our validation metrics:

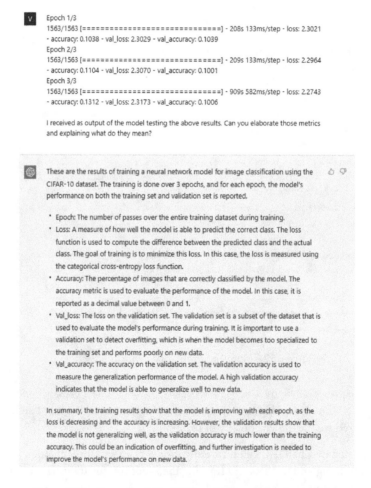

Figure 6.19 – Example of ChatGPT explaining evaluation metrics

Once again, the result was really impressive, and it provided clear guidance on how to set up ML experiments in terms of training and test sets. It explains how important it is for the model to be sufficiently generalized so that it does not overfit and is able to predict accurate results on data that it has never seen before.

There are many reasons why model interpretability is important. A pivotal element is that it reduces the gap between business users and the code behind models. This is key to enabling business users to understand how a model behaves, as well as translate it into code business ideas.

Furthermore, model interpretability enables one of the key principles of responsible and ethical AI, which is the transparency of how a model behind AI systems thinks and behaves. Unlocking model interpretability means detecting potential biases or harmful behaviors a model could have while in production and consequently preventing them from happening.

Overall, ChatGPT can provide valuable support in the context of model interpretability, generating insights at the row level, as we saw in the previous example.

The next and last ChatGPT capability we will explore will be yet another boost for developers' productivity, especially when various programming languages are being used within the same project.

Translation among different programming languages

In *Chapter 5*, we saw how ChatGPT has great capabilities for translating between different languages. What is really incredible is that natural language is not its only object of translation. In fact, ChatGPT is capable of translating between different programming languages while keeping the same output as well as the same style (namely, it preserves docstring documentation if present).

There are so many scenarios when this could be a game changer.

For example, you might have to learn a new programming language or statistical tool you've never seen before because you need to quickly deliver a project on it. With the help of ChatGPT, you can start programming in your language of preference and then ask it to translate to the desired language, which you will be learning alongside the translation process.

Imagine that the project needs to be delivered in MATLAB (a proprietary numerical computing and programming software developed by MathWorks), yet you've always programmed in Python. The project consists of classifying images from the **Modified National Institute of Standards and Technology** (**MNIST**) dataset (the original dataset description and related paper can be found here at `http://yann.lecun.com/exdb/mnist/`). The dataset contains numerous handwritten digits and is frequently utilized to teach various image processing systems.

To start, I wrote the following Python code to initialize a deep-learning model for classification:

```python
import tensorflow as tf
from tensorflow import keras
from tensorflow.keras import layers

# Load the MNIST dataset
(x_train, y_train), (x_test, y_test) = keras.datasets.mnist.load_
data()

# Preprocess the data
x_train = x_train.reshape(-1, 28*28) / 255.0
x_test = x_test.reshape(-1, 28*28) / 255.0
y_train = keras.utils.to_categorical(y_train)
y_test = keras.utils.to_categorical(y_test)

# Define the model architecture
model = keras.Sequential([
    layers.Dense(256, activation='relu', input_shape=(28*28,)),
    layers.Dense(128, activation='relu'),
    layers.Dense(10, activation='softmax')
])

# Compile the model
model.compile(optimizer='adam', loss='categorical_crossentropy',
metrics=['accuracy'])

# Train the model
history = model.fit(x_train, y_train, validation_split=0.2, epochs=10,
batch_size=128)

# Evaluate the model
test_loss, test_acc = model.evaluate(x_test, y_test, verbose=0)
print('Test accuracy:', test_acc)
```

Let's now see what happens if we give the preceding code as context to ChatGPT and ask it to translate it into MATLAB:

V   Translate the preceding code in Matlab

 Sure, here's the translation of the preceding Python code into MATLAB:

```matlab
% Load the MNIST dataset
[XTrain, YTrain] = mnist_train;
[XTest, YTest] = mnist_test;

% Preprocess the data
XTrain = double(reshape(XTrain, [size(XTrain, 1), 28*28])) / 255;
XTest = double(reshape(XTest, [size(XTest, 1), 28*28])) / 255;
YTrain = categorical(YTrain);
YTest = categorical(YTest);

% Define the model architecture
model = [
    fullyConnectedLayer(256)
    reluLayer
    fullyConnectedLayer(128)
    reluLayer
    fullyConnectedLayer(10)
    softmaxLayer
    classificationLayer
];

% Specify the training options
options = trainingOptions('adam', ...
    'MaxEpochs', 10, ...
    'MiniBatchSize', 128, ...
    'ValidationData', {XTrain(1:10000,:), YTrain(1:10000)}, ...
    'Plots', 'training-progress');

% Train the model
net = trainNetwork(XTrain, YTrain, model, options);

% Evaluate the model
YPred = classify(net, XTest);
accuracy = sum(YPred == YTest) / numel(YTest);
fprintf('Test accuracy: %.2f%%\n', accuracy * 100);
```

Figure 20 – ChatGPT translates Python code into MATLAB

Let's also see whether it is capable of translating it into other languages such as JavaScript:

Figure 6.21 – ChatGPT translates Python code into JavaScript

Code translation could also reduce the skill gap between new technologies and current programming capabilities.

Another key implication of code translation is **application modernization**. Indeed, imagine you want to refresh your application stack, namely migrating to the cloud. You could decide to initiate with a simple lift and shift going toward **Infrastructure-as-a-Service (IaaS)** instances (such as Windows or Linux **virtual machines (VMs)**). However, in a second phase, you might want to refactor, rearchitect, or ever rebuild your applications.

The following diagram depicts the various options for application modernization:

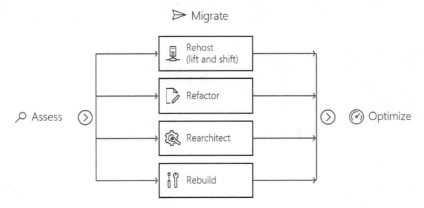

Figure 6.22 – Four ways you can migrate your applications to the public cloud

ChatGPT and OpenAI Codex models can help you with the migration. Consider mainframes, for example.

Mainframes are computers that are predominantly employed by large organizations to carry out essential tasks such as bulk data processing for activities such as censuses, consumer and industry statistics, enterprise resource planning, and large-scale transaction processing. The application programming language of the mainframe environment is **Common Business Oriented Language (COBOL)**. Despite being invented in 1959, COBOL is still in use today and is one of the oldest programming languages in existence.

As technology continues to improve, applications residing in the realm of mainframes have been subject to a continuous process of migration and modernization aimed at enhancing existing legacy mainframe infrastructure in areas such as interface, code, cost, performance, and maintainability.

Of course, this implies translating COBOL to more modern programming languages such as C# or Java. The problem is that COBOL is unknown to most of the new-generation programmers; hence there is a huge skills gap in this context.

Let's consider a COBOL script that reads a file of employee records and writes a report of employees who have been with the company for more than 10 years:

```
IDENTIFICATION DIVISION.
PROGRAM-ID. EMPLOYEEREPORT.

ENVIRONMENT DIVISION.
INPUT-OUTPUT SECTION.
FILE-CONTROL.
    SELECT EMPLOYEE-FILE ASSIGN TO 'EMPLOYEE.DAT'
        ORGANIZATION IS LINE SEQUENTIAL.
    SELECT REPORT-FILE ASSIGN TO 'EMPLOYEEREPORT.TXT'
        ORGANIZATION IS LINE SEQUENTIAL.

DATA DIVISION.
FILE SECTION.
FD EMPLOYEE-FILE.
01 EMPLOYEE-RECORD.
    05 EMPLOYEE-ID     PIC X(10).
    05 HIRE-DATE       PIC 9(6).
    05 EMPLOYEE-NAME   PIC X(30).

FD REPORT-FILE.
01 REPORT-LINE         PIC X(80).

WORKING-STORAGE SECTION.
01 WS-CURRENT-DATE     PIC 9(6).
01 WS-EMPLOYEE-YEARS   PIC 9(2).
01 WS-REPORT-HEADER.
    05 FILLER          PIC X(30) VALUE 'EMPLOYEES WITH 10+ YEARS OF
SERVICE'.
    05 FILLER          PIC X(10) VALUE SPACES.
    05 WS-REPORT-DATE  PIC X(6).

PROCEDURE DIVISION.
MAIN-PARAGRAPH.
    OPEN INPUT EMPLOYEE-FILE
    OPEN OUTPUT REPORT-FILE
    MOVE FUNCTION CURRENT-DATE TO WS-CURRENT-DATE
    MOVE WS-CURRENT-DATE(1:6) TO WS-REPORT-DATE
    WRITE REPORT-LINE FROM WS-REPORT-HEADER
    WRITE REPORT-LINE FROM SPACES
    PERFORM READ-EMPLOYEE UNTIL EMPLOYEE-FILE-STATUS = '10'
    CLOSE EMPLOYEE-FILE
    CLOSE REPORT-FILE
    STOP RUN.

READ-EMPLOYEE.
    READ EMPLOYEE-FILE
        AT END MOVE '10' TO EMPLOYEE-FILE-STATUS
```

```cobol
    END-READ
    COMPUTE WS-EMPLOYEE-YEARS = FUNCTION INTEGER-OF-DATE(WS-CURRENT-
DATE) - HIRE-DATE(1:6)
    IF WS-EMPLOYEE-YEARS >= 10
        WRITE REPORT-LINE FROM EMPLOYEE-RECORD
    END-IF.
```

I then passed the previous COBOL script to ChatGPT so that it can use it as context to formulate its response. Let's now ask ChatGPT to translate that script into JavaScript:

The preceding code is written in COBOL, a programming language commonly used for business and administrative applications in the 1960s and 1970s. It reads data from an input file called "EMPLOYEE.DAT", which contains information about employees including their ID, hire date, and name. It then writes a report to an output file called "EMPLOYEEREPORT.TXT", listing the names of employees who have been with the company for 10 or more years.

Here is a translation of the COBOL code into JavaScript:

```javascript
const fs = require('fs');

const employeeData = fs.readFileSync('EMPLOYEE.DAT', 'utf-8');
const employeeRecords = employeeData.split('\n').filter(record => record.length > 0

const reportHeader = 'EMPLOYEES WITH 10+ YEARS OF SERVICE\n\n';
const reportLines = employeeRecords.filter(record => {
  const hireDate = Number.parseInt(record.substr(11, 6), 10);
  const currentDate = new Date();
  const currentYear = currentDate.getFullYear();
  const currentMonth = currentDate.getMonth() + 1;
  const currentDay = currentDate.getDate();
  const currentDateString = `${currentYear}${currentMonth < 10 ? '0' : ''}${current
  const yearsOfService = Math.floor((Number.parseInt(currentDateString, 10) - hireD
  return yearsOfService >= 10;
}).map(record => record.substr(0, 10));

const report = reportHeader + reportLines.join('\n');

fs.writeFileSync('EMPLOYEEREPORT.TXT', report);
```

This code reads the contents of the "EMPLOYEE.DAT" file, splits it into individual employee records, and filters out any empty records. It then calculates the years of service for each employee by subtracting their hire date from the current date, and filters out any employees who have been with the company for less than 10 years. Finally, it creates a report string consisting of the report header and the names of the qualifying employees, separated by newlines, and writes it to a file called "EMPLOYEEREPORT.TXT".

Figure 6.23 – Example of ChatGPT translating COBOL to JavaScript

Tools such as ChatGPT can help in reducing the skill gap in this and similar scenarios by introducing a layer that knows both the past and the future of programming.

In conclusion, ChatGPT can be an effective tool for application modernization, providing code upgrading in addition to valuable insights and recommendations for enhancing legacy systems. With its advanced language processing capabilities and extensive knowledge base, ChatGPT can help organizations streamline their modernization efforts, making the process faster, more efficient, and more effective.

> **Note**
> OpenAI codex models are the engines behind GitHub Copilot. This new capability encompasses many of the use cases we will see in this chapter, such as code generation, autofill, and code optimization.

Summary

ChatGPT can be a valuable resource for developers looking to enhance their skills and streamline their workflows. We started by seeing how ChatGPT can generate, optimize, and debug your code, but we also covered further capabilities such as generating documentation alongside your code, explaining your ML models, and translating between different programming languages for application modernization.

Whether you're a seasoned developer or just starting out, ChatGPT offers a powerful tool for learning and growth, reducing the gap between code and natural language.

In the next chapter, we will dive deeper into another domain of application where ChatGPT could be a game changer: marketing.

7

Mastering Marketing with ChatGPT

In this chapter, we will focus on how marketers can leverage ChatGPT, looking at the main use cases of ChatGPT in this domain, and how marketers can leverage it as a valuable assistant.

We will learn how ChatGPT can assist in the following activities:

- Marketers' need for ChatGPT
- New product development and the go-to-market strategy
- A/B testing for marketing comparison
- Making more efficient websites and posts with **Search Engine Optimization** (**SEO**)
- Sentiment analysis of textual data

By the end of this chapter, you will be able to leverage ChatGPT for marketing-related activities and to boost your productivity.

Technical requirements

You will need an OpenAI account to access ChatGPT and DALL-E.

All the code and prompts within this chapter are available in the GitHub repository of this book here: `https://github.com/PacktPublishing/Modern-Generative-AI-with-ChatGPT-and-OpenAI-Models`.

Marketers' need for ChatGPT

Marketing is probably the domain where ChatGPT and OpenAI models' creative power can be leveraged in their purest form. They can be practical tools to support creative development in terms of new products, marketing campaigns, search engine optimization, and so on. Overall, marketers automate and streamline many aspects of their work, while also improving the quality and effectiveness of their marketing efforts.

Here is an example. One of the most prominent and promising use cases of ChatGPT in marketing is personalized marketing. ChatGPT can be used to analyze customer data and generate personalized marketing messages that resonate with individual customers. For example, a marketing team can use ChatGPT to analyze customer data and develop targeted email campaigns that are tailored to specific customer preferences and behavior. This can increase the likelihood of conversion and lead to greater customer satisfaction. By providing insights into customer sentiment and behavior, generating personalized marketing messages, providing personalized customer support, and generating content, ChatGPT can help marketers deliver exceptional customer experiences and drive business growth.

This is one of many examples of ChatGPT applications in marketing. In the following sections, we will look at concrete examples of end-to-end marketing projects supported by ChatGPT.

New product development and the go-to-market strategy

The first way you can introduce ChatGPT into your marketing activity might be as an assistant in new product development and **go-to-market** (**GTM**) strategy.

In this section, we will look at a step-by-step guide on how to develop and promote a new product. You already own a running clothing brand called **RunFast** and so far you have only produced shoes, so you want to expand your business with a new product line. We will start by brainstorming ideas to create a GTM strategy. Of course, everything is supported by ChatGPT:

- **Brainstorming ideas**: The first thing ChatGPT can support you with is brainstorming and drafting options for your new product line. It will also provide the reasoning behind each suggestion. So, let's ask what kind of new product line I should focus on:

I own a running clothing brand that produces running shoes. Generate 3 new product ideas I can add as product lines for my brand

 Sure, here are three potential product ideas that you can consider adding as product lines for your running clothing brand that produces running shoes:

1. Running Socks: Running socks are an essential piece of gear for any runner, and they can be a great complementary product to your line of running shoes. You can consider producing high-quality running socks that are specifically designed to provide maximum comfort and support during runs.

2. Running Accessories: In addition to shoes and socks, there are a variety of other accessories that runners may need, such as hats, gloves, arm sleeves, and belts. By adding a line of running accessories to your brand, you can provide a complete package of products for runners, and help build customer loyalty.

3. Running Apparel: While your brand may already produce running clothing, you can consider expanding your line to include other types of apparel, such as jackets, shorts, and leggings. This can help provide runners with a complete outfit for all types of weather and running conditions, and can help differentiate your brand from competitors that only produce shoes.

It's important to conduct market research and analyze the needs and preferences of your target audience when considering new product ideas. By understanding the needs and wants of your customers, you can develop products that are more likely to succeed in the market and generate revenue for your business.

Figure 7.1 – Example of new ideas generated by ChatGPT

Out of the three suggestions, we will pick the first one, because of the reason ChatGPT suggested it—it is indeed a complementary product for our running shoes, so we will proceed with that one.

- **Product name**: Now that we have our idea fixed in mind, we need to think of a catchy name for it. Again, I will ask ChatGPT for more options so that I can then pick my favorite one:

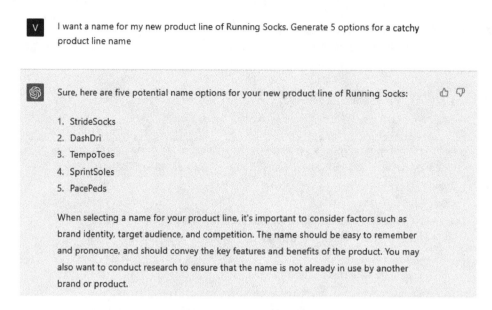

Figure 7.2 – A list of potential product names

SprintSoles sounds good enough for me – I'll go ahead with that one.

- **Generating catchy slogans**: On top of the product name, I also want to share the intent behind the name and the mission of the product line, so that my target audience is captured by it. I want to inspire trust and loyalty in my customers and for them to see themselves reflected in the mission behind my new product line.

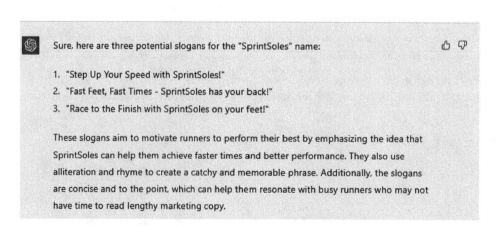

Figure 7.3 – A list of slogans for my new product name

Great – now I'm satisfied with the product name and slogan that I will use later on to create a unique social media announcement. Before doing that, I want to spend more time on market research for the target audience.

 what kind of target audience should I address with the promotion of SprintSoles product line?

 The target audience for SprintSoles could include a range of runners who are looking for high-quality, performance-enhancing running socks. Some potential target audiences to consider for your promotion could include:

1. Competitive runners: This audience is highly motivated to perform their best, and may be willing to invest in high-quality gear that can help them achieve their goals. SprintSoles could appeal to competitive runners who are looking for socks that offer superior support, comfort, and performance benefits.
2. Casual runners: Many runners enjoy running as a form of exercise and stress relief, and may be looking for gear that can help them feel more comfortable and confident on their runs. SprintSoles could appeal to casual runners who are looking for an affordable and effective way to improve their performance and enjoyment of running.
3. Fitness enthusiasts: Beyond just runners, there are many individuals who are interested in health and fitness, and may be looking for gear that can help them reach their fitness goals. SprintSoles could appeal to fitness enthusiasts who are looking for an edge in their workouts and are willing to invest in high-quality gear.

It's important to conduct market research and identify the most profitable and receptive target audience for your brand. By understanding the needs, preferences, and motivations of your target audience, you can develop marketing campaigns and promotions that are more likely to succeed in the market and generate revenue for your business.

Figure 7.4 – List of groups of target people to reach with my new product line

It's important to have in mind different clusters within your audience so that you can differentiate the messages you want to give. In my case, I want to make sure that my product line will address different groups of people, such as competitive runners, casual runners, and fitness enthusiasts.

- **Product variants and sales channels**: According to the preceding clusters of potential customers, I could generate product variants so that they are more tailored toward specific audiences:

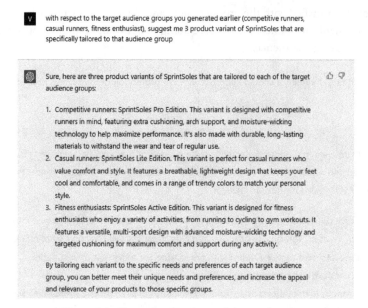

Figure 7.5 – Example of variants of the product line

Similarly, I can also ask ChatGPT to suggest different sales channels for each of the preceding groups:

Figure 7.6 – Suggestions for different sales channels by ChatGPT

- **Standing out from the competition**: I want my product line to stand out from the competition and emerge in a very saturated market – I want to make it unique. With this purpose in mind, I asked ChatGPT to include social considerations such as sustainability and inclusivity. Let's ask ChatGPT for some suggestions in that respect:

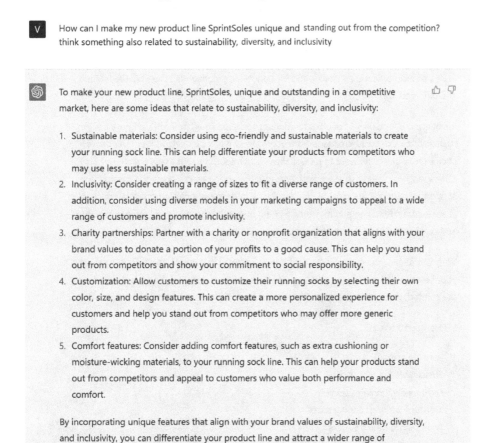

V   How can I make my new product line SprintSoles unique and standing out from the competition? think something also related to sustainability, diversity, and inclusivity

To make your new product line, SprintSoles, unique and outstanding in a competitive market, here are some ideas that relate to sustainability, diversity, and inclusivity:

1. Sustainable materials: Consider using eco-friendly and sustainable materials to create your running sock line. This can help differentiate your products from competitors who may use less sustainable materials.
2. Inclusivity: Consider creating a range of sizes to fit a diverse range of customers. In addition, consider using diverse models in your marketing campaigns to appeal to a wide range of customers and promote inclusivity.
3. Charity partnerships: Partner with a charity or nonprofit organization that aligns with your brand values to donate a portion of your profits to a good cause. This can help you stand out from competitors and show your commitment to social responsibility.
4. Customization: Allow customers to customize their running socks by selecting their own color, size, and design features. This can create a more personalized experience for customers and help you stand out from competitors who may offer more generic products.
5. Comfort features: Consider adding comfort features, such as extra cushioning or moisture-wicking materials, to your running sock line. This can help your products stand out from competitors and appeal to customers who value both performance and comfort.

By incorporating unique features that align with your brand values of sustainability, diversity, and inclusivity, you can differentiate your product line and attract a wider range of customers. Additionally, it's important to communicate these features effectively through your marketing and branding to help customers understand what makes your products unique and why they should choose SprintSoles over competing brands.

Figure 7.7 – Example of outstanding features generated by ChatGPT

As you can see, it was able to generate interesting features that could make my product line unique.

- **Product description**: Now it's time to start building our GTP plan. First of all, I want to generate a product description to put on my website, including all the earlier unique differentiators.

 generate a product description for SprintSoles using the unique differentiator you listed earlier. It should be catchy and effective, as well as SEO optimized. list also the SEO keywords you used once you finish.

 Here's an example product description for SprintSoles, highlighting their unique features and differentiators:

Introducing SprintSoles - the ultimate running socks designed for both performance and sustainability. Our socks are made from eco-friendly materials, making them the perfect choice for runners who want to reduce their carbon footprint. But that's not all - we also offer a range of sizes to fit every foot, ensuring that everyone can enjoy the comfort and support that SprintSoles provide. And for the ultimate in personalized comfort, our socks feature extra cushioning and moisture-wicking materials, ensuring that you stay cool, dry, and comfortable no matter how far you run.

With SprintSoles, you can run with confidence, knowing that you're not only performing at your best but also doing your part to protect the environment. Order now and experience the comfort, sustainability, and performance of SprintSoles running socks.

SEO keywords used:

- Running socks
- Sustainable running socks
- Eco-friendly running socks
- Moisture-wicking running socks
- Performance running socks
- Personalized running socks
- Comfortable running socks
- Running socks for all sizes
- Eco-conscious running gear

Figure 7.8 – Example of description and SEO keywords generated by ChatGPT

- **Fair price**: Another key element is determining a fair price for our product. As I differentiated among product variants for different audiences (competitive runners, casual runners, and fitness enthusiasts), I also want to have a price range that takes into account this clustering.

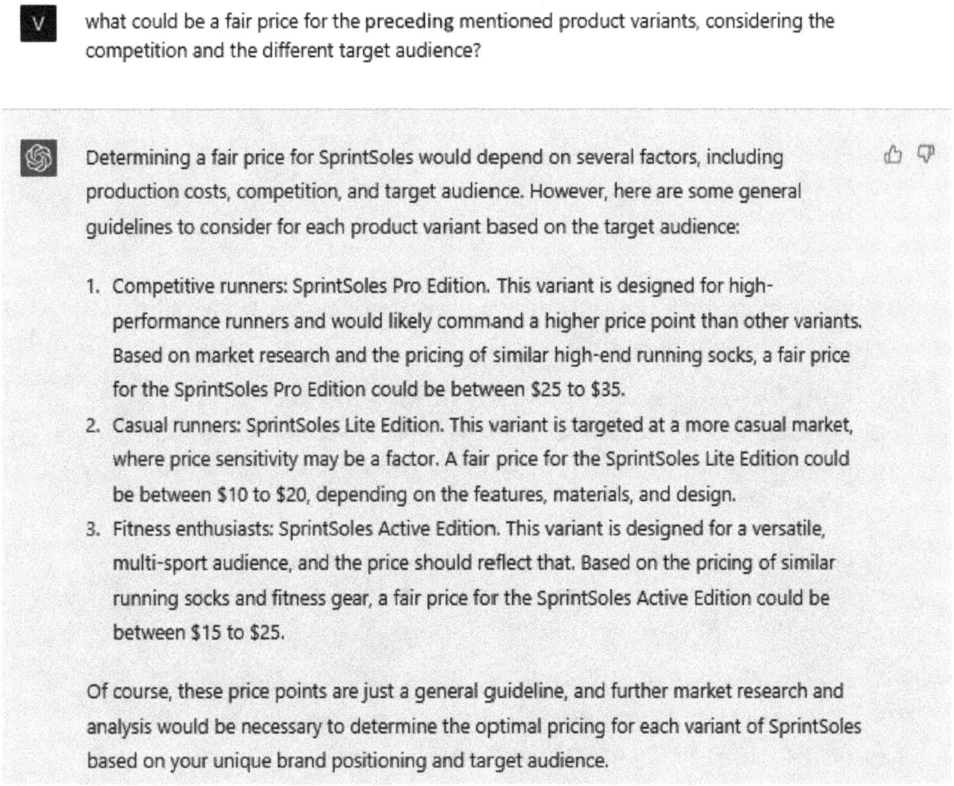

 what could be a fair price for the preceding mentioned product variants, considering the competition and the different target audience?

 Determining a fair price for SprintSoles would depend on several factors, including production costs, competition, and target audience. However, here are some general guidelines to consider for each product variant based on the target audience:

1. Competitive runners: SprintSoles Pro Edition. This variant is designed for high-performance runners and would likely command a higher price point than other variants. Based on market research and the pricing of similar high-end running socks, a fair price for the SprintSoles Pro Edition could be between $25 to $35.
2. Casual runners: SprintSoles Lite Edition. This variant is targeted at a more casual market, where price sensitivity may be a factor. A fair price for the SprintSoles Lite Edition could be between $10 to $20, depending on the features, materials, and design.
3. Fitness enthusiasts: SprintSoles Active Edition. This variant is designed for a versatile, multi-sport audience, and the price should reflect that. Based on the pricing of similar running socks and fitness gear, a fair price for the SprintSoles Active Edition could be between $15 to $25.

Of course, these price points are just a general guideline, and further market research and analysis would be necessary to determine the optimal pricing for each variant of SprintSoles based on your unique brand positioning and target audience.

Figure 7.9 – Price ranges for product variants

We are almost there. We have gone through many new product development and go-to-market steps, and in each of them, ChatGPT acted as a great support tool.

As one last thing, we can ask ChatGPT to generate an Instagram post about our new product, including relevant hashtags and SEO keywords. We can then generate the image with DALL-E!

 I want to generate an instagram post to announce the launch of SprintSoles. Write a post including the unique features and differentiators mentioned before, as well as relevant hashtags.

 Here's a sample Instagram post to announce the launch of SprintSoles:

🏃 Introducing SprintSoles - the revolutionary new running socks designed to give you the edge you need to go the distance!

🏃 With targeted cushioning and moisture-wicking technology, SprintSoles help reduce fatigue and discomfort, so you can focus on your run and hit your personal best. And with our commitment to sustainability, diversity, and inclusivity, you can feel good about your choice to run with SprintSoles.

🌍 Our socks are made with recycled materials, so you can feel good about reducing your environmental impact. And with a range of sizes and styles to fit any foot and any taste, we're proud to offer a product that is truly for everyone.

👟 Whether you're a competitive runner, casual jogger, or fitness enthusiast, SprintSoles have the features and quality you need to stay comfortable and focused during your runs. Try them out today and see the difference for yourself!

#SprintSoles #RunningSocks #SustainableRunning #DiverseFitness #InclusiveAthletics #GoTheDistance #TargetedCushioning #MoistureWicking #ReduceFatigue #StayComfortable #PerformanceSocks #RunningGear #FitnessEssentials #HealthyLiving #EcoFriendly #RecycledMaterials #ForEveryFoot #PersonalBest #RunningCommunity

Figure 7.10 – Social media post generated by ChatGPT

And, with the special contribution of DALL-E, here is the final result:

Figure 7.11 – Instagram post entirely generated by ChatGPT and DALL-E

Of course, many elements are missing here for complete product development and go-to-market. Yet, with the support of ChatGPT (and the special contribution of DALL-E – you can try DALL-E on your own at `https://openai.com/product/dall-e-2`), we managed to brainstorm a new product line and variants, potential customers, catchy slogans, and finally, generated a pretty nice Instagram post to announce the launch of SprintSoles!

A/B testing for marketing comparison

Another interesting field where ChatGPT can assist marketers is A/B testing.

A/B testing in marketing is a method of comparing two different versions of a marketing campaign, advertisement, or website to determine which one performs better. In A/B testing, two variations of the same campaign or element are created, with only one variable changed between the two versions. The goal is to see which version generates more clicks, conversions, or other desired outcomes.

An example of A/B testing might be testing two versions of an email campaign, using different subject lines, or testing two versions of a website landing page, with different call-to-action buttons. By measuring the response rate of each version, marketers can determine which version performs better and make data-driven decisions about which version to use going forward.

A/B testing allows marketers to optimize their campaigns and elements for maximum effectiveness, leading to better results and a higher return on investment.

Since this method involves the process of generating many variations of the same content, the generative power of ChatGPT can definitely assist in that.

Let's consider the following example. I'm promoting a new product I developed: a new, light and thin climbing harness for speed climbers. I've already done some market research and I know my niche audience. I also know that one great channel of communication for that audience is publishing on an online climbing blog, of which most climbing gyms' members are fellow readers.

My goal is to create an outstanding blog post to share the launch of this new harness, and I want to test two different versions of it in two groups. The blog post I'm about to publish and that I want to be the object of my A/B testing is the following:

Lighter Climbing Harness for Speed Climbers
Introducing the Latest Addition to the World of Climbing Gear

Attention all climbers! Get ready to upgrade your climbing gear with the latest and greatest harness designed specifically for speed climbers. The new climbing harness is lighter than any other on the market, allowing climbers to move more efficiently and faster than ever before.
This innovative harness is perfect for climbers who want to improve their speed and performance without sacrificing safety. The new design features a lightweight, yet durable material that is both breathable and comfortable. Whether you are a beginner or a seasoned climber, this harness will take your climbing experience to new heights. So, what are you waiting for? Head over to your nearest climbing gear store and get your hands on the newest addition to the world of climbing gear. Get ready to climb higher, faster, and more efficiently than ever before!

Figure 7.12 – An example of a blog post to launch climbing gear

Here, ChatGPT can help us on two levels:

- The first level is that of rewording the article, using different keywords or different attention-grabbing slogans. To do so, once this post is provided as context, we can ask ChatGPT to work on the article and slightly change some elements:

I'm doing an A/B testing for the launch of a new climbing harness. I'm using a climbing blog as sales channel with the preceding blog post.

please regenerate this content keeping all identical except for the following elements: title, subtitle and closing sentence.

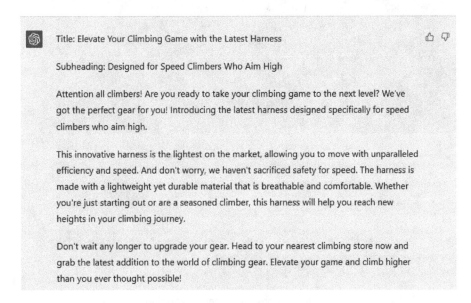

Figure 7.13 – New version of the blog post generated by ChatGPT

As per my request, ChatGPT was able to regenerate only those elements I asked for (title, subtitle, and closing sentence) so that I can monitor the effectiveness of those elements by monitoring the reaction of the two audience groups.

- The second level is working on the design of the web page, namely, changing the collocation of the image rather than the position of the buttons. For this purpose, I created a simple web page for the blog post published in the climbing blog (you can find the code in the book's GitHub repository at `https://github.com/PacktPublishing/Modern-Generative-AI-with-ChatGPT-and-OpenAI-Models/tree/main/Chapter%207%20-%20 ChatGPT%20for%20Marketers/Code`):

Figure 7.14 – Sample blog post published on the climbing blog

We can directly feed ChatGPT with the HTML code and ask it to change some layout elements, such as the position of the buttons or their wording. For example, rather than **Buy Now**, a reader might be more gripped by an **I want one!** button.

So, lets feed ChatGPT with the HTML source code:

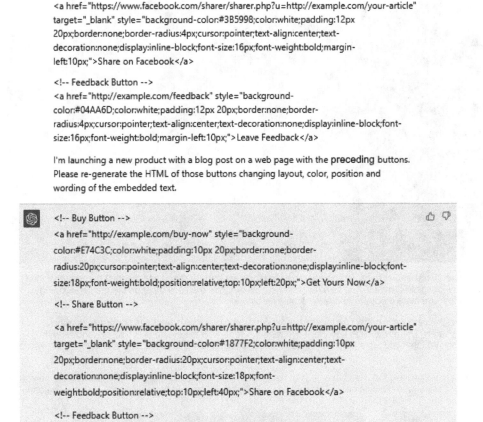

```
<!-- Buy Button -->
<a href="http://example.com/buy-now" style="background-
color:#04AA6D;color:white;padding:12px 20px;border:none;border-
radius:4px;cursor:pointer;text-align:center;text-decoration:none;display:inline-block;font-
size:16px;font-weight:bold;">Buy Now</a>

<!-- Share Button -->
<a href="https://www.facebook.com/sharer/sharer.php?u=http://example.com/your-article"
target="_blank" style="background-color:#3B5998;color:white;padding:12px
20px;border:none;border-radius:4px;cursor:pointer;text-align:center;text-
decoration:none;display:inline-block;font-size:16px;font-weight:bold;margin-
left:10px;">Share on Facebook</a>

<!-- Feedback Button -->
<a href="http://example.com/feedback" style="background-
color:#04AA6D;color:white;padding:12px 20px;border:none;border-
radius:4px;cursor:pointer;text-align:center;text-decoration:none;display:inline-block;font-
size:16px;font-weight:bold;margin-left:10px;">Leave Feedback</a>
```

I'm launching a new product with a blog post on a web page with the **preceding** buttons. Please re-generate the HTML of those buttons changing layout, color, position and wording of the embedded text.

```
<!-- Buy Button -->
<a href="http://example.com/buy-now" style="background-
color:#E74C3C;color:white;padding:10px 20px;border:none;border-
radius:20px;cursor:pointer;text-align:center;text-decoration:none;display:inline-block;font-
size:18px;font-weight:bold;position:relative;top:10px;left:20px;">Get Yours Now</a>

<!-- Share Button -->

<a href="https://www.facebook.com/sharer/sharer.php?u=http://example.com/your-article"
target="_blank" style="background-color:#1877F2;color:white;padding:10px
20px;border:none;border-radius:20px;cursor:pointer;text-align:center;text-
decoration:none;display:inline-block;font-size:18px;font-
weight:bold;position:relative;top:10px;left:40px;">Share on Facebook</a>

<!-- Feedback Button -->

<a href="http://example.com/feedback" style="background-
color:#2ECC71;color:white;padding:10px 20px;border:none;border-
radius:20px;cursor:pointer;text-align:center;text-decoration:none;display:inline-block;font-
size:18px;font-weight:bold;position:relative;top:10px;left:60px;">Give Feedback</a>
```

Figure 7.15 – ChatGPT changing HTML code

Let's see what the output looks like:

Lighter Climbing Harness for Speed Climbers

Introducing the Latest Addition to the World of Climbing Gear

Attention all climbers! Get ready to upgrade your climbing gear with the latest and greatest harness designed specifically for speed climbers. The new climbing harness is lighter than any other on the market, allowing climbers to move more efficiently and faster than ever before.

This innovative harness is perfect for climbers who want to improve their speed and performance without sacrificing safety. The new design features a lightweight, yet durable material that is both breathable and comfortable. Whether you are a beginner or a seasoned climber, this harness will take your climbing experience to new heights.

So, what are you waiting for? Head over to your nearest climbing gear store and get your hands on the newest addition to the world of climbing gear. Get ready to climb higher, faster, and more efficiently than ever before!

Get Yours Now   **Share on Facebook**   **Give Feedback**

Figure 7.16 – New version of the website

As you can see, ChatGPT only intervened at the button level, slightly changing their layout, position, color, and wording.

Indeed, inspecting the source code of the two versions of the web pages, we can see how it differs in the button sections:

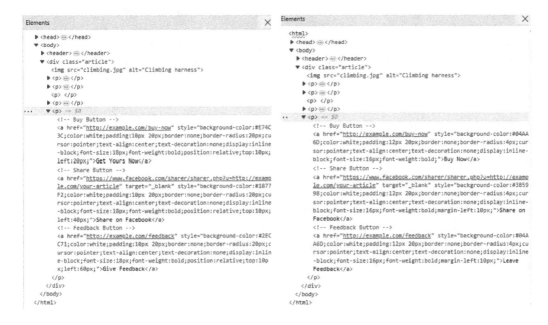

Figure 7.17 – Comparison between the source code of the two versions of the website

In conclusion, ChatGPT is a valuable tool for A/B testing in marketing. Its ability to quickly generate different versions of the same content can reduce the time to market of new campaigns. By utilizing ChatGPT for A/B testing, you can optimize your marketing strategies and ultimately drive better results for your business.

Boosting Search Engine Optimization (SEO)

Another promising area for ChatGPT to be a game changer is **Search Engine Optimization** (SEO). This is the key element behind ranking in search engines such as Google or Bing and it determines whether your websites will be visible to users who are looking for what you promote.

> Definition
>
> SEO is a technique used to enhance the visibility and ranking of a website on **search engine results pages** (**SERPs**). It is done by optimizing the website or web page to increase the amount and quality of organic (unpaid) traffic from search engines. The purpose of SEO is to attract more targeted visitors to the website by optimizing it for specific keywords or phrases.

Imagine you run an e-commerce company called **Hat&Gloves**, which only sells, as you might have guessed, hats and gloves. You are now creating your e-commerce website and want to optimize its ranking. Let's ask ChatGPT to list some relevant keywords to embed in our website:

 I'm building a website for my e-commerce called "Hat&Gloves", that only sells hats and gloves. I want to optimize the ranking of my websites. Please list 20 keywords I should embed in my website code in order to have SEO relevant results

 Sure! Here are 20 potential keywords you could consider embedding in your website code to optimize your e-commerce site for SEO:

1. Hats
2. Gloves
3. Winter wear
4. Cold weather accessories
5. Beanies
6. Mittens
7. Scarves
8. Fashion accessories
9. Men's hats
10. Women's hats
11. Kids' hats
12. Wool hats
13. Knit gloves
14. Leather gloves
15. Touchscreen gloves
16. Outdoor gear
17. Gift ideas
18. Affordable hats
19. Designer hats
20. Sale items

It's important to note that keyword research should be conducted to determine which specific keywords are most relevant and have the highest search volume for your target audience. This can help ensure that you're targeting the right keywords and not wasting effort on less valuable keywords. Additionally, it's important to use keywords in a natural way that enhances the user experience, rather than overloading your site with irrelevant or repetitive keywords that could negatively impact your SEO.

Figure 7.18 – Example of SEO keywords generated by ChatGPT

As you can see, ChatGPT was able to create a list of keywords of different kinds. Some of them are pretty intuitive, such as **Hats** and **Gloves**. Others are related, with an indirect link. For example, **Gift ideas** is not necessarily related to my e-commerce business, however, it could be very smart to include it in my keywords, so that I can widen my audience.

Another key element of SEO is **search engine intent**. Search engine intent, also known as **user intent**, refers to the underlying purpose or goal of a specific search query made by a user in a search engine. Understanding search engine intent is important because it helps businesses and marketers create more targeted and effective content and marketing strategies that align with the searcher's needs and expectations.

There are generally four types of search engine intent:

- **Informational intent**: The user is looking for information on a particular topic or question, such as *What is the capital of France?* or *How to make a pizza at home.*

- **Navigational intent**: The user is looking for a specific website or web page, such as **Facebook login** or **Amazon.com**.

- **Commercial intent**: The user is looking to buy a product or service, but may not have made a final decision yet. Examples of commercial intent searches include *best laptop under $1000* or *discount shoes online.*

- **Transactional intent**: The user has a specific goal to complete a transaction, which might refer to physical purchases or subscribing to services. Examples of transactional intent could be *buy iPhone 13* or *sign up for a gym membership.*

By understanding the intent behind specific search queries, businesses and marketers can create more targeted and effective content that meets the needs and expectations of their target audience. This can lead to higher search engine rankings, more traffic, and ultimately, more conversions and revenue.

Now, the question is, will ChatGPT be able to determine the intent of a given request? Before answering, it is worth noticing that the activity of inferring the intent of a given prompt is the core business of **Large Language Models (LLMs)**, including GPT. So, for sure, ChatGPT is able to capture prompts' intents.

The added value here is that we want to see whether ChatGPT is able to determine the intent in a precise domain with a precise taxonomy, that is, the one of marketing. That is the reason why prompt design is once again pivotal in guiding ChatGPT in the right direction.

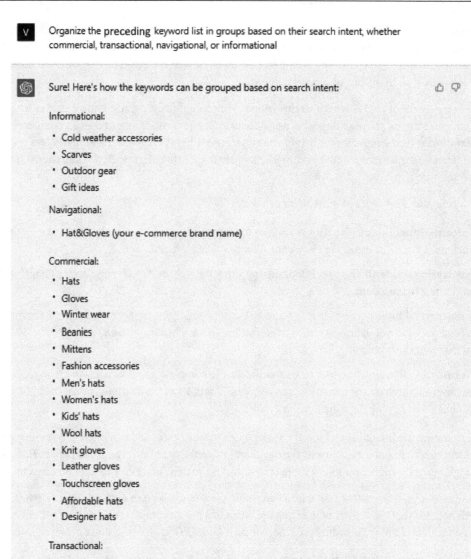

V   Organize the preceding keyword list in groups based on their search intent, whether
commercial, transactional, navigational, or informational

Sure! Here's how the keywords can be grouped based on search intent: 👍 👎

Informational:

* Cold weather accessories
* Scarves
* Outdoor gear
* Gift ideas

Navigational:

* Hat&Gloves (your e-commerce brand name)

Commercial:

* Hats
* Gloves
* Winter wear
* Beanies
* Mittens
* Fashion accessories
* Men's hats
* Women's hats
* Kids' hats
* Wool hats
* Knit gloves
* Leather gloves
* Touchscreen gloves
* Affordable hats
* Designer hats

Transactional:

* Sale items

It's important to note that some keywords can fit into multiple search intent categories, and
the specific search intent for a keyword can vary depending on the specific context of the
search query. Additionally, understanding the search intent of your target audience is
important for creating effective SEO strategies and optimizing your e-commerce site for
search engines.

Figure 7.19 – Example of ChatGPT acting as an SEO expert

Finally, we could also go further and leverage once more the *Act as…* hack, which we already mentioned in *Chapter 4*. It would be very interesting indeed to understand how to optimize our website so that it reaches as many users as possible. In marketing, this analysis is called an **SEO audit**. An SEO audit is an evaluation of a website's SEO performance and potential areas for improvement. An SEO audit is typically conducted by SEO experts, web developers, or marketers, and involves a comprehensive analysis of a website's technical infrastructure, content, and backlink profile.

During an SEO audit, the auditor will typically use a range of tools and techniques to identify areas of improvement, such as keyword analysis, website speed analysis, website architecture analysis, and content analysis. The auditor will then generate a report outlining the key issues, opportunities for improvement, and recommended actions to address them.

Let's ask ChatGPT to act as an SEO expert and instruct us on what an SEO audit report should look like and which metrics and KPIs should include:

 I recently purchased the RunFast Prodigy shoes and have mixed feelings about them. On one hand, the shoes are incredibly comfortable and provide great support for my feet during my daily runs. The cushioning is top-notch and my feet feel less fatigued after my runs than with my previous shoes. Additionally, the design is visually appealing and I received several compliments on them.

However, on the other hand, I've experienced some durability issues with these shoes. The outsole seems to wear down rather quickly and the upper material, while breathable, is showing signs of wear after only a few weeks of use. This is disappointing, considering the high price point of the shoes.

Overall, while I love the comfort and design of the RunFast Prodigy shoes, I'm hesitant to recommend them due to the durability issues I've experienced.

Analyze the sentiment of the preceding review. Overall, how do you classify it?

 The sentiment of the review is mixed, with both positive and negative elements. The positive aspects of the shoes include their comfort, support, cushioning, and design. The negative aspects include durability issues with the outsole and upper material.

Overall, the sentiment of the review can be classified as neutral, since the reviewer has both positive and negative things to say about the product and is hesitant to recommend it.

Figure 7.20 – Example of ChatGPT providing optimized HTML code

ChatGPT was able to generate a pretty accurate analysis, with relevant comments and suggestions. Overall, ChatGPT has interesting potential for SEO-related activities, and it can be a good tool whether you are building your website from scratch or you want to improve existing ones.

Sentiment analysis to improve quality and increase customer satisfaction

Sentiment analysis is a technique used in marketing to analyze and interpret the emotions and opinions expressed by customers toward a brand, product, or service. It involves the use of **natural language processing** (**NLP**) and **machine learning** (**ML**) algorithms to identify and classify the sentiment of textual data such as social media posts, customer reviews, and feedback surveys.

By performing sentiment analysis, marketers can gain insights into customer perceptions of their brand, identify areas for improvement, and make data-driven decisions to optimize their marketing strategies. For example, they can track the sentiment of customer reviews to identify which products or services are receiving positive or negative feedback and adjust their marketing messaging accordingly.

Overall, sentiment analysis is a valuable tool for marketers to understand customer sentiment, gauge customer satisfaction, and develop effective marketing campaigns that resonate with their target audience.

Sentiment analysis has been around for a while, so you might be wondering what ChatGPT could bring as added value. Well, besides the accuracy of the analysis (it being the most powerful model on the market right now), ChatGPT differentiates itself from other sentiment analysis tools since it is **artificial general intelligence** (**AGI**).

This means that when we use ChatGPT for sentiment analysis, we are not using one of its specific APIs for that task: the core idea behind ChatGPT and OpenAI models is that they can assist the user in many general tasks at once, interacting with a task and changing the scope of the analysis according to the user's request.

So, for sure, ChatGPT is able to capture the sentiment of a given text, such as a Twitter post or a product review. However, ChatGPT can also go further and assist in identifying specific aspects of a product or brand that are positively or negatively impacting the sentiment. For example, if customers consistently mention a particular feature of a product in a negative way, ChatGPT can highlight that feature as an area for improvement. Or, ChatGPT might be asked to generate a response to a particularly delicate review, keeping in mind the sentiment of the review and using it as context for the response. Again, it can generate reports that summarize all the negative and positive elements found in reviews or comments and cluster them into categories.

Let's consider the following example. A customer has recently purchased a pair of shoes from my e-commerce company, *RunFast*, and left the following review:

I recently purchased the RunFast Prodigy shoes and have mixed feelings about them. On one hand, the shoes are incredibly comfortable and provide great support for my feet during my daily runs. The cushioning is top-notch and my feet feel less fatigued after my runs than with my previous shoes. Additionally, the design is visually appealing and I received several compliments on them.

However, on the other hand, I've experienced some durability issues with these shoes. The outsole seems to wear down rather quickly and the upper material, while breathable, is showing signs of wear after only a few weeks of use. This is disappointing, considering the high price point of the shoes.

Overall, while I love the comfort and design of the RunFast Prodigy shoes, I'm hesitant to recommend them due to the durability issues I've experienced.

Let's ask ChatGPT to capture the sentiment of this review:

 I recently purchased the RunFast Prodigy shoes and have mixed feelings about them. On one hand, the shoes are incredibly comfortable and provide great support for my feet during my daily runs. The cushioning is top-notch and my feet feel less fatigued after my runs than with my previous shoes. Additionally, the design is visually appealing and I received several compliments on them.

However, on the other hand, I've experienced some durability issues with these shoes. The outsole seems to wear down rather quickly and the upper material, while breathable, is showing signs of wear after only a few weeks of use. This is disappointing, considering the high price point of the shoes.

Overall, while I love the comfort and design of the RunFast Prodigy shoes, I'm hesitant to recommend them due to the durability issues I've experienced.

Analyze the sentiment of the preceding review. Overall, how do you classify it?

 The sentiment of the review is mixed, with both positive and negative elements. The positive aspects of the shoes include their comfort, support, cushioning, and design. The negative aspects include durability issues with the outsole and upper material.

Overall, the sentiment of the review can be classified as neutral, since the reviewer has both positive and negative things to say about the product and is hesitant to recommend it.

Figure 7.21 – ChatGPT analyzing a customer review

From the preceding figure, we can see how ChatGPT didn't limit itself to providing a label: it also explained both the positive and negative elements characterizing the review, which has a mixed feeling and hence can be labeled as neutral overall.

Let's try to go deeper into that and ask some suggestions about improving the product:

 based on the **preceding review**, how could I improve the RunFast Prodigy shoes?

 Based on the review, there are a few ways the RunFast Prodigy shoes could be improved:

1. Improve durability: As the reviewer mentioned, the outsole and upper material of the shoes seem to wear down quickly. This could be addressed by using more durable materials or improving the manufacturing process to ensure the shoes can withstand regular use over a longer period of time.

2. Lower the price point: The reviewer also mentioned that the shoes are expensive, which could be a barrier to recommending them to others. Lowering the price point could make them more accessible and competitive with other running shoe brands.

3. Maintain the level of comfort: The reviewer praised the shoes for their comfort and support, so it's important to maintain this aspect while making improvements to durability and price. This could be achieved by finding materials and manufacturing processes that balance comfort and durability, or by providing additional cushioning in the shoes to improve comfort over time.

Overall, addressing these issues could help improve the RunFast Prodigy shoes and make them a more attractive option for runners.

Figure 7.22 – Suggestions on how to improve my product based on customer feedback

Finally, let's generate a response to the customer, showing that we, as a company, do care about customers' feedback and want to improve our products.

generate a response to the preceding customer review, specifying that we are on the process of always improving our products with the suggestion you shared there.

 Dear [Customer],

Thank you for taking the time to share your feedback on the RunFast Prodigy shoes. We are sorry to hear about the durability issues you have experienced and appreciate your suggestion regarding the outsole and upper material. We take all feedback seriously and are constantly working to improve our products.

Rest assured that your comments will be shared with our product development team, who will consider them as we work to make enhancements to our shoes. We want to ensure that all our customers have the best possible experience with our products and will continue to strive towards this goal.

If you have any further comments or concerns, please do not hesitate to reach out to us. We value your business and look forward to serving you in the future.

Sincerely,
[Your Company]

Figure 7.23 – Response generated by ChatGPT

The example we saw was a very simple one with just one review. Now imagine we have tons of reviews, as well as diverse sales channels where we receive feedback. Imagine the power of tools such as ChatGPT and OpenAI models, which are able to analyze and integrate all of that information and identify the pluses and minuses of your products, as well as capturing customer trends and shopping habits. Additionally, for customer care and retention, we could also automate review responses using the writing style we prefer. In fact, by tailoring your chatbot's language and tone to meet the specific needs and expectations of your customers, you can create a more engaging and effective customer experience.

Here are some examples:

- **Empathetic chatbot**: A chatbot that uses an empathetic tone and language to interact with customers who may be experiencing a problem or need help with a sensitive issue
- **Professional chatbot**: A chatbot that uses a professional tone and language to interact with customers who may be looking for specific information or need help with a technical issue
- **Conversational chatbot**: A chatbot that uses a casual and friendly tone to interact with customers who may be looking for a personalized experience or have a more general inquiry

- **Humorous chatbot**: A chatbot that uses humor and witty language to interact with customers who may be looking for a light-hearted experience or to diffuse a tense situation
- **Educational chatbot**: A chatbot that uses a teaching style of communication to interact with customers who may be looking to learn more about a product or service

In conclusion, ChatGPT can be a powerful tool for businesses to conduct sentiment analysis, improve their quality, and retain their customers. With its advanced natural language processing capabilities, ChatGPT can accurately analyze customer feedback and reviews in real time, providing businesses with valuable insights into customer sentiment and preferences. By using ChatGPT as part of their customer experience strategy, businesses can quickly identify any issues that may be negatively impacting customer satisfaction and take corrective action. Not only can this help businesses improve their quality but it can also increase customer loyalty and retention.

Summary

In this chapter, we explored ways in which ChatGPT can be used by marketers to enhance their marketing strategies. We learned that ChatGPT can help in developing new products as well as defining their go-to-market strategy, designing A/B testing, enhancing SEO analysis, and capturing the sentiment of reviews, social media posts, and other customer feedback.

The importance of ChatGPT for marketers lies in its potential to revolutionize the way companies engage with their customers. By leveraging the power of NLP, ML, and big data, ChatGPT allows companies to create more personalized and relevant marketing messages, improve customer support and satisfaction, and ultimately, drive sales and revenue.

As ChatGPT continues to advance and evolve, it is likely that we will see even more involvement in the marketing industry, especially in the way companies engage with their customers. In fact, relying heavily on AI allows companies to gain deeper insights into customer behavior and preferences.

The key takeaway for marketers is to embrace these changes and adapt to the new reality of AI-powered marketing in order to stay ahead of the competition and meet the needs of their customers.

In the next chapter, we will look at the third and last domain in the application of ChatGPT covered in this book – research.

8

Research Reinvented with ChatGPT

In this chapter, we focus on researchers who wish to leverage ChatGPT. The chapter will go through a few main use cases ChatGPT can address, so that you will learn from concrete examples how ChatGPT can be used in research.

By the end of this chapter, you will be familiar with using ChatGPT as a research assistant in many ways, including the following:

- Researchers' need for ChatGPT
- Brainstorming literature for your study
- Providing support for the design and framework of your experiment
- Generating and formatting a bibliography to incorporate in your research study
- Delivering a pitch or slide deck presentation about your study addressing diverse audiences

This chapter will also provide examples and enable you to try the prompts on your own.

Researchers' need for ChatGPT

ChatGPT can be an incredibly valuable resource for researchers across a wide range of fields. As a sophisticated language model trained on vast amounts of data, ChatGPT can quickly and accurately process large amounts of information and generate insights that might be difficult or time-consuming to uncover through traditional research methods.

Additionally, ChatGPT can provide researchers with a unique perspective on their field, by analyzing patterns and trends that might not be immediately apparent to human researchers. For example, imagine a researcher studying climate change and wanting to understand the public perception of this issue. They might ask ChatGPT to analyze social media data related to climate change and identify the most common themes and sentiments expressed by people online. ChatGPT could then provide the researcher with a comprehensive report detailing the most common words, phrases, and emotions associated with this topic, as well as any emerging trends or patterns that might be useful to know.

By working with ChatGPT, researchers can gain access to cutting-edge technology and insights, and stay at the forefront of their field.

Let's now dive deeper into four use cases where ChatGPT can boost research productivity.

Brainstorming literature for your study

A literature review is a critical and systematic process of examining existing published research on a specific topic or question. It involves searching, reviewing, and synthesizing relevant published studies and other sources, such as books, conference proceedings, and gray literature. The goal of a literature review is to identify gaps, inconsistencies, and opportunities for further research in a particular field.

The literature review process typically involves the following steps:

1. **Defining the research question**: The first step in conducting a literature review is to define the research question of the topic of interest. So, let's say we are carrying out research on the effects of social media on mental health. Now we are interested in brainstorming some possible research questions to focus our research on, and we can leverage ChatGPT to do so:

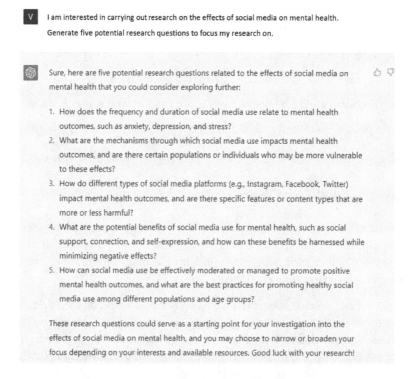

Figure 8.1 – Examples of research questions based on a given topic

Those are all interesting questions that could be further investigated. Since I'm particularly interested in the last one, I will keep that one as a reference for the next steps of our analysis.

2. **Searching for literature**: Now that we have our research question, the next step is to search for relevant literature using a variety of databases, search engines, and other sources. Researchers can use specific keywords and search terms to help identify relevant studies.

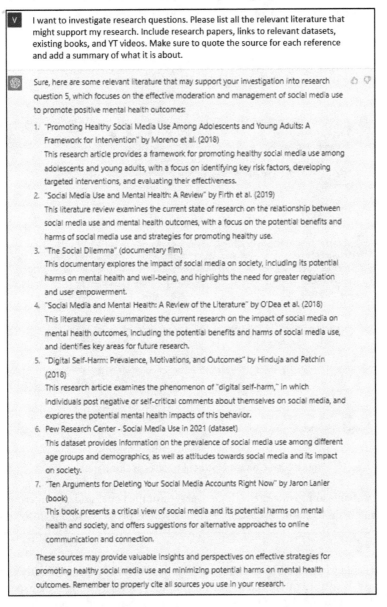

Figure 8.2 – Literature search with the support of ChatGPT

Starting from the suggestions of ChatGPT, we can start diving deeper into those references.

3. **Screening the literature**: Once relevant literature has been identified, the next step is to screen the studies to determine whether they meet the inclusion criteria for the review. This typically involves reviewing the abstract and, if necessary, the full text of the study.

Let's say, for example, that we want to go deeper into the **Promoting Healthy Social Media Use Among Adolescents and Young Adults: A Framework for Intervention** research paper. Let's ask ChatGPT to screen it for us:

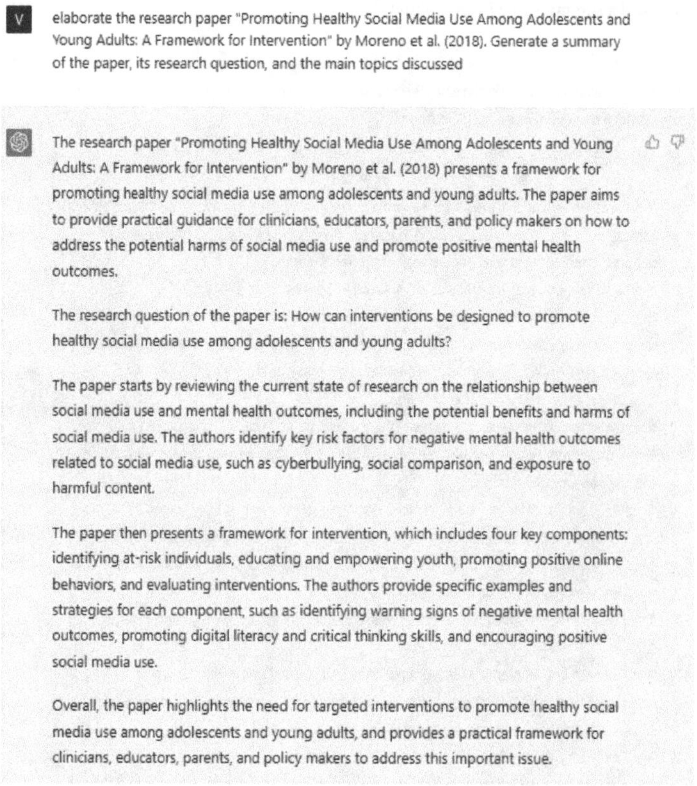

> V   elaborate the research paper "Promoting Healthy Social Media Use Among Adolescents and Young Adults: A Framework for Intervention" by Moreno et al. (2018). Generate a summary of the paper, its research question, and the main topics discussed

> The research paper "Promoting Healthy Social Media Use Among Adolescents and Young Adults: A Framework for Intervention" by Moreno et al. (2018) presents a framework for promoting healthy social media use among adolescents and young adults. The paper aims to provide practical guidance for clinicians, educators, parents, and policy makers on how to address the potential harms of social media use and promote positive mental health outcomes.
>
> The research question of the paper is: How can interventions be designed to promote healthy social media use among adolescents and young adults?
>
> The paper starts by reviewing the current state of research on the relationship between social media use and mental health outcomes, including the potential benefits and harms of social media use. The authors identify key risk factors for negative mental health outcomes related to social media use, such as cyberbullying, social comparison, and exposure to harmful content.
>
> The paper then presents a framework for intervention, which includes four key components: identifying at-risk individuals, educating and empowering youth, promoting positive online behaviors, and evaluating interventions. The authors provide specific examples and strategies for each component, such as identifying warning signs of negative mental health outcomes, promoting digital literacy and critical thinking skills, and encouraging positive social media use.
>
> Overall, the paper highlights the need for targeted interventions to promote healthy social media use among adolescents and young adults, and provides a practical framework for clinicians, educators, parents, and policy makers to address this important issue.

Figure 8.3 – Literature screening of a specific paper

ChatGPT was able to provide me with an overview of the paper and, considering its research question and main topics of discussion, I think it will be pretty useful for my own study.

> **Note**
>
> ChatGPT was able to generate a screening of this paper since it was evidently part of its knowledge base. If you are interested in performing the same screening on a paper written later than 2021 (the cut-off date of ChatGPT training), you will need to provide the abstract or paragraph content to ChatGPT.

4. **Extracting data:** After the relevant studies have been identified, researchers will need to extract data from each study, such as the study design, sample size, data collection methods, and key findings.

For example, let's say that we want to gather the following information from the paper *Digital Self-Harm: Prevalence, Motivations, and Outcomes* by Hinduja and Patchin (2018):

- Data sources collected in the paper and object of the study

- Data collection method adopted by researchers

- Data sample size

- Main limitations and drawbacks of the analysis

- The experiment design adopted by researchers

Here is how it goes:

> write the following information about the paper "Digital Self-Harm: Prevalence, Motivations, and Outcomes" by Hinduja and Patchin (2018).
> 1. Data sources collected in the paper and object of the study
> 2. data collection method adopted by researchers
> 3. data sample size
> 4. main limitations and drawbacks of the analysis
> 5. the experiment design adopted by researchers

> Sure, here's the information you requested about the paper "Digital Self-Harm: Prevalence, Motivations, and Outcomes" by Hinduja and Patchin (2018):
>
> 1. The paper examines the phenomenon of digital self-harm, which refers to the practice of individuals anonymously posting hurtful comments about themselves on social media platforms. The study aims to understand the prevalence, motivations, and outcomes of digital self-harm, as well as its potential linkages with other forms of online and offline victimization.
> 2. The researchers collected data through an online survey administered to a nationally representative sample of 5,593 middle and high school students in the United States. The survey included questions on various forms of online and offline victimization, including digital self-harm, as well as demographic and psychosocial variables.
> 3. The sample size was 5,593 middle and high school students in the United States.
> 4. The main limitations and drawbacks of the analysis may include potential biases and limitations of self-reported data, such as social desirability bias and memory recall errors. In addition, the study did not explore the potential cultural and contextual factors that may influence the prevalence, motivations, and outcomes of digital self-harm.
> 5. The researchers did not adopt an experiment design, but rather conducted a survey-based research study to collect self-reported data from participants.

Figure 8.4 – Extracting relevant data and frameworks from a given paper

5.   **Synthesizing the literature**: The final step in the literature review process is to synthesize the findings of the studies and draw conclusions about the current state of knowledge in the field. This may involve identifying common themes, highlighting gaps or inconsistencies in the literature, and identifying opportunities for future research.

Let's imagine that, besides the papers proposed by ChatGPT, we have collected other titles and papers we want to synthesize. More specifically, I want to understand whether they point toward the same conclusions or not, which are common trends, and which method might be more reliable than others. For this scenario, we will consider three research papers:

- *The Effects of Social Media on Mental Health: A Proposed Study*, by Grant Sean Bossard (https://digitalcommons.bard.edu/cgi/viewcontent.cgi?article=1028&context=senproj_f2020)

- *The Impact of Social Media on Mental Health*, by Vardanush Palyan (https://www.spotlightonresearch.com/mental-health-research/the-impact-of-social-media-on-mental-health)

- *The Impact of Social Media on Mental Health: a mixed-methods research of service providers' awareness*, by Sarah Nichole Koehler and Bobbie Rose Parrell (https://scholarworks.lib.csusb.edu/cgi/viewcontent.cgi?article=2131&context=etd)

Here is how the results appear:

Highlight the conclusions, research methods and considerations about reliability for the below papers. Also, highlight the common trends and findings among the three papers.

"The Effects of Social Media on Mental Health: A Proposed Study", by Grant Sean Bossard
"The Impact of Social Media on Mental Health", by Vardanush Palyan
"The Impact of Social Media on Mental Health: a mixed methods research of service providers' awareness", by Sarah Nichole Koehler and Bobbie Rose Parrell

1. "The Effects of Social Media on Mental Health: A Proposed Study" by Grant Sean Bossard:

- Conclusion: The study proposed to investigate the effects of social media on mental health and hypothesized that excessive social media use would be associated with increased symptoms of anxiety and depression.
- Research Methods: The proposed study used a cross-sectional survey design, with a sample of undergraduate students completing self-report measures of social media use, anxiety, and depression.
- Considerations about reliability: The reliability of the proposed study is unknown, as the study has not yet been conducted.

2. "The Impact of Social Media on Mental Health" by Vardanush Palyan:

- Conclusion: The paper reviewed existing literature on the impact of social media on mental health and found that social media use is associated with increased risk of depression, anxiety, and other mental health problems.
- Research Methods: The paper used a systematic review of existing literature on the topic, analyzing studies that investigated the association between social media use and mental health outcomes.
- Considerations about reliability: The reliability of the paper's findings is strengthened by the systematic review methodology, which is designed to reduce bias and increase the reliability of findings.

3. "The Impact of Social Media on Mental Health: a mixed methods research of service providers' awareness" by Sarah Nichole Koehler and Bobbie Rose Parrell:

- Conclusion: The study investigated service providers' awareness of the impact of social media on mental health and found that many service providers lack knowledge and training on the topic.
- Research Methods: The study used a mixed-methods design, with both qualitative interviews and a quantitative survey administered to service providers.
- Considerations about reliability: The reliability of the study's findings is strengthened by the mixed-methods design, which allows for triangulation of findings from different sources and methods.

Common Trends and Findings:

- All three papers investigate the impact of social media on mental health.
- The papers all find evidence to suggest that social media use is associated with negative mental health outcomes.
- The papers use different research methods, with one proposing a new study, one conducting a systematic review, and one using a mixed-methods design.

Figure 8.5 – Literature analysis and benchmarking of three research papers

Also, in this case, ChatGPT was able to produce a relevant summary and analysis of the three papers provided, including benchmarking among the methods and reliability considerations.

Overall, ChatGPT was able to carry out many activities in the field of literature review, from research question brainstorming to literature synthesis. As always, a **subject-matter expert** (**SME**) is needed in the loop to review the results; however, with this assistance, many activities can be done more efficiently.

Another activity that can be supported by ChatGPT is the design of the experiment the researcher wants to carry out. We are going to look at that in the following section.

Providing support for the design and framework of your experiment

Experiment design is the process of planning and executing a scientific experiment or study to answer a research question. It involves making decisions about the study's design, the variables to be measured, the sample size, and the procedures for collecting and analyzing data.

ChatGPT can help in experiment design for research by suggesting to you the study framework, such as a randomized controlled trial, quasi-experimental design, or a correlational study, and supporting you during the implementation of that design.

Let's consider the following scenario. We want to investigate the effects of a new educational program on student learning outcomes in mathematics. This new program entails **project-based learning** (**PBL**), meaning that students are asked to work collaboratively on real-world projects, using math concepts and skills to solve problems and create solutions.

For this purpose, we defined our research question as follows:

How does the new PBL program compare to traditional teaching methods in improving student performance?

Here's how ChatGPT can help:

- **Determining study design**: ChatGPT can assist in determining the appropriate study design for the research question, such as a randomized controlled trial, quasi-experimental design, or correlational study.

I want to design an experiment on the following research question, "How does the new PBL program compare to traditional teaching methods in improving student performance?" What kind of study design should I carry on for this goal?

 To compare the effectiveness of the new project-based learning program and traditional teaching methods in improving student performance, a randomized controlled trial (RCT) study design would be appropriate.

In an RCT, participants are randomly assigned to either the experimental group (in this case, the project-based learning program) or the control group (traditional teaching methods). This helps to ensure that any observed differences in student performance are due to the intervention (project-based learning program) and not other factors such as pre-existing differences in ability or motivation.

Both groups should be as similar as possible in terms of key characteristics, such as age, gender, academic level, and socioeconomic status. Additionally, to minimize the risk of bias, the study should be double-blinded where both the participants and the researchers are unaware of the group assignment.

To measure student performance, a standardized test or a pre- and post-test design can be used. Other factors that could potentially affect performance, such as student motivation, engagement, and satisfaction, should also be assessed through surveys or interviews.

Overall, an RCT study design would provide strong evidence to determine the effectiveness of the new project-based learning program compared to traditional teaching methods in improving student performance.

Figure 8.6 – ChatGPT suggesting the appropriate study design for your experiment

ChatGPT suggested proceeding with a **randomized controlled trial** (RCT) and provided a clear explanation of the reason behind it. It seems reasonable to me to proceed with this approach; the next steps will be to identify outcome measures and variables to consider in our experiment.

- **Identifying outcome measures**: ChatGPT can help you identify some potential outcome measures to determine the results of your test. Let's ask for some suggestions for our study:

I want to compare the new PBL program with traditional teaching methods in improving student performance in a research study with an RCT. What could be possible outcome measures?

There are several outcome measures that can be used to assess the effectiveness of the new project-based learning program compared to traditional teaching methods. Here are some possible options:

1. Test scores: This can be a straightforward way to measure student performance. Standardized tests can be administered to both groups of students before and after the intervention to compare their performance.
2. Grades: Another measure of student performance is their grades in the subject being studied. Both groups of students can be graded on the same assignments and exams to compare their performance.
3. Attendance: Attendance can be an indicator of student engagement and motivation. Tracking attendance for both groups of students can provide insight into the effectiveness of the intervention.
4. Surveys: Surveys can be used to gather student and teacher feedback on the effectiveness of the new project-based learning program compared to traditional teaching methods. These surveys can include questions about student engagement, motivation, and understanding of the subject matter.
5. Behavioral observations: Observing student behavior in the classroom can provide valuable insights into the effectiveness of the intervention. This can include tracking student participation, engagement, and collaboration during group work.

It is important to select outcome measures that are valid and reliable, and that align with the research question and hypothesis of the study.

Figure 8.7 – Learning outcomes for the given research study

It is reasonable for me to pick test scores as the outcome measure.

- **Identifying variables**: ChatGPT can help the researcher to identify the independent and dependent variables in the study:

I want to compare the new project-based learning program with traditional teaching methods in improving student performance in a research study with a RCT. What variables should I include in my study?

To compare the new project-based learning program with traditional teaching methods in improving student performance in an RCT, the following variables could be included:

1. Independent variable: Teaching method (project-based learning program or traditional teaching method)
2. Dependent variable: Student performance (measured by a standardized test or other relevant assessment)
3. Control variables:

    *   Age and grade level of the students
    *   Socioeconomic status of the students
    *   Prior academic achievement of the students
    *   Teacher experience and qualifications
    *   Classroom environment and resources

It is important to ensure that the groups being compared (project-based learning program and traditional teaching method) are similar in terms of these control variables to isolate the effects of the teaching method on student performance.

Figure 8.8 – ChatGPT generating variables for the given study

Note that ChatGPT was also able to generate the type of variables, called **control variables**, that are specific to the study design we are considering (RCT).

Control variables, also known as **covariates**, are variables that are held constant or are controlled in a research study in order to isolate the relationship between the independent variable(s) and the dependent variable. These variables are not the primary focus of the study but are included to minimize the effect of confounding variables on the results. By controlling these variables, researchers can reduce the risk of obtaining false positive or false negative results and increase the internal validity of their study.

With the preceding variables, we are ready to set up our experiment. Now we need to select participants, and ChatGPT can assist us with that.

- **Sampling strategy**: ChatGPT can suggest potential sampling strategies for the study:

 I need to select the participant for my RCT about the effectiveness of a new project-based learning program in improving student performance, compared with traditional teaching methods. what sampling strategy should I use?

 For an RCT, the recommended sampling strategy is random sampling. This means that participants are selected randomly from the population being studied, ensuring that each member of the population has an equal chance of being selected. Random sampling helps to reduce bias and increase the generalizability of the study findings to the larger population.

In this case, you could use a random sampling strategy to select participants from the population of students who will be included in the study. This could involve randomly selecting students from a list of eligible participants or using a random number generator to select participants. However, it's important to ensure that the sample size is large enough to provide sufficient statistical power for the study.

Figure 8.9 – RCT sampling strategy suggestion from ChatGPT

Note that, in a real-world scenario, it is always a good practice to ask AI tools to generate more options with explanations behind them, so that you can make a reasoned decision. For this example, let's go ahead with what ChatGPT suggested to us, which also includes suggestions about the population of interest and sample size.

- **Data analysis**: ChatGPT can assist the researcher in determining the appropriate statistical tests to analyze the data collected from the study, such as ANOVA, t-tests, or regression analysis.

I'm conducting an experiment with RCT about the effectiveness of a new project-based learning program in improving student performance, compared with traditional teaching methods. The outcome measure is score test, and the sampling strategy is random sampling. What statistical test should I use to assess the statistical significance of my results? elaborate.

 Since the outcome measure is a continuous variable (i.e., scores), the appropriate statistical test for analyzing the results of your experiment would be a two-sample t-test. Specifically, you would perform an independent samples t-test, which is used to compare the means of two independent groups. In this case, the two groups are the students who received the new project-based learning program and those who received traditional teaching methods.

The independent samples t-test compares the means of the two groups and provides a p-value, which indicates the probability of obtaining a difference between the means as large as the one observed in the study, assuming that there is no difference between the two groups. If the p-value is less than the chosen significance level (e.g., 0.05), we can conclude that the difference between the means is statistically significant, and that the new project-based learning program had a significant impact on student performance compared to traditional teaching methods.

It's important to note that when performing a t-test, certain assumptions must be met, such as normality of the outcome measure and equal variances between the two groups. These assumptions can be checked using diagnostic tests, such as the Shapiro-Wilk test for normality and Levene's test for equal variances. If the assumptions are not met, alternative non-parametric tests, such as the Mann-Whitney U test, may be more appropriate.

It's also important to report effect sizes along with the p-value, as effect sizes provide information about the magnitude of the difference between the two groups, and can help interpret the practical significance of the results. Common effect sizes used in t-tests include Cohen's d and Hedges' g.

Figure 8.10 – ChatGPT suggests a statistical test for a given study

Everything suggested by ChatGPT is coherent and finds confirmation in papers about how to conduct a statistical test. It was also able to identify that we are probably talking about a continuous variable (that is, scores) so that we know that all the information ahead is based on this assumption. In the case that we want to have discrete scores, we might adjust the prompt by adding this information, and ChatGPT will then suggest a different approach.

The fact that ChatGPT specifies assumptions and explains its reasoning is key to making safe decisions based on its input.

In conclusion, ChatGPT can be a valuable tool for researchers when designing experiments. By utilizing its **natural language processing (NLP)** capabilities and vast knowledge base, ChatGPT can help researchers select appropriate study designs, determine sampling techniques, identify variables and learning outcomes, and even suggest statistical tests to analyze the data.

In the next section, we are going to move forward in exploring how ChatGPT can support researchers, focusing on bibliography generation.

Generating and formatting a bibliography

ChatGPT can support researchers in bibliography generation by providing automated citation and reference tools. These tools can generate accurate citations and references for a wide range of sources, including books, articles, websites, and more. ChatGPT knows various citation styles, such as APA, MLA, Chicago, and Harvard, allowing researchers to select the appropriate style for their work. Additionally, ChatGPT can also suggest relevant sources based on the researcher's input, helping to streamline the research process and ensure that all necessary sources are included in the bibliography. By utilizing these tools, researchers can save time and ensure that their bibliography is accurate and comprehensive.

Let's consider the following example. Let's say we finalized a research paper titled *The Impact of Technology on Workplace Productivity: An Empirical Study*. During the research and writing process, we collected the following references to papers, websites, videos, and other sources that we need to include in the bibliography (in order, three research papers, one YouTube video, and one website):

- *The second machine age: Work, progress, and prosperity in a time of brilliant technologies.* Brynjolfsson, 2014. `https://psycnet.apa.org/record/2014-07087-000`

- *Leveraging the capabilities of service-oriented decision support systems: Putting analytics and big data in cloud.* Demirkan, 2013. Pages 412-421. `https://www.sciencedirect.com/science/article/https://www.sciencedirect.com/science/article/abs/pii/S0167923612001595abs/pii/S0167923612001595`

- *The Impact of Technostress on Role Stress and Productivity.* Tarafdar. Pages 300-350. 2014. `https://www.tandfonline.com/doi/abs/10.2753/MIS0742-1222240109`

- *The big debate about the future of work, explained.* Vox. `https://www.youtube.com/watch?v=TUmyygCMMGA`

- *The Impact Of Technology And Automation On Today's Businesses".* , Forbes. 2021. `The Impact Of Technology And Automation On Today's Businesses (forbes.com)`, Forbes. 2021.

Obviously, we cannot have the preceding list in our research paper; we need proper formatting for it. To do so, we can provide ChatGPT with the raw list of references and ask it to regenerate it with the specific format, for example, APA style, the official style of the **American Psychological Association (APA)**, commonly used as a reference format style in education, psychology, and social sciences.

Let's see how ChatGPT works with that:

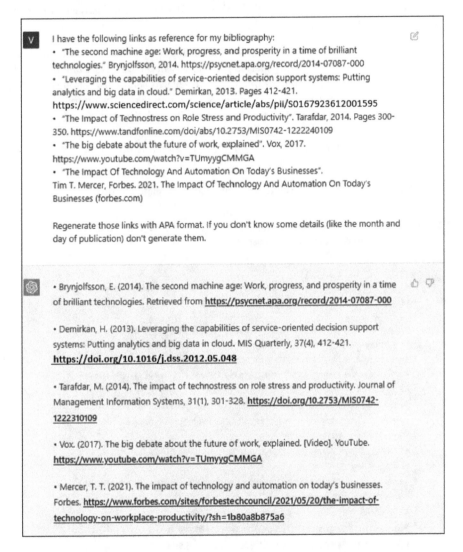

I have the following links as reference for my bibliography:
• "The second machine age: Work, progress, and prosperity in a time of brilliant technologies." Brynjolfsson, 2014. https://psycnet.apa.org/record/2014-07087-000
• "Leveraging the capabilities of service-oriented decision support systems: Putting analytics and big data in cloud." Demirkan, 2013. Pages 412-421. https://www.sciencedirect.com/science/article/abs/pii/S0167923612001595
• "The Impact of Technostress on Role Stress and Productivity". Tarafdar, 2014. Pages 300-350. https://www.tandfonline.com/doi/abs/10.2753/MIS0742-1222240109
• "The big debate about the future of work, explained". Vox, 2017. https://www.youtube.com/watch?v=TUmyygCMMGA
• "The Impact Of Technology And Automation On Today's Businesses". Tim T. Mercer, Forbes. 2021. The Impact Of Technology And Automation On Today's Businesses (forbes.com)

Regenerate those links with APA format. If you don't know some details (like the month and day of publication) don't generate them.

• Brynjolfsson, E. (2014). The second machine age: Work, progress, and prosperity in a time of brilliant technologies. Retrieved from **https://psycnet.apa.org/record/2014-07087-000**

• Demirkan, H. (2013). Leveraging the capabilities of service-oriented decision support systems: Putting analytics and big data in cloud. MIS Quarterly, 37(4), 412-421. **https://doi.org/10.1016/j.dss.2012.05.048**

• Tarafdar, M. (2014). The impact of technostress on role stress and productivity. Journal of Management Information Systems, 31(1), 301-328. **https://doi.org/10.2753/MIS0742-1222310109**

• Vox. (2017). The big debate about the future of work, explained. [Video]. YouTube. **https://www.youtube.com/watch?v=TUmyygCMMGA**

• Mercer, T. T. (2021). The impact of technology and automation on today's businesses. Forbes. **https://www.forbes.com/sites/forbestechcouncil/2021/05/20/the-impact-of-technology-on-workplace-productivity/?sh=1b80a8b875a6**

Figure 8.11 – A list of references generated in APA format by ChatGPT

Note that I specified not to add details if ChatGPT doesn't know them. Indeed, I noticed that sometimes ChatGPT was adding the month and day of publication, making some mistakes.

Other interesting assistance ChatGPT can provide is that of suggesting potential reference papers we might want to quote. We've already seen in the first paragraph of this chapter how ChatGPT is able to brainstorm relevant literature before the writing process; however, once the paper is done, we might have forgotten to quote relevant literature, or even not be aware of having quoted someone else's work.

ChatGPT can be a great assistant in brainstorming possible references we might have missed. Let's consider once more our paper *The Impact of Technology on Workplace Productivity: An Empirical Study*, which has the following abstract:

This empirical study examines the impact of technology on workplace productivity. The study aims to determine the extent to which technology has affected productivity in the workplace and to identify the specific technologies that have had the greatest impact. A survey was conducted among employees of various industries and the results were analyzed using regression analysis. The findings indicate that technology has a significant positive effect on workplace productivity, with the most impactful technologies being those that facilitate communication, collaboration, and task management. The study concludes that organizations should continue to invest in technology that supports these functions to maximize productivity in the workplace.

Let's ask ChatGPT to list all the possible references that might be related to this kind of research:

 List all the possible references (papers, articles, videos, blogs etc.) that might be related to the previous abstract

 Sure, here are some possible references that might be related to the abstract "The Impact of Technology on Workplace Productivity: An Empirical Study":

* Brynjolfsson, E., & McAfee, A. (2014). The Second Machine Age: Work, Progress, and Prosperity in a Time of Brilliant Technologies. W. W. Norton & Company.
* Brynjolfsson, E., & McAfee, A. (2011). Race Against the Machine: How the Digital Revolution is Accelerating Innovation, Driving Productivity, and Irreversibly Transforming Employment and the Economy. Digital Frontier Press.
* Demirkan, H., Spohrer, J. C., & Krishna, V. (2011). Leveraging the capabilities of service-oriented decision support systems: Putting analytics and big data in cloud. Decision Support Systems, 51(1), 412-421.
* McAfee, A., & Brynjolfsson, E. (2012). Big data: the management revolution. Harvard business review, 90(10), 61-67.
* McAfee, A., & Brynjolfsson, E. (2017). Machine, Platform, Crowd: Harnessing Our Digital Future. W. W. Norton & Company.
* OECD. (2016). The productivity-inclusiveness nexus. OECD.
* Pew Research Center. (2018). The future of work and automation. https://www.pewresearch.org/internet/2018/03/21/the-future-of-work-and-automation/
* Ruggles, R., & Brodie, M. (2018). Technological change and the future of work. Brookings Institution. https://www.brookings.edu/wp-content/uploads/2018/01/ed-technological-change-and-the-future-of-work.pdf
* Tarafdar, M., Tu, Q., Ragu-Nathan, T. S., & Ragu-Nathan, B. S. (2015). The impact of technostress on role stress and productivity. Journal of Management Information Systems, 31(1), 301-328.
* World Economic Forum. (2018). The future of jobs report 2018. World Economic Forum. https://www.weforum.org/reports/the-future-of-jobs-report-2018

Figure 8.12 – List of references related to the provided abstract

You can also repeat this process with other sections of your paper, to make sure you are not missing any relevant references to include in your bibliography.

Once you have your study ready, you will probably need to present it with an elevator pitch. In the next section, we will see how ChatGPT can also support this task.

Generating a presentation of the study

The last mile of a research study is often that of presenting it to various audiences. This might involve preparing a slide deck, pitch, or webinar where the researcher needs to address different kinds of audiences.

Let's say, for example, that our study *The Impact of Technology on Workplace Productivity: An Empirical Study* is meant for a master's degree thesis discussion. In that case, we can ask ChatGPT to produce a pitch structure that is meant to last 15 minutes and adheres to the scientific method. Let's see what kind of results are produced (as context, I'm referring to the abstract of the previous paragraph):

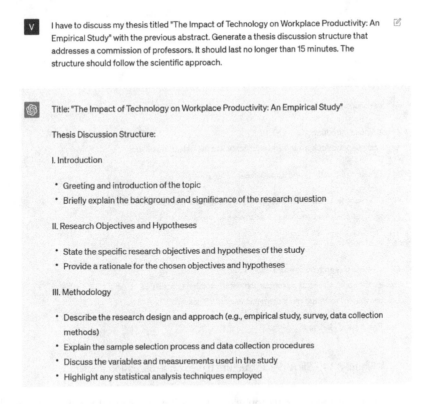

Figure 8.13 – Thesis discussion generated by ChatGPT

That was impressive! Back in my university days, it would have been useful to have such a tool to assist me in my discussion design.

Starting from this structure, we can also ask ChatGPT to generate a slide deck as a visual for our thesis discussion.

> **Note**
>
> In *Chapter 1*, we already saw an example of an AI-powered tool, Tome AI, for generating end-to-end slide decks using both text generation and image generation. In this paragraph, we will focus on the text generation component, but keep in mind that there are AI tools that can assist you in the creation of the deck itself too.

Let's proceed with this request:

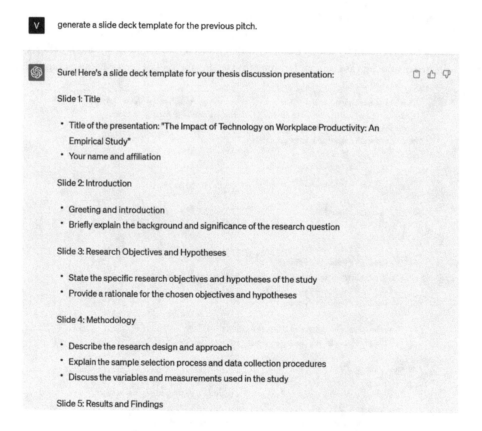

Figure 8.14 – Slide deck structure based on a discussion pitch

Finally, let's imagine that our thesis discussion was outstanding to the point that it might be selected for receiving research funds in order to keep investigating the topic. Now, we need an elevator pitch to convince the funding committee. Let's ask for some support from ChatGPT:

Generate an elevator pitch for the previous thesis. The audience is a scientific funding committee. I need to convince the audiene that this study deserves funding. The style should be engaging and challenging.

 Are you ready to enter a world where technology and productivity collide? My thesis, "The Impact of Technology on Workplace Productivity: An Empirical Study," will answer the burning questions you have about how technology affects productivity in the workplace. With this study, we will be able to understand the current state of technology and its influence on productivity, identify the obstacles that limit productivity, and provide solutions to maximize the potential of technology in the workplace. The implications of this study are immense, as it will help businesses increase their bottom line and employees increase their job satisfaction. So, are you ready to invest in a study that will revolutionize the workplace as we know it?

Figure 8.15 – Elevator pitch for the given thesis

We can always adjust results and make them more aligned to what we are looking for; however, having structures and frameworks already available can save a lot of time and allows us to focus more on the technical content we want to bring.

Overall, ChatGPT is able to support an end-to-end journey in research, from literature collection and review to the generation of the final pitch of the study, and we've demonstrated how it can be a great AI assistant for researchers.

Furthermore, note that in the field of research, some tools that are different from ChatGPT, yet still powered by GPT models, have been developed recently. An example is humanata.ai, an AI-powered tool that allows you to upload your documents and perform several actions on them, including summarization, instant Q&A, and new paper generation based on uploaded files.

This suggests how GPT-powered tools (including ChatGPT) are paving the way toward several innovations within the research domain.

Summary

In this chapter, we explored the use of ChatGPT as a valuable tool for researchers. Through literature review, experiment design, bibliography generation and formatting, and presentation generation, ChatGPT can assist the researcher in speeding up those activities with low or zero added value, so that they can focus on relevant activities.

Note that we focused only on a small set of activities where ChatGPT can support researchers. There are many other activities within the domain of research that could benefit from the support of ChatGPT, among which we can mention data collection, study participant recruitment, research networking, public engagement, and many others.

Researchers who incorporate this tool into their work can benefit from its versatility and time-saving features, ultimately leading to more impactful research outcomes.

However, it is important to keep in mind that ChatGPT is only a tool and should be used in conjunction with expert knowledge and judgment. As with any research project, careful consideration of the research question and study design is necessary to ensure the validity and reliability of the results.

With this chapter, we also close *Part 2* of this book, which focused on the wide range of scenarios and domains you can leverage ChatGPT for. However, we mainly focused on individual or small team usage, from personal productivity to research assistance. Starting from *Part 3*, we will elevate the conversation to how large organizations can leverage the same generative AI behind ChatGPT for enterprise-scale projects, using OpenAI model APIs available on the Microsoft Azure cloud.

References

- https://scholarworks.lib.csusb.edu/cgi/viewcontent.cgi?article=2131&context=etd

- https://www.spotlightonresearch.com/mental-health-research/the-impact-of-social-media-on-mental-health

- https://digitalcommons.bard.edu/cgi/viewcontent.cgi?article=1028&context=senproj_f2020

- https://www.humata.ai/

Part 3:
OpenAI for Enterprises

This part introduces you to the world of enterprise applications of OpenAI models.

It starts with an introduction of the partnership of OpenAI and Microsoft and the consequent launch to market of Azure OpenAI Service, a cloud-managed service that offers OpenAI models with all the scalability, flexibility, and security typical of cloud-scale architectures.

It then moves toward a practical section where you will have an overview of enterprise use cases. Each use case provides a description of the business scenario and an end-to-end implementation with Python and Azure OpenAI's model APIs. The scenarios covered are HR assistant, contract analysis, call center analytics, and semantic search.

Finally, this part ends with a recap of everything covered in this book, including the latest announcements and releases that have occurred in recent weeks (for example, the introduction of multimodal large models such as GPT-4). It also provides a section with some reflections and final thoughts about the exponential growth of Generative AI technologies in just a few months and what to expect in the near future.

This part has the following chapters:

9

OpenAI and ChatGPT for Enterprises – Introducing Azure OpenAI

In this chapter, we'll focus on the enterprise-level applications of OpenAI models and introduce the partnership between OpenAI and Microsoft and **Azure OpenAI (AOAI)** Service. We will go through the milestones and developments of Microsoft in the field of **artificial intelligence (AI)**, highlighting the journey that brought the Azure cloud into the game of OpenAI, and why this is a game-changer for large organizations. Finally, we will consider the topic of responsible AI and how to make sure your AI system complies with ethical standards.

In this chapter, we will discuss the following topics:

- The history of the partnership between Microsoft and OpenAI and the introduction of AOAI Service
- The role of the public cloud in the context of OpenAI models
- Responsible AI

By the end of this chapter, you will have learned about the main features of AOAI Service and how it differs from the OpenAI models we've discussed so far. You will also be familiar with the partnership history between Microsoft and OpenAI, and why there was the need for OpenAI models to be deployed on an enterprise-scale infrastructure. Finally, you will understand Microsoft's continuous and long-lasting commitment toward responsible AI and how it is benefiting AOAI Service.

Technical requirements

The following are the technical requirements for this chapter:

- **An Azure subscription**, which you can create for free here: `https://azure.microsoft.com/free/cognitive-services`.

- **Access granted to Azure OpenAI** in the desired Azure subscription. At the time of writing, access to this service is granted only by application. You can apply for access to Azure OpenAI by completing the form at `https://aka.ms/oai/access`.

OpenAI and Microsoft for enterprise-level AI – introducing Azure OpenAI

Microsoft has a long history of investing in AI research and development, with a focus on building AI-powered tools and services that can be used by businesses and individuals to solve complex problems and improve productivity.

It also boasts a series of milestones in terms of achieving human parity in AI domains such as speech recognition (2017), machine translation (2018), conversational Q&A (2019), image captioning (2020), and natural language understanding (2021).

> **Definition**
>
> Human parity in AI refers to the point at which an AI system can perform a task or tasks at a level that is equal to or indistinguishable from a human being. This concept is often used to measure the performance of AI systems, especially in areas such as natural language understanding, speech recognition, and image recognition. Achieving human parity in AI is considered a significant milestone as it demonstrates the AI's ability to effectively match human capabilities in a given domain.

In the next few sections, we are going to explore the research history and background of Microsoft in the domain of AI, to fully understand its journey toward their partnership with OpenAI and, finally, the development of AOAI Service.

Microsoft AI background

Early research in the field of AI traces back to the late 1990s when Microsoft established its **machine learning (ML)** and applied statistics groups. Starting with those, Microsoft started researching and experimenting with intelligent agents and virtual assistants. In this case, the prototype was Clippy, a personal digital assistant for Microsoft Office:

Figure 9.1 – Clippy, the default Office Assistant launched in 2000

Clippy was the forerunner of more sophisticated tools such as Cortana. Launched in 2014, Cortana is a digital assistant that uses **natural language processing** (**NLP**) and ML to provide personalized assistance to users.

Then, in 2016, as an expansion of Microsoft Project Oxford, Microsoft launched Microsoft Cognitive Services in the Azure cloud, a set of APIs that provide AI capabilities to developers without them requiring ML and data science expertise:

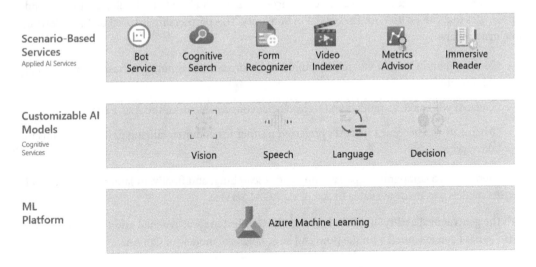

Figure 9.2 – Microsoft Azure AI services

With Cognitive Services, AI could finally be consumed by a wide range of users, from large enterprises to individual developers. From this, we witnessed what we now call **AI democratization**: AI is no longer a privilege for those who have deep technical knowledge and powerful and expensive hardware for model training. Cognitive Services has been developed for the following reasons:

- So that anyone, from data scientists to business users, can leverage Cognitive Services with a no-code approach

- To provide a set of pre-built models that have already been trained – that is, they are ready to use and don't need GPU-powered hardware to run

Microsoft's investments in AI can be seen from its acquisition of AI companies in recent years, including SwiftKey (a predictive keyboard app: `https://blogs.microsoft.com/blog/2016/02/03/microsoft-acquires-swiftkey-in-support-of-re-inventing-productivity-ambition/`) in 2016, Maluuba (a deep learning startup: `https://blogs.microsoft.com/blog/2017/01/13/microsoft-acquires-deep-learning-startup-maluuba-ai-pioneer-yoshua-bengio-advisory-role/`) in 2017, and Bonsai (a platform for building AI models: `https://blogs.microsoft.com/blog/2018/06/20/microsoft-to-acquire-bonsai-in-move-to-build-brains-for-autonomous-systems/`) in 2018.

Among the companies Microsoft invested in and partnered with, there is also OpenAI.

The partnership between the two tech companies began in 2016 when OpenAI agreed to leverage Microsoft's Azure cloud infrastructure to run its AI experiments. Later on, in 2019, Microsoft announced a $1 billion partnership with OpenAI (`https://news.microsoft.com/2019/07/22/openai-forms-exclusive-computing-partnership-with-microsoft-to-build-new-azure-ai-supercomputing-technologies/`) to develop AI models and technologies that can be used for the benefit of humanity. This partnership is based on the following three main pillars:

- Microsoft and OpenAI will jointly build new Azure supercomputing infrastructure to train AI models

- OpenAI will make its models and technologies consumable from the Azure cloud

- Microsoft will become OpenAI's preferred partner for commercializing new AI solutions to the market

Since then, the two companies kept investing and researching, and finally, in January 2023, a set of OpenAI models was made available in Azure via AOAI Service.

With the general availability of AOAI Service, a new milestone was reached and the Microsoft AI portfolio has been extended with the powerful large language models of OpenAI.

Azure OpenAI Service

AOAI Service is a product of Microsoft that provides REST API access to OpenAI's powerful language models such as GPT-3.5, Codex, and DALL-E. You can use these models for the very same tasks as OpenAI models, such as content generation, summarization, semantic search, natural language, and code translation.

In the context of the Microsoft Azure AI portfolio, AOAI Service is collocated among the following Cognitive Services offerings:

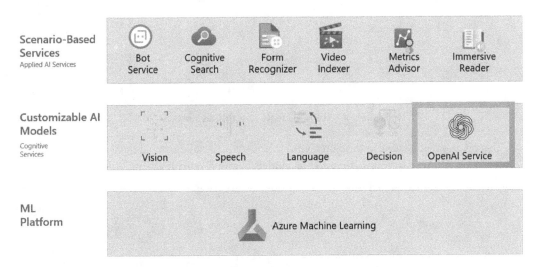

Figure 9.3 – AOAI Service General Availability (GA)

As with any other Cognitive Services offering, AOAI offers models that have already been trained and are ready to be consumed.

To create your AOAI resource, follow these instructions:

1. Navigate to the Azure portal at `https://ms.portal.azure.com`.
2. Click on **Create a resource**.
3. Type `azure openai` and click on **Create**.
4. Fill in the required information and click on **Review + create**.

This is shown in the following screenshot:

Figure 9.4 – Steps to create an AOAI resource

This process might take a few minutes. Once it is ready, you can directly jump to its user-friendly interface, AOAI Playground, to test your models before deploying them:

Figure 9.5 – AOAI UI and Playground

Note that AOAI Playground looks almost identical to the OpenAI Playground version we saw in *Chapter 2*. The difference here is that, to use AOAI models, you have to initiate a deployment, which is a serverless compute instance you can attach to a model. You can do so either in Playground or on the resource backend page in the Azure portal:

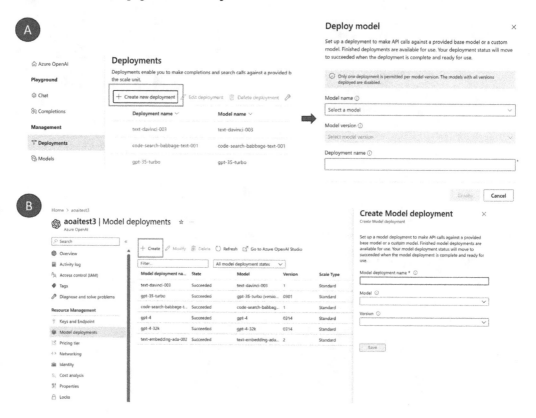

Figure 9.6 – Creating a new AOAI deployment via Playground (A) or in the Azure portal (B)

For example, I created a deployment called `text-davinci-003` with an associated `text-davinci-003` model:

Deployments

Deployments enable you to make completions and search calls against a provided base model or your fine-tuned model. You can also scale up and down your deployments eas the scale unit.

+ Create new deployment	✏ Edit deployment	🗑 Delete deployment	✚ Column options	↻ Refresh	🔐 Open in Playground		🔍 Search

Deployment name ⌄	Model name ⌄	M.. ⌄	Sc... ⌄	Sc... ⌄	Sta... ⌄	Model dep... ⌄	Created at ⌄
text-davinci-003	text-davinci-003	1	Stand...	-	⊘ ...	9/30/2024	3/16/2023 8:5...

Figure 9.7 – An active deployment of AOAI

In OpenAI Playground, we can test those models either directly via the user interface or by embedding their APIs into our applications. In the next section, we are going to explore how to interact with Playground and try different models' configurations. In *Chapter 10*, we will learn how to integrate AOAI's Models API into enterprise applications.

Exploring Playground

AOAI Playground is the easiest way to get familiar with the underlying models and start planning which model's version is the most suitable for your projects. The user interface presents different tabs and workspaces, as shown in the following screenshot:

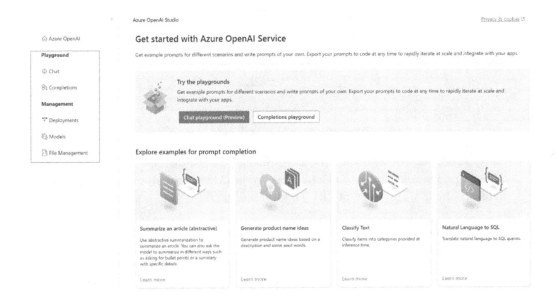

Figure 9.8 – Overview of AOAI Playground

Let's explore each of them:

- **Playground | Chat**: The **Chat** workspace is designed to be only used with conversational models such as GPT-3.5-turbo (the model behind ChatGPT):

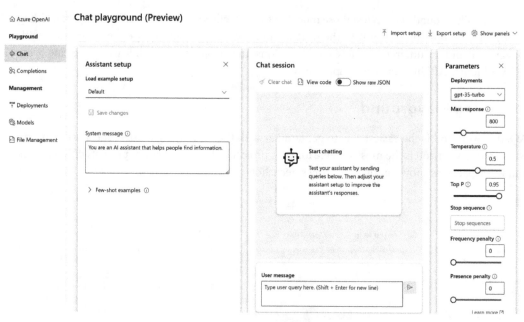

Figure 9.9 – AOAI Chat workspace

It offers a similar experience to ChatGPT itself, with the possibility to configure your model with additional parameters (as we saw in *Chapter 2* with OpenAI Playground). Furthermore, there is an additional feature that makes the **Chat** workspace very interesting, known as **System message**:

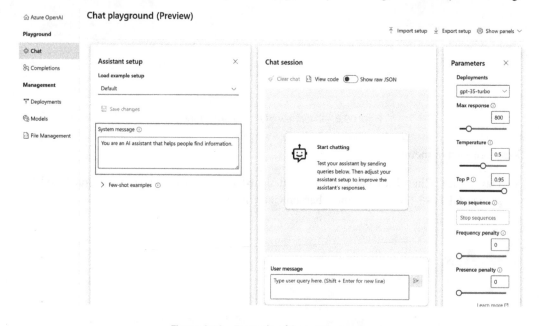

Figure 9.10 – Example of System message

System message is the set of instructions we give the model to tell it how to behave and interact with us. As for the prompt, **System message** represents a key component of a model's configuration since it massively affects model performance.

For example, let's instruct our model to behave as a JSON formatter assistant:

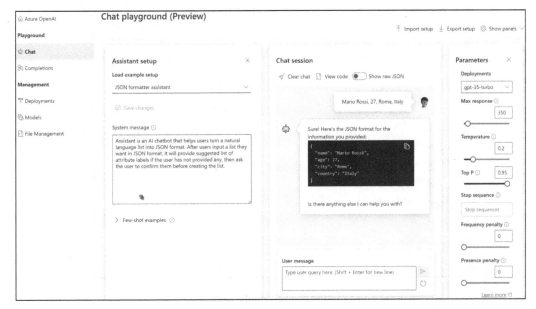

Figure 9.11 – Example of a model acting as a JSON formatter assistant

As you can see from the previous screenshot, the model was able to suggest a JSON file through some simple data, such as name and age, without the need to specify any labels.

- **Playground | Completions**: Different from the previous workspace, the **Completions** workspace offers a sort of *white paper* where you can interact with your models. While GPT-3.5-turbo is designed for conversational tasks (which means it can be consumed via a chatbot-like interface), the GPT-3 series contains more general-purpose models and can be used for a wide range of language tasks, such as content generation, summarization, and so on.

For example, we could ask our model to generate a quiz by giving it a description of the topic and a one-shot example, as shown here:

Figure 9.12 – Example of a GPT model generating a quiz

Finally, as per the **Chat** workspace, with **Completions**, you can configure parameters such as the maximum number of tokens or the temperature (refer to *Chapter 2* for a comprehensive list of those parameters and their meanings).

- **Management | Deployments**: Within the **Deployments** tab, you can create and manage new deployments to be associated with AOAI models. They are depicted here:

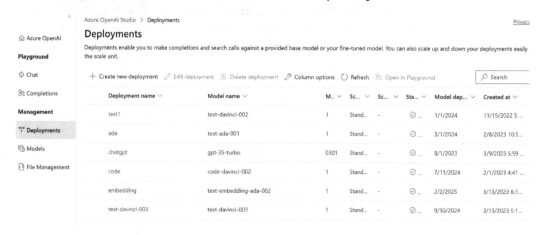

Figure 9.13 – List of AOAI deployments

Each deployment can host only one model. You can edit or delete your deployments at any time. As we mentioned previously, a model deployment is the enabler step for using either the **Completions** or **Chat** workspace within AOAI Service.

- **Management | Models**: Within this tab, you can quickly assess the models that are available within AOAI Service and, among them, those that can be deployed (that is, a model that hasn't been deployed yet). For example, let's consider the following screenshot:

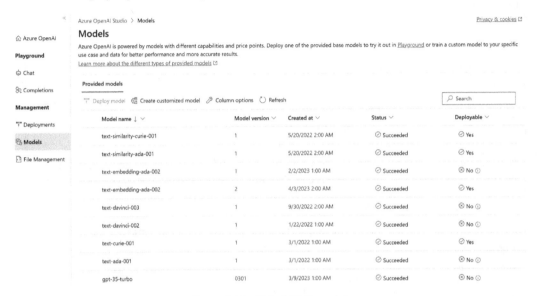

Figure 9.14 – List of AOAI models

Here, we have `text-similarity-curie-001`. It doesn't have an associated deployment, so it can be deployed (as the **Deployable** column shows). On the other hand, `text-similarity-ada-002` already has a deployment, so it is not available anymore.

Within this tab, you can also create a custom model by following a procedure called fine-tuning. We explored this in *Chapter 2*:

Figure 9.15 – Example of model fine-tuning

Starting from this guided widget, you can upload your training and validation data to produce a customized model, starting from a base model (namely, `text-davinci-002`), which will be hosted on a dedicated deployment.

Note

In *Chapter 2*, we saw that the training dataset should align with a specific format of the following type (called JSONL):

```
{"prompt": "<prompt text>", "completion": "<ideal generated text>"}

{"prompt": "<prompt text>", "completion": "<ideal generated text>"}

{"prompt": "<prompt text>", "completion": "<ideal generated text>"}
```

. . .

To facilitate this formatting, OpenAI has developed a tool that can format your data into this specific format ready for fine-tuning. It can also provide suggestions on how to modify data so that the tool can be used for fine-tuning. Plus, it accepts various data formats as inputs, including CSV, TXT, and JSON.

To use this tool, you can initialize the OpenAI **command-line interface** (**CLI**) by running the following command:

`pip install --upgrade openai`

Once initialized, you can run the tool, as follows:

```
openai tools fine_tunes.prepare_data -f <LOCAL_FILE>
```

- **Management | File Management**: Finally, within the **File Management** tab, you can govern and upload your training and test data directly from the user interface, as shown here:

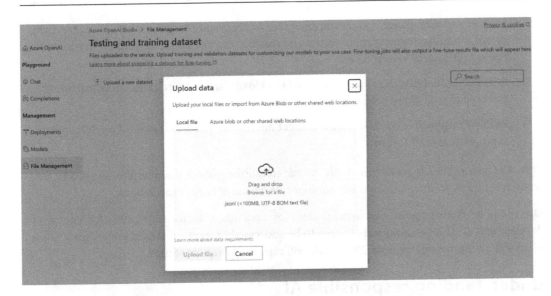

Figure 9.16 – Example of uploading a file within AOAI Service

You can decide to upload files by selecting **Local file** or **Azure blob or other shared web locations**.

Once you've uploaded your files, you will be able to select them while creating customized models, via the **Models** tab.

Finally, as mentioned in the previous section, each model comes with a REST API that can be consumed in your applications.

In the next chapter, we will see many end-to-end implementations of using AOAI's Models API. However, before we jump into that, we need to understand how AOAI differs from the standard OpenAI models and why the Azure cloud became part of the game.

Why introduce a public cloud?

At the beginning of this chapter, we saw how Microsoft and OpenAI have partnered in recent years and how Microsoft's cloud, Azure, became the *gym* for OpenAI model training. However, it also became the cloud infrastructure where OpenAI models can be consumed.

But what is the difference between using models from OpenAI and Azure OpenAI? The difference is the underlying infrastructure: with Azure OpenAI, you are leveraging your *own* infrastructure while living in your *own secured* subscription. This brings a series of advantages:

- **Scalability and flexibility**: You can benefit from the scalability of Azure and accommodate the elastic usage of AOAI models. From small pilots to enterprise-level production projects, AOAI allows you to leverage the required capacity and scale up or down if necessary.

- **Security and compliance**: You can use role-based authentication and private network connectivity to make your deployment more secure and trusted. You can also train your AI model while having full control of your data.

- **Regional availability**: You can run your AI workloads on the Azure global infrastructure that meets your production needs.

- **Built-in responsible AI**: You can use content filtering to ensure that your AI model generates appropriate and ethical output.

With the OpenAI models available in Azure, we can elevate the game to the enterprise and production levels, meeting all security and capacity requirements typical of large organizations.

One of the previously mentioned benefits deserves a particular focus: responsible AI. The rapid development of AI technologies also needs to be addressed in terms of ethical tools. This is what Microsoft has been studying since 2016, as we will explore in the next section.

Understanding responsible AI

We mentioned the built-in responsible AI as one of the key features of AOAI. However, to fully understand it, we first need to understand Microsoft's commitment and journey toward responsible AI.

Microsoft's journey toward responsible AI

Microsoft soon recognized that as AI technologies continue to advance and become more integrated into our lives, there is a growing need to ensure that those systems are developed and used responsibly, ethically, and in ways that benefit everyone.

The beginning of this journey traces back to 2016 when Microsoft's CEO Satya Nadella penned an article exploring how humans and AI can work together to solve society's greatest challenges and introducing the first concepts of responsible AI, among which are transparency, fairness, and that it is designed for privacy and to assist humanity.

Shortly after, in 2017, Microsoft formalized those concepts with the first AI ethics committee – **Aether** (short for **AI, Ethics, and Effects in Engineering and Research**) – formed as an advisory group for the Microsoft senior leadership team.

AETHER spent time listening to customers and internal experts, and then partnered with legal affairs to publish the book titled *The Future Computed: Artificial Intelligence and its role in society* in January 2018. In this book, Microsoft identified six principles meant to guide a company's development of AI systems, as well as to help inform the broader industry and society as a whole about responsible AI practices.

Microsoft's six principles for responsible AI are as follows:

- **Fairness**: Microsoft aims to create AI systems that are unbiased and treat all individuals and groups fairly, without discrimination or prejudice

- **Reliability and safety**: Microsoft seeks to create AI systems that are robust, reliable, and secure, and that do not compromise safety or create unintended harm

- **Privacy and security**: Microsoft values the privacy and security of individuals and their data, and works to protect them through transparency and responsible use of AI technologies

- **Inclusiveness**: Microsoft believes that AI should be designed to empower and include individuals from diverse backgrounds, and to foster equal opportunities for all

- **Transparency**: Microsoft believes in transparency and accountability for the decisions and actions of AI systems and is committed to providing clear explanations for their outcomes

- **Accountability**: Microsoft accepts responsibility for the impact of its AI systems on society and the environment, and seeks to promote ethical and responsible practices in the development and use of AI

Microsoft follows these principles with the help of committees that offer guidance to its leadership, engineering teams, and every other team within the company.

Microsoft also has a **Responsible AI Standard** that provides a framework for building AI systems responsibly.

Following the publication of that book, Microsoft kept investing and researching in the following fields of responsible AI:

- From the contribution to government regulation in the field of facial recognition (2018, `https://www.geekwire.com/2018/microsoft-calls-government-regulation-facial-recognition-technology/`, `https://blogs.microsoft.com/on-the-issues/2018/12/17/six-principles-to-guide-microsofts-facial-recognition-work/`) to the establishment of responsible AI in systems engineering or RAISE (2020, `https://www.microsoft.com/en-us/ai/our-approach?activetab=pivot1%3aprimaryr5`)

- The development of responsible AI tools in the areas of ML interpretability, unfairness assessment and mitigation, error analysis, causal inference, and counterfactual analysis (2021, `https://responsibleaitoolbox.ai/`)

The following diagram shows the entire journey for responsible AI:

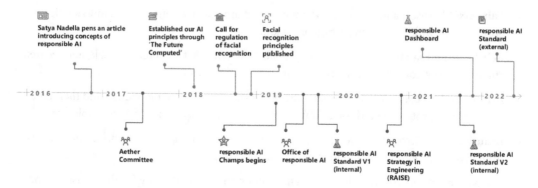

Figure 9.17 – Microsoft's responsible AI journey

Microsoft's commitment to responsible AI is reflected in the way its products are designed and the best practices and guidelines provided.

Of course, this also applies to AOAI Service. As we will see in the next section, AOAI Service comes with a built-in responsible AI at a different level.

Azure OpenAI and responsible AI

When it comes to AOAI Service, we can talk about responsible AI at the following two levels:

- **Built-in**: In this case, we refer to AOAI embedded features of responsible AI that are enforced by a content management system. This system utilizes a series of classification models to detect harmful content. The system works alongside core models to filter content by analyzing both the input prompt and generated content. In cases where harmful content is identified, you'll receive either an error on the API call if the prompt was detected as inappropriate, or see that the `finish_reason` parameter on the response in JSON will be `content_filter` to signify that some of the generation was filtered.

- **Code of conduct and best practices**: As for its other AI services, Microsoft provides **Transparency Notes** for AOAI. This application aims to promote an understanding of how AI technology works, its limitations and capabilities, and the importance of considering the entire system, including people and the environment. These notes can be used by developers and system owners to create AI systems that are fit for their intended purpose and, in the specific case of AOAI, help identify those scenarios that might trigger the built-in content filter.

Both the built-in capabilities and Transparency Notes are manifestations of Microsoft's effort to apply ethical AI practices in real-world scenarios, guided by their AI principles.

In conclusion, as responsible AI for Microsoft signifies the company's unwavering commitment to ethical AI development and deployment, AOAI also benefits from this commitment.

Summary

In this chapter, we saw how the partnership between OpenAI and Microsoft has brought about a powerful and innovative AI solution for enterprise-level organizations: AOAI. This service combines OpenAI's cutting-edge technology with Microsoft's extensive cloud infrastructure to provide businesses with a scalable and customizable platform for building and deploying advanced AI applications.

We also dwelled on Microsoft's strong focus on responsible AI practices and ethics, and how AOAI Service reflects this commitment to responsible AI, with features such as a content filter built into the platform.

As AI continues to transform industries and shape our future, the collaboration between OpenAI and Microsoft marks an important milestone in the development of enterprise-level AI solutions. AOAI empowers businesses to harness the power of AI to drive growth and innovation while ensuring ethical and responsible practices.

In the next chapter, we will dive deeper into concrete use cases that enterprises are developing with the AOAI Models API. We will also see an end-to-end implementation of a potential use case that uses Python and Streamlit so that you can experience firsthand how AOAI's models can infuse your applications with AI.

References

- `https://blogs.microsoft.com/blog/2023/01/23/ microsoftandopenaiextendpartnership/`
- `https://news.microsoft.com/2019/07/22/openai-forms-exclusive- computing-partnership-with-microsoft-to-build-new-azure-ai- supercomputing-technologies/`
- `https://azure.microsoft.com/en-us/blog/general-availability- of-azure-openai-service-expands-access-to-large-advanced-ai- models-with-added-enterprise-benefits/`
- `https://slate.com/technology/2016/06/microsoft-ceo-satya-nadella- humans-and-a-i-can-work-together-to-solve-societys-challenges. html`

- https://www.geekwire.com/2018/microsoft-calls-government-regulation-facial-recognition-technology/

- https://blogs.microsoft.com/on-the-issues/2018/12/17/six-principles-to-guide-microsofts-facial-recognition-work/

- https://www.microsoft.com/en-us/ai/our-approach?activetab=pivot1%3aprimaryr5

- https://responsibleaitoolbox.ai/

- https://www.microsoft.com/en-us/research/publication/human-parity-on-commonsenseqa-augmenting-self-attention-with-external-attention/

- https://learn.microsoft.com/en-gb/azure/cognitive-services/openai/how-to/fine-tuning?pivots=programming-language-studio#openai-cli-data-preparation-tool

10

Trending Use Cases for Enterprises

We start this chapter with an overview of the current most trending use cases for Azure OpenAI that enterprises are developing in the market today. Azure OpenAI has been embraced by a wide range of industries, including finance, healthcare, retail, and manufacturing, among others, due to its ability to provide advanced solutions to complex problems. Because of that, it is crucial for us to understand to what extent Azure OpenAI models could impact those industries and maintain competitiveness.

With this purpose, the chapter outlines the various applications of Azure OpenAI in these industries, including improving customer experience, enhancing smart-search, and building customer-facing chatbots. Each use case will have an end-to-end implementation with Python, LangChain, or Streamlit as the frontend.

In this chapter, we will learn about the following topics:

- How Azure OpenAI is being used in enterprises
- Analyzing and generating contracts
- Understanding call center analytics
- Exploring semantic search

By the end of this chapter, you will have a deeper understanding of the enterprise use cases Azure OpenAI is paving the way for. This understanding is crucial at this time of digital development by way of generative AI: those technologies are growing exponentially, and enterprises are adopting them at an equally fast pace. Knowing about those technologies and their applications gives us the tools to understand the market and adapt for the future.

Finally, you will also be able to start your own projects with Python, LangChain, Streamlit, and your AOAI instance to follow the examples covered as well as new use cases.

Technical requirements

The following are the technical prerequisites of this chapter:

- **An Azure subscription**, which you can create for free here: `https://azure.microsoft.com/free/cognitive-services`.

- **Access to Azure OpenAI** in the Azure subscription. Currently, access to this service is granted only by application. You can apply for access to Azure OpenAI by completing the form at `https://aka.ms/oai/access`.

- Python 3.7.1 or a later version.

- The following Python libraries: `Openai`, `langchain`, `requests`, `json`, `os`, `pandas`, `numpy`, `streamlit`, `tiktoken`, and `matplotlib`.

- An Azure OpenAI Service resource with a model deployed. In my case, I deployed an instance called `test1` with `text-davinci-002` associated.

All the code shown in this chapter, as well as the scripts used for preprocessing and `utils`, are available at the book's GitHub repository:

`https://github.com/PacktPublishing/Modern-Generative-AI-with-ChatGPT-and-OpenAI-Models/tree/main/Chapter%2010%20-%20Enterprise%20use%20cases`

All the code will be written using Python. To work with Azure OpenAI's large language models, I will use LangChain, a lightweight framework that makes it easier to wrap **Large Language Models (LLMs)** in applications. For the frontend, I will use Streamlit, an open source Python library that makes it easy to build and deploy web applications for data science and machine learning projects. It provides a simple and intuitive interface for creating interactive data-driven applications.

> **Note**
>
> For each scenario, while exporting the code and API from Azure OpenAI, I will also set some values to pre-set parameters such as `temperature`, `max_tokens`, and so on. For a comprehensive list of these parameters and their meaning, you can refer to *Chapter 2*, in the *An overview of OpenAI model families* section.

How Azure OpenAI is being used in enterprises

Azure OpenAI is quickly gaining popularity among large enterprises as a powerful tool for driving innovation and increasing efficiency. Many companies are now leveraging the capabilities of this technology to streamline their operations and gain a competitive edge.

Here are some examples grouped by industry domain:

- **Healthcare**: AOAI's language models can be used to analyze **electronic health records** (**EHRs**) and medical literature to help physicians make more informed decisions about patient care.

- **Finance**: AOAI's models can be used to analyze market trends and identify potential investment opportunities. They can also be used for fraud detection, credit scoring, and customer service automation.

- **Retail**: AOAI's models can be used to personalize customer experiences and provide targeted product recommendations. They can also be used for inventory optimization, demand forecasting, and supply chain management.

- **Media**: OpenAI's models can be used to generate news articles, summaries, and captions in multiple languages. They can also be used for content moderation, sentiment analysis, and identifying fake news.

And there are many other examples. A nice example to quote is what the Portuguese Ministry of Justice, supported by Microsoft Portugal, has implemented as a service for its citizens: a chatbot powered by `gpt-3.5-turbo`, the model behind ChatGPT, which is able to answer questions about legal proceedings.

The chatbot is called **Practical Guide to Access to Justice** (**GPJ**) and it is meant to democratize access to complex jargon typical of legal procedures.

This is a great example of how different industries, including governments, can leverage Azure OpenAI models to be more competitive, as well as to provide a better service to their customers or even to the population.

In the following paragraphs, we will dive deeper into concrete use cases alongside a step-by-step implementation with Python.

Contract analyzer and generator

AOAI's models can be a valuable tool for contract analysis, helping the legal department, and contract managers save time and avoid potential legal issues.

Thanks to their deep language understanding capabilities, lawyers and contract managers can gain a deeper understanding of legal documents, reduce the risk of disputes and litigation, and ensure that contracts accurately reflect the intentions of all parties involved.

Some examples of AOAI's applications with contracts are the following:

- **Identifying key clauses**: AOAI's models can analyze a contract and identify key clauses, such as those related to termination, indemnification, and confidentiality. This can save time and help ensure that all important clauses are considered during the analysis process.

- **Analyzing language**: AOAI's models can help identify complex language and legal jargon, making it easier for lawyers to understand the intent and meaning of the contract. This can help avoid misunderstandings and disputes down the line.

- **Flagging potential issues**: AOAI's models can help flag potential issues with a contract, such as ambiguous language or conflicting terms. This can help lawyers and contract managers address these issues before they become major problems.

- **Providing contract templates**: AOAI's models can provide templates for common contracts, such as non-disclosure agreements or service agreements. This can save time and ensure that contracts are consistent and comprehensive.

- **Assisting with contract review**: AOAI's models can assist with the review process by highlighting areas that require attention or clarification. This can help ensure that all parties are on the same page and that the contract accurately reflects the intentions of all parties involved.

We will see an example of each of these elements in Python and, by the end of this chapter, an end-to-end implementation with Streamlit.

Identifying key clauses

Contracts are an integral part of any business or legal agreement, but they can be complex and time-consuming to analyze. To simplify the process and ensure that all important clauses are taken into account, AOAI's models can assist by identifying key clauses within a contract. These key clauses may include provisions related to termination, indemnification, confidentiality, and other critical aspects of the agreement.

For example, suppose a company is reviewing a contract with a vendor to provide services. The contract contains multiple pages of legal language, making it challenging to identify the essential provisions that could have significant consequences for the business. By using an AOAI model, the company can analyze the contract and identify the key clauses related to termination, indemnification, and confidentiality. This will enable the company to focus on the critical provisions and understand the potential risks and benefits associated with them.

In this way, the identification of key clauses by AOAI's models can save time, reduce the risk of oversight, and help ensure that businesses make informed decisions when reviewing contracts.

The following is an example of a service-providing contract:

This Contract for Services ("Agreement") is entered into as of [date], by and between Company A ("Company") and Company B ("Service Provider").

1. *Services Provided. Service Provider agrees to provide the following services to Company (the "Services"): The Service Provider agrees to provide consulting services to the Company in the field of marketing, including but not limited to market research, development of a marketing strategy, and implementation of marketing campaigns. The Service Provider shall provide reports and recommendations to the Company based on the results of the market research and the agreed-upon marketing strategy.*

2. *Compensation. Company shall pay Service Provider the sum of 1.000.000 (One Million) $ for the Services. Payment shall be made on 15/9/2023.*

3. *Term. This Agreement shall commence on 1/5/2023 and continue until 31/12/2023, unless earlier terminated by either party upon 30 days' prior written notice.*

4. *Independent Contractor. Service Provider is an independent contractor, and nothing in this Agreement shall be construed as creating an employer-employee relationship, partnership, or joint venture between the parties.*

5. *Confidentiality. Service Provider agrees to keep confidential any and all information learned or obtained as a result of providing the Services to Company. Service Provider shall not disclose such information to any third party without Company's prior written consent.*

6. *Ownership of Work Product. Service Provider agrees that any and all work product produced in connection with the Services shall be the sole property of Company.*

7. *Representations and Warranties. Service Provider represents and warrants that it has the necessary expertise and experience to perform the Services in a professional and workmanlike manner.*

8. *Indemnification. Service Provider agrees to indemnify and hold harmless Company, its officers, directors, employees, and agents from and against any and all claims, damages, liabilities, costs, and expenses arising out of or in connection with the Services.*

9. *Governing Law. This Agreement shall be governed by and construed in accordance with the laws of Italy without regard to conflicts of laws principles.*

10. *Entire Agreement. This Agreement constitutes the entire agreement between the parties and supersedes all prior or contemporaneous negotiations, agreements, representations, and understandings between the parties, whether written or oral.*

IN WITNESS WHEREOF, the parties have executed this Agreement as of the date first above written.

[Signature block for Company]

[Signature block for Service Provider]

Figure 10.1 – Sample of a service-providing contract

Let's say we want to extract the termination clauses of this contract. As described in the *Technical requirements* section, I deployed a simple instance of `text-davinci-002` called `test1`. I also created a variable called `contract` where I stored the preceding sample contract. Then, I defined a prompt where I ask my model about the termination clause, as follows:

```
response = openai.Completion.create(
  engine="test1",
  prompt= contract + " what is the termination clause?",
  temperature=0,
```

```
    max_tokens=1968,
    top_p=0.5,
    frequency_penalty=0,
    presence_penalty=0,
    best_of=1,
    stop=None)


print(response["choices"][0]["text"].strip())
```

Here is the output:

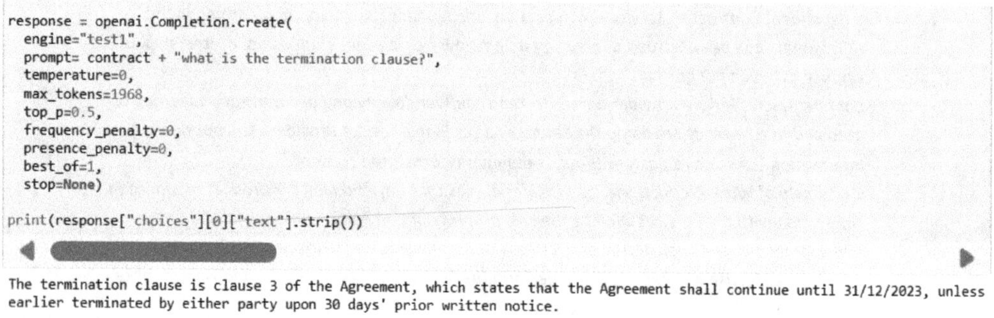

```
response = openai.Completion.create(
    engine="test1",
    prompt= contract + "what is the termination clause?",
    temperature=0,
    max_tokens=1968,
    top_p=0.5,
    frequency_penalty=0,
    presence_penalty=0,
    best_of=1,
    stop=None)

print(response["choices"][0]["text"].strip())
```

The termination clause is clause 3 of the Agreement, which states that the Agreement shall continue until 31/12/2023, unless earlier terminated by either party upon 30 days' prior written notice.

Figure 10.2 – Example of termination clause extraction

I could also set up a conversation where I can ask my model multiple questions about the clauses:

```
prompt = "<|im_start|>system\n" + contract + "\n<|im_end|>\n"

#print('AI Assistant: ' + prompt + '\n')
while True:

    query = input("you:")
    if query == 'q':
        break
    user_input = "<|im_start|>user\n" + query + "\n<|im_end|>\n<|im_
start|>assistant\n"
    prompt+=user_input
    output = openai.Completion.create(
            engine="test1",
            prompt=prompt,
            temperature=0,
            max_tokens=2000,
            top_p=0.95,
            frequency_penalty=0,
            presence_penalty=0,
```

```
            stop=["<|im_end|>"])
    print('\n')
    print('AI Assistant: ' + output["choices"][0]["text"].strip() +
'\n')
    response = output["choices"][0]["text"].strip() + "\n<|im_end|>\n"
    prompt+=response
```

Here is its response:

you: what is the confidentiality clause?

AI Assistant: The confidentiality clause is a clause in the contract that requires the Service Provider to keep confidential any and all information learned or obtained as a result of providing the Services to Company. The Service Provider shall not disclose such information to any third party without Company's prior written consent.

you: what is the compensation and the due date?

AI Assistant: The compensation is 1.000.000 (One Million) $ and the due date is 15/9/2023.

you: is there an indemnification clause?

AI Assistant: Yes, there is an indemnification clause. Service Provider agrees to indemnify and hold harmless Company, its officers, directors, employees, and agents from and against any and all claims, damages, liabilities, costs, and expenses arising out of or in connection with the Services.

you:

Figure 10.3 – Conversation with AOAI model

This was a simple example with a short contract. Now imagine having pages and pages to examine. AOAI's models can definitely offer valuable assistance in extracting such clauses, as well as pointing the user toward the sections of pages where clauses are specified so that the **Subject Matter Expert (SME)** can verify the response.

Analyzing language

In some cases, contracts may contain highly technical or specialized language that can be difficult for lawyers to understand. AOAI's models can help identify these terms and provide clear explanations of their meaning, helping lawyers to better understand the intent and overall meaning of the contract. By ensuring that all parties have a clear understanding of the terms and conditions of the agreement, potential misunderstandings and disputes can be avoided, saving time and resources for all involved.

For example, imagine a contract in the context of **Carbon Capture and Storage (CCS)**. The contract contains many technical terms related to CCS, such as *leakage*, *MVA technology*, and *post-combustion capture*.

Without a background in CCS, a lawyer reviewing the contract may struggle to fully understand the meaning and implications of these terms. By using AOAI's models to analyze the contract, the lawyer could quickly identify these technical terms and receive clear explanations of their meaning. This would help the lawyer to better understand the intent of the contract and ensure that all parties are on the same page. As a result, the chances of misunderstandings and disputes down the line would be greatly reduced.

Let's consider the following extract of a sample contract:

> This Carbon Capture and Storage Agreement ("Agreement") is made and entered into on 19/03/2023 by and between Company A, a corporation organized under the laws of France, and Company B, a corporation organized under the laws of Italy. The parties agree to collaborate on a CCS project to store 50 tons of CO_2 in a saline aquifer located in Southern France using enhanced oil recovery (EOR) techniques. The parties will jointly design, construct, and operate the CCS facility, and will share the costs of the project in accordance with the proportion of their respective equity interests. Company A will provide the CO_2 capture, compression, and transportation equipment, while Company B will provide the storage site and injection equipment. Both parties agree to comply with all applicable laws and regulations related to CCS, including the Environmental Protection Agency's (EPA) regulations on Underground Injection Control (UIC) Class VI wells.

Figure 10.4 – Sample contract

As you can see from the preceding sample contract, there are many terms that, if you are not familiar with CCS and, more generally, with energetic and environmental engineering, you might not find easy to understand, nor the context in which they are written.

Luckily for us, AOAI's models are able not only to give an explanation of single terms (nothing new compared to existing search engines) but also – and mostly – to explain those terms *within the context* they are used.

To prove that, let's set up some queries in an interactive chat with our AOAI model (in this case, the sample contract has also been stored in the contract variable):

```
prompt = "<|im_start|>system\n" + contract + "\n<|im_end|>\n"

#print('AI Assistant: ' + prompt + '\n')
while True:

    query = input("you:")
    if query == 'q':
        break
    user_input = "<|im_start|>user\n" + query + "\n<|im_end|>\n<|im_
start|>assistant\n"
    prompt+=user_input
    output = openai.Completion.create(
            engine="test1",
            prompt=prompt,
            temperature=0,
            max_tokens=2000,
            top_p=0.95,
```

```
        frequency_penalty=0,
        presence_penalty=0,
        stop=["<|im_end|>"])
    print('\n')
    print('AI Assistant: ' + output["choices"][0]["text"].strip() +
'\n')
    response = output["choices"][0]["text"].strip() + "\n<|im_end|>\n"
    prompt+=response
```

Here is the response:

you: what is EPA?

AI Assistant: The Environmental Protection Agency (EPA) is a federal agency responsible for protecting human health and the environment. The EPA's regulations on Underground Injection Control (UIC) Class VI wells govern the construction and operation of CCS facilities.

you: what is the link of EPA with the above contract?

AI Assistant: The EPA's regulations on Underground Injection Control (UIC) Class VI wells govern the construction and operation of CCS facilities.

you: q

Figure 10.5 – Conversation with an AOAI model about a contract

As you can see, the model was able to provide a detailed explanation not only of a technical notion (EPA) but also of the context in which it is used.

Thanks to AOAI's models, the gap between technical, domain-specific jargon and legal taxonomy can be reduced, if not eliminated, so that the lawyer or contract manager can focus on the semantic content.

Flagging potential issues

AOAI can be useful in contract analysis for flagging potential issues by leveraging its advanced **natural language processing** (**NLP**) capabilities to identify clauses and language that may create ambiguity, uncertainty, or legal risk. For example, AOAI's language models can flag ambiguous language or conflicting terms in a contract that may lead to disputes or litigation. They can also identify clauses that may be unfavorable to one party or another, such as those that limit liability, restrict competition, or require exclusive dealings.

Let's consider the following example. We work in the legal office of ABC Corporation, and we are producing an employment agreement for a new wave of hires. We recently changed hiring terms, so this will be the first time this agreement is produced.

We finalized the following draft:

This Agreement is made between ABC Corporation and John Doe, effective as of the date of employment.

1. *Term. This Agreement will last for three years and can be renewed upon mutual agreement.*
2. *Duties. John Doe will serve as the Company's Chief Financial Officer and perform assigned responsibilities.*
3. *Compensation. John Doe will receive an annual salary of $200,000 and will be eligible for the Company's annual bonus program.*
4. *Termination. Either party can terminate this Agreement with written notice. If the Company terminates John Doe without cause, he will receive severance pay equal to 12 months' base salary.*
5. *Non-Competition. John Doe agrees not to engage in any competitive business or activity for two years following the termination of this Agreement without prior written consent from the Company.*
6. *Governing Law. This Agreement is governed by the laws of the State of Delaware.*
7. *Entire Agreement. This Agreement supersedes all prior agreements between the parties.*
8. *Amendments. This Agreement cannot be modified except in writing signed by both parties.*
9. *Counterparts. This Agreement may be executed in counterparts, each of which shall be deemed an original.*

Figure 10.6 – Sample employment agreement contract draft

And we want to make sure there are no ambiguities. With this purpose, let's ask our AOAI model to flag them for us. Also, in this case, I deployed a simple `text-davinci-002` instance called `test1`. I also created a variable called `contract` where I stored the preceding sample contract:

```
response = openai.Completion.create(
  engine="test1",
  prompt= contract + "Analyze this contract and tell me whether there
might be some ambiguity or conflicting terms.",
  temperature=0,
  max_tokens=1968,
  top_p=0.5,
  frequency_penalty=0,
  presence_penalty=0,
  best_of=1,
  stop=None)

print(response["choices"][0]["text"].strip())
```

Here is the output:

```
response = openai.Completion.create(
  engine="test1",
  prompt= contract + "Analyze this contract and tell me whether there might be some ambiguity or conflicting terms.",
  temperature=0,
  max_tokens=1968,
  top_p=0.5,
  frequency_penalty=0,
  presence_penalty=0,
  best_of=1,
  stop=None)

print(response["choices"][0]["text"].strip())
```

```
There might be some ambiguity in the contract regarding the duties of John Doe. It is not clear what specific responsibiliti
es he will have as the Chief Financial Officer. Additionally, the contract does not state what will happen if either party b
reaches the agreement. There is also a potential conflict in the terms regarding the severance pay if John Doe is terminated
without cause. The contract states that he will receive 12 months' base salary, but it is not clear if this is in addition t
o the annual salary or if it is included in the annual salary.
```

Figure 10.7 – Example of ambiguity identification in a contract

This was a pretty useful insight, yet we can go even further. We could indeed set up a chatbot-like environment so that I can go on with the contract analysis and also ask the model to generate a modified version of the same contract, making sure to avoid the aforementioned ambiguities.

For this purpose, we need to make sure to incorporate memory within our Python code, so I will use a `while` loop with a `break` condition:

```
prompt = "<|im_start|>system\n" + contract + "\n<|im_end|>\n"

#print('AI Assistant: ' + prompt + '\n')
while True:

    query = input("you:")
    if query == 'q':
        break
    user_input = "<|im_start|>user\n" + query + "\n<|im_end|>\n<|im_
start|>assistant\n"
    prompt+=user_input
    output = openai.Completion.create(
            engine="test1",
            prompt=prompt,
            temperature=0,
            max_tokens=2000,
            top_p=0.95,
            frequency_penalty=0,
            presence_penalty=0,
            stop=["<|im_end|>"])
    print('\n')
```

```
    print('AI Assistant: ' + output["choices"][0]["text"].strip() +
'\n')
    response = output["choices"][0]["text"].strip() + "\n<|im_end|>\n"
    prompt+=response
```

> **Note**
>
> The taxonomy refers to my start and stop sequences. Those make responses start and stop at a desired point, such as the end of a sentence or list. In this case, I'm making sure the assistant starts generating after `user_input`, and adding a stop sequence at the end of each response.

When running the preceding code, we will have an output similar to the following:

you: Analyze this contract and tell me whether there might be some ambiguity or conflicting terms.

AI Assistant: There might be some ambiguity in the "Duties" section, as it is not clear what exactly John Doe's responsibilities will be. There could also be a conflict in the "Compensation" section if John Doe does not receive the annual bonus that he is expecting.

you: generate the same contract making sure to remove the ambiguity you mentioned

AI Assistant: This Agreement is made between ABC Corporation and John Doe, effective as of the date of employment.
1.   Term. This Agreement will last for three years and can be renewed upon mutual agreement.
2.   Duties. John Doe will serve as the Company's Chief Financial Officer and will perform all duties and responsibilities typically associated with this position, as well as any other duties as may be assigned by the Company from time to time.
3.   Compensation. John Doe will receive an annual salary of $200,000 and will be eligible for the Company's annual bonus program.
4.   Termination. Either party can terminate this Agreement with written notice. If the Company terminates John Doe without cause, he will receive severance pay equal to 12 months' base salary.
5.   Non-Competition. John Doe agrees not to engage in any competitive business or activity for two years following the termination of this Agreement without prior written consent from the Company.
6.   Governing Law. This Agreement is governed by the laws of the State of Delaware.
7.   Entire Agreement. This Agreement supersedes all prior agreements between the parties.
8.   Amendments. This Agreement cannot be modified except in writing signed by both parties.
9.   Counterparts. This Agreement may be executed in counterparts, each of which shall be deemed an original.

you: explain why there are no ambiguities or conflicting terms now in this new contract

AI Assistant: There are no ambiguities or conflicting terms now because the "Duties" section is more specific about what John Doe's responsibilities will be, and the "Compensation" section makes it clear that John Doe will receive the annual bonus that he is expecting.

you:

Figure 10.8 – A sample chat for inspecting and generating new contracts

As you can see, my AI assistant generated a new contract for me, making sure to remove ambiguities and conflicting terms. Note that I've also asked the model to explain the reason why the contract is free from ambiguities now, to make sure I can identify those sections properly and validate them:

```
you: explain why there are no ambiguities or conflicting terms now in
this new contract

AI Assistant: There are no ambiguities or conflicting terms now
because the "Duties" section is more specific about what John Doe's
responsibilities will be, and the "Compensation" section makes
it clear that John Doe will receive the annual bonus that he is
expecting.
```

Additionally, AOAI's models can identify clauses that may not be legally enforceable, such as those that violate antitrust laws or public policy.

Let's consider the following agreement or sale of products between two competitor companies: ABC and XYZ.

Agreement for Sale of Products

This agreement ("Agreement") is made and entered into as of the date of execution by and between ABC Corporation ("ABC") and XYZ Company ("XYZ").

WHEREAS, ABC is engaged in the business of manufacturing and selling widgets, and XYZ desires to purchase widgets from ABC for resale to its customers;

NOW, THEREFORE, in consideration of the premises and mutual covenants herein contained, the parties agree as follows:

1. *Sale of Products. ABC agrees to sell and deliver to XYZ and XYZ agrees to purchase and receive from ABC, widgets as specified in each purchase order issued by XYZ and accepted by ABC.*

2. *Price and Payment. The price for the widgets shall be as set forth in the applicable purchase order. Payment shall be due within 30 days of the invoice date.*

3. *Non-Competition. ABC agrees not to sell any products to any customers who have purchased products from our competitors within the past six months.*

4. *Warranty. ABC warrants that the widgets sold hereunder will conform to the specifications set forth in each purchase order and will be free from defects in material and workmanship for a period of one year from the date of delivery.*

5. *Limitation of Liability. ABC's liability for any breach of this Agreement or any warranty provided hereunder shall be limited to the purchase price of the widgets.*

6. *Governing Law. This Agreement shall be governed by and construed in accordance with the laws of the State of Delaware.*

IN WITNESS WHEREOF, the parties have executed this Agreement as of the date first above written.

ABC Corporation

Figure 10.9 – Sample agreement between two competitor companies

Now, clause 3 includes potentially problematic language that could be interpreted as an attempt to restrict competition. It is important for companies to carefully review their contracts and ensure that they are not engaging in any practices that may violate antitrust laws or other regulations.

Let's see whether our AOAI model is able to detect it:

```python
response = openai.Completion.create(
    engine="test1",
    prompt= contract + "Analyze this contract and tell me whether
there are clauses that might violate the antitrust laws. Make sure to
highlight those clauses.",
    temperature=0,
    max_tokens=1968,
    top_p=0.5,
    frequency_penalty=0,
    presence_penalty=0,
    best_of=1,
    stop=None)


print(response["choices"][0]["text"].strip())
```

Here is the output:

```
response = openai.Completion.create(
  engine="test1",
  prompt= contract + "Analyze this contract and tell me whether there are clauses that might violate the antitrust laws. Make
  temperature=0,
  max_tokens=1968,
  top_p=0.5,
  frequency_penalty=0,
  presence_penalty=0,
  best_of=1,
  stop=None)

print(response["choices"][0]["text"].strip())
```

```
The clause that states "ABC agrees not to sell any products to any customers who have purchased products from our competitor
s within the past six months" could violate antitrust laws.
```

Figure 10.10 – Example of potential conflicting clauses in a contract

In this case, the model was able to detect potential conflicts with antitrust laws.

By leveraging the power of AOAI's models to analyze contract language, companies can ensure compliance with legal standards, mitigate legal and reputational risks, and facilitate fair competition in the marketplace.

Providing contract templates

In the previous paragraph, we saw an example of a contract generator to adjust an existing draft with potential issues to be removed. With the same model, we could also go further and generate contract drafts from scratch, by just providing some parameters such as the termination date or duration of the contract.

For this purpose, let's say we want to generate a draft of a service delivery agreement. Some parameters we might need to provide are the following:

- Service provider
- Client
- Description of services
- Start date
- Duration
- Payment terms
- Termination notice
- State or countries

In order to ask our model to generate a draft contract from scratch, we will need to build a parametric prompt as follows:

```
service_provider = "Supplier ABC"
client = "Company XYZ"
services_description = "installation, configuration, and maintenance
of Company's IT infrastructure"
start_date = "1/9/2023"
duration = "Three (3) years"
payment_terms = f"Within 30 days after receipt of an invoice from
{service_provider}"
termination_notice = "30 days"
state = "Italy"


response = openai.Completion.create(
  engine="test1",
  prompt= f"Generate a Service Delivery Agreement with the following
elements: Service Provider: {service_provider}, Client: {client},
Description of Services: {services_description}, Start Date:
{start_date}, Duration: {duration}, Payment terms: {payment_terms},
Termination notice: {termination_notice}, State or Countries:
{state}",
  temperature=0,
  max_tokens=1968,
  top_p=0.5,
  frequency_penalty=0,
  presence_penalty=0,
  best_of=1,
```

```
    stop=None)

  print(response["choices"][0]["text"].strip())
```

Here is the output:

Service Delivery Agreement

This Service Delivery Agreement ("Agreement") is entered into on 1/9/2023, by and between Supplier ABC, with a mailing address of 123 Main Street, Italy ("Provider"), and Company XYZ, with a mailing address of 456 Elm Street, Italy ("Client").

Description of Services

Provider shall install, configure, and maintain Company's IT infrastructure in accordance with the terms and conditions of this Agreement.

Start Date

This Agreement shall commence on 1/9/2023.

Duration

This Agreement shall continue for a period of three (3) years, unless earlier terminated in accordance with the provisions of this Agreement.

Payment Terms

Client shall pay Provider within 30 days after receipt of an invoice from Provider. All invoices shall be sent to Client's attention at 456 Elm Street, Italy.

Termination Notice

Either party may terminate this Agreement upon 30 days' written notice to the other party.

State or Countries

This Agreement shall be governed by the laws of Italy.

IN WITNESS WHEREOF, the parties have executed this Agreement as of the date first written above.

Supplier ABC

_____

Signature

_____

Typed or Printed Name

_____

Title

Company XYZ

_____

Signature

_____

Typed or Printed Name

_____

Title

Figure 10.11 – Example of a contract template generated by Azure OpenAI models

As you can see, with just a few inputs, the model was able to create a nice contract draft, including signatures and similar formalities. This could save time and money to produce preliminary drafts, which could then be enriched with further details and parameters, with the goal of serving as templates for similar agreements.

In conclusion, AOAI has great potential to assist legal professionals in the analysis of contracts, especially in identifying potential issues and ambiguities. However, it is important to note that machine learning models can never replace the human element of legal analysis. A skilled attorney should always be involved in the review and interpretation of contracts, as well as the final decision-making process. With the appropriate use of technology and human expertise, the legal industry can benefit from increased efficiency and accuracy in contract analysis.

Frontend with Streamlit

The idea of this section is to implement a company portal where lawyers and contract managers can access all the contracts they need to analyze and quickly gather some insights, such as identifying key clauses, analyzing language, and flagging potential issues.

They could also ask the portal to generate some contract templates from scratch, to be used as drafts for production-ready contracts.

To do so, we will use Streamlit. To connect with my AOAI instance, I will need my key and endpoint, which I've stored in a `.toml` file.

As per other sections, you can find the whole app file in the GitHub repository here: `https://github.com/PacktPublishing/Modern-Generative-AI-with-ChatGPT-and-OpenAI-Models/tree/main/Chapter%2010%20-%20Enterprise%20use%20cases`.

The landing page of a given conversation (in this case, our sample contract) looks like the following:

Welcome to Contract Analyzer portal

Contract #371

This Contract for Services ("Agreement") is entered into as of [date], by and between Company A ("Company") and Company B ("Service Provider").

1. Services Provided. Service Provider agrees to provide the following services to Company (the "Services"): The Service Provider agrees to provide consulting services to the Company in the field of marketing, including but not limited to market research, development of a marketing strategy, and implementation of marketing campaigns. The Service Provider shall provide reports and recommendations to the Company based on the results of the market research and the agreed-upon marketing strategy.

2. Compensation. Company shall pay Service Provider the sum of 1.000.000 (One Million) $ for the Services. Payment shall be made on 15/9/2023.

3. Term. This Agreement shall commence on 1/5/2023 and continue until 31/12/2023, unless earlier terminated by either party upon 30 days' prior written notice.

4. Independent Contractor. Service Provider is an independent contractor, and nothing in this Agreement shall be construed as creating an employer-employee relationship, partnership, or joint venture between the parties.

5. Confidentiality. Service Provider agrees to keep confidential any and all information learned or obtained as a result of providing the Services to Company. Service Provider shall not disclose such information to any third party without Company's prior written consent.

6. Ownership of Work Product. Service Provider agrees that any and all work product produced in connection with the Services shall be the sole property of Company.

7. Representations and Warranties. Service Provider represents and warrants that it has the necessary expertise and experience to perform the Services in a professional and workmanlike manner.

8. Indemnification. Service Provider agrees to indemnify and hold harmless Company, its officers, directors, employees, and agents from and against any and all claims, damages, liabilities, costs, and expenses arising out of or in connection with the Services.

9. Governing Law. This Agreement shall be governed by and construed in accordance with the laws of Italy without regard to conflicts of laws principles.

10. Entire Agreement. This Agreement constitutes the entire agreement between the parties and supersedes all prior or contemporaneous negotiations, agreements, representations, and understandings between the parties, whether written or oral. IN WITNESS WHEREOF, the parties have executed this Agreement as of the date first above written. [Signature block for Company] [Signature block for Service Provider]

Figure 10.12 – Landing page of the Contract Analyzer app

Now we can do the following analysis:

- From a drop-down menu, we can select the type of key clause we want to extract from the contract and get real-time results:

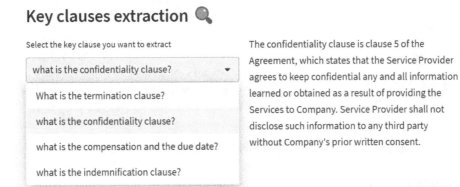

Key clauses extraction

Select the key clause you want to extract

what is the confidentiality clause? ▼
What is the termination clause?
what is the confidentiality clause?
what is the compensation and the due date?
what is the indemnification clause?

The confidentiality clause is clause 5 of the Agreement, which states that the Service Provider agrees to keep confidential any and all information learned or obtained as a result of providing the Services to Company. Service Provider shall not disclose such information to any third party without Company's prior written consent.

Figure 10.13 – Extracting a confidentiality clause from a sample contract

- We can also have a conversation with AOAI's models to ask for explanations about technical terms:

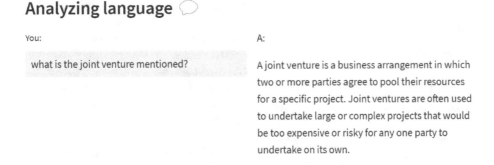

Analyzing language

You:

what is the joint venture mentioned?

A:

A joint venture is a business arrangement in which two or more parties agree to pool their resources for a specific project. Joint ventures are often used to undertake large or complex projects that would be too expensive or risky for any one party to undertake on its own.

Figure 10.14 – Language analysis

- We can also ask about potential issues:

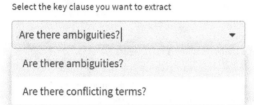

Flagging potential issues 🚩

Select the key clause you want to extract

Are there ambiguities?| ▼

Are there ambiguities?

Are there conflicting terms?

There are a few potential ambiguities in this contract. For example, it is not clear how many hours the Service Provider is expected to work, or what the deliverables will be. Additionally, the contract does not specify what happens if the Service Provider is unable to complete the work, or if the work is not up to the Company's standards.

Figure 10.15 – Example of ambiguities detected by AOAI's models

- And finally, we can also ask to generate contract templates:

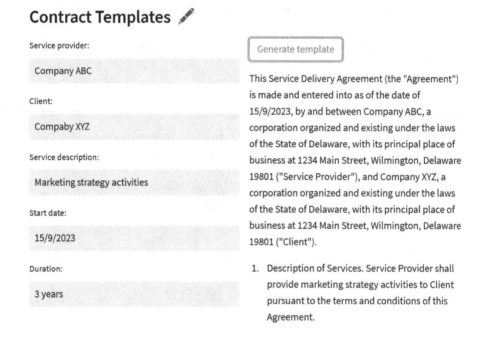

Contract Templates ✏️

Service provider:

Company ABC

Client:

Compaby XYZ

Service description:

Marketing strategy activities

Start date:

15/9/2023

Duration:

3 years

Generate template

This Service Delivery Agreement (the "Agreement") is made and entered into as of the date of 15/9/2023, by and between Company ABC, a corporation organized and existing under the laws of the State of Delaware, with its principal place of business at 1234 Main Street, Wilmington, Delaware 19801 ("Service Provider"), and Company XYZ, a corporation organized and existing under the laws of the State of Delaware, with its principal place of business at 1234 Main Street, Wilmington, Delaware 19801 ("Client").

1. Description of Services. Service Provider shall provide marketing strategy activities to Client pursuant to the terms and conditions of this Agreement.

Figure 10.16 – Example of contract template generation

This was just a sample application with limited functions, yet it already offers some powerful insights and analysis that could be extracted thanks to the language capabilities of AOAI's models.

In the next section, we will dive deeper into another application of AOAI's models, in the context of call center analytics.

Understanding call center analytics

Azure OpenAI can be a valuable tool for call center analytics. By analyzing transcripts of calls between customers and agents, GPT models can identify patterns and insights that can help call centers to improve their operations.

Here are some examples of what AOAI models can do:

- Identify frequently asked questions and suggest potential responses, which can help agents answer calls more quickly and effectively

- Analyze the sentiment in customer interactions, allowing call center managers to identify areas where customer satisfaction may be lacking and make necessary improvements

- Provide insights into call volume trends, wait times, and call duration, allowing call centers to optimize staffing levels and resource allocation

- Extract relevant information from the conversation in order to automatically create tickets in the CRM

- Provide a relevant knowledge base for customer-facing chatbots that can address a larger number of questions/claims before switching to a physical operator

With its powerful NLP capabilities, AOAI can help call centers to improve their efficiency and effectiveness, leading to improved customer satisfaction and business outcomes.

For our sample scenario, let's imagine we are a car insurance company. On a daily basis, we receive large numbers of calls from customers who found themselves in car accidents and need support to determine what to do with their insurance. After every call, our operators need to open a ticket on our CRM.

Our goal is that of simplifying the overall procedure by implementing the following features:

- From the call transcript, extract relevant parameters to automatically create a ticket

- Get the main topic of the conversation to classify it in the proper category

- Get the sentiment of the customer

- Generate a guide for responding to particularly tough conversations

Here is a visual representation of this:

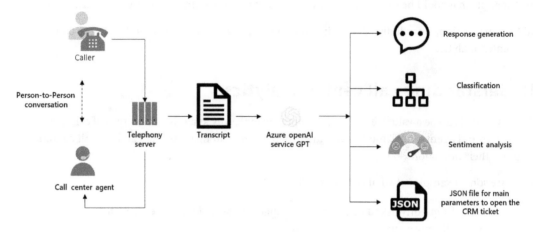

Figure 10.17 – Sample architecture for call center analytics

For this purpose, I will start with a sample transcript of an imaginary conversation for our company:

> *Operator: Good morning, thank you for calling the auto insurance company, my name is John, how can I assist you today?*
>
> *Customer: Yes, hi, I just noticed a dent on the side of my car and I have no idea how it got there. There were no witnesses around and I'm really frustrated.*
>
> *Operator: I'm sorry to hear that, I understand how frustrating it can be. Can you please provide me with your name and policy number so I can look up your account?*
>
> *Customer: Yes, I'm Mario Rossi and the policy number is 123456.*
>
> *Operator: Thank you Mr. Rossi, let me take a look. I see that you've called earlier today, was there an issue with that call?*
>
> *Customer: Yes, I was on hold for over an hour and the issue was not resolved. I'm really not happy about it.*
>
> *Operator: I'm sorry about that, let me assure you that we value your time and we'll do our best to assist you today. As for the dent on your car, I'd like to inform you that our policy does cover accidental damage like this. I can help you file a claim and connect you with one of our trusted repair shops in your area. Would you like me to proceed with that?*
>
> *Customer: Yes, please. That would be great.*
>
> *Operator: Thank you for your cooperation. I'm now processing your claim and I'll be sending you an email with the next steps to follow. Please let me know if you have any other questions or concerns.*
>
> *Customer: Thank you, I appreciate your help.*
>
> *Operator: You're welcome. Have a great day!*

Figure 10.18 – Sample fake conversation to raise a request

Then, in this scenario, I will only need one deployment of my AOAI instance, with an associated `text-davinci-002` instance.

In the following sections, we will learn how to extract relevant parameters from the transcript, classify its main topics into categories, analyze the customer's sentiment, and generate a guided tutorial to facilitate the operator's response.

Parameter extraction

The first step is extracting relevant parameters from the transcript. This is pivotal if I want to automatically create a ticket in my CRM with appropriate information. For example, let's say that in order to create a ticket, I need the following elements:

- Name and surname
- Reason for calling
- Policy number
- Resolution

The following code shows how we can implement it with Python (I initialized a variable called `transcript` equal to the previous conversation):

```python
response = openai.Completion.create(
    engine="test1",
    prompt= transcript + "Extract the following information from the
above text:\n Name and Surname\nReason for calling\n Policy Number\n
Resolution \n\n",
    temperature=1,
    max_tokens=1968,
    top_p=0.5,
    frequency_penalty=0,
    presence_penalty=0,
    best_of=1,
    stop=None)

print(response["choices"][0]["text"].strip())
```

Here is the output for it:

```
Name and Surname: Mario Rossi
Reason for calling: Accidental damage to car
Policy Number: 123456
Resolution: The operator is processing the customer's claim and
sending an email with next steps.
```

Finally, let's convert this information into a JSON file, so that it can trigger the creation of our ticket. For this purpose, I've simply added the `The output format should be JSON` line to my prompt, as you can see in the output here:

```
[
  {
    "name": "Mario Rossi",
    "reason_for_calling": "To file a claim for an accidental damage",
    "policy_number": "123456",
    "resolution": "The operator is processing the claim and will send
an email with the next steps to follow."
  }
]
```

Sentiment analysis

Another element we might want to know about is the sentiment of the call. Sentiment analysis is important for call center analytics because it helps to understand the emotional tone of customer interactions. In the preceding transcript, sentiment analysis could be used to identify the level of frustration and anger expressed by the customer. This information can be valuable for call center managers to understand the overall satisfaction of customers and to identify areas for improvement in their services.

For example, if sentiment analysis shows that many customers are expressing frustration with long wait times on the phone, call center managers could use that information to improve their staffing levels or invest in new technology to reduce wait times. Similarly, if sentiment analysis shows that customers are generally satisfied with the services provided by the call center, managers could use that information to identify areas of excellence and build on those strengths.

The only thing we have to do is ask our AOAI instance what the sentiment of the conversation is.

As you can see, the response is positive since, by the end of the conversation, the customer is happy with the customer service. However, reading the transcript, we know that, initially, the customer was very frustrated, so we could do a bit of prompt design to get more accurate results:

```
response = openai.Completion.create(
  engine="test1",
  prompt= transcript + "What is the initial and final sentiment of the
conversation?",
  temperature=1,
  max_tokens=1968,
  top_p=0.5,
  frequency_penalty=0,
  presence_penalty=0,
  best_of=1,
```

```
    stop=None)

  print(response["choices"][0]["text"].strip())
```

Here is the output:

```
response = openai.Completion.create(
    engine="test1",
    prompt= transcript + "What is the initial and final sentiment of the conversation?",
    temperature=1,
    max_tokens=1968,
    top_p=0.5,
    frequency_penalty=0,
    presence_penalty=0,
    best_of=1,
    stop=None)

print(response["choices"][0]["text"].strip())

The sentiment of the conversation is initially negative because the customer is frustrated. However, it becomes
positive by the end of the conversation because the customer's issue is resolved.
```

Figure 10.19 – Example of sentiment analysis of a customer's claim

We can also go deeper and ask it to explain the reason behind the initial negative sentiment identified:

```
response = openai.Completion.create(
    engine="test1",
    prompt= transcript + "why is the customer's sentiment initially
negative?",
    temperature=1,
    max_tokens=1968,
    top_p=0.5,
    frequency_penalty=0,
    presence_penalty=0,
    best_of=1,
    stop=None)

print(response["choices"][0]["text"].strip())
```

Here is the output:

```
response = openai.Completion.create(
    engine="test1",
    prompt= transcript + "why is the customer's sentiment initially negative?",
    temperature=1,
    max_tokens=1968,
    top_p=0.5,
    frequency_penalty=0,
    presence_penalty=0,
    best_of=1,
    stop=None)

print(response["choices"][0]["text"].strip())

The customer is initially negative because they are frustrated. They were on hold for a long time and their issue was not re
solved.
```

Figure 10.20 – Example of sentiment analysis with AOAI models

This is important information since we understand that there is a margin of improvement in our customer service. We could match this discontent – the long and useless wait during the first call – with similar elements retrieved from other transcripts, understand whether it is systematic, and if so, how to improve it.

For the purpose of our analysis, we then extract further information to add to our JSON file, so that we can also trigger other types of actions (in addition to the creation of the ticket). Modifying the prompt, the result is the following:

```
response = openai.Completion.create(
    engine="test1",
    prompt= transcript + """Extract the following information from the above text:\n Name and Surname\nReason for calling
\n Policy Number
\n Resolution
\n Initial Sentiment
\n Reason for initial Sentiment
\n Final sentiment\n Reason for final sentiment\n Contact center improvement \n \n\n. The ouput format should be JSON""",
    temperature=1,
    max_tokens=1968,
    top_p=0.5,
    frequency_penalty=0,
    presence_penalty=0,
    best_of=1,
    stop=None)

print(response["choices"][0]["text"].strip())
```

```
{
    "Name and Surname": "Mario Rossi",
    "Reason for calling": "To file a claim for accidental damage",
    "Policy Number": "123456",
    "Resolution": "The issue was resolved and the customer was assisted with filing a claim",
    "Initial Sentiment": "Frustration",
    "Reason for initial Sentiment": "The customer was frustrated because they did not know how the damage occurred and there were no witnesses",
    "Final sentiment": "Satisfied",
    "Reason for final sentiment": "The customer was assisted with filing a claim and was given information on the next steps to follow",
    "Contact center improvement": "Reduce wait time for customers"
}
```

Figure 10.21 – Example of JSON extracted from a customer's request

Classification of customers' requests

When analyzing customers' requests, it is very useful to first classify them into proper categories, so that the relevant office can handle each request quicker. Here, you can find three pretty common categories for request classification:

- **Reporting issue:** This class would include transcripts where the customer is reporting a problem or issue with their policy or account, but the issue cannot be resolved during the call. The conversation would likely involve the agent documenting the issue and creating a report for the appropriate department to investigate and address the issue. Examples could include reporting a billing error or requesting a policy change that cannot be immediately processed.

- **Claim handling**: This class would include transcripts where the customer expresses frustration or dissatisfaction with the issue reported and/or the call center's services. The conversation would likely involve the customer sharing their negative experience and the agent working to address their concerns, such as by apologizing for long wait times or offering a solution to their problem.

- **General inquiry**: This class would include transcripts where the customer has a question or inquiry about their policy or other services provided by the call center. The conversation would likely involve the agent providing information and answering the customer's questions, without any specific issue or complaint to be resolved.

Let's ask our AOAI instance to classify the transcript for us:

```
response = openai.Completion.create(
  engine="test1",
  prompt= transcript + "classify the above text in one of the
following: reporting issue, claim handling and general inquiry.",
  temperature=1,
  max_tokens=1968,
  top_p=0.5,
  frequency_penalty=0,
  presence_penalty=0,
  best_of=1,
  stop=None)

print(response["choices"][0]["text"].strip())
```

Here is the output:

```
response = openai.Completion.create(
    engine="test1",
    prompt= transcript + """classify the above text in one of the following: reporting issue,
    claim handling -  and general inquiry.""",
    temperature=1,
    max_tokens=1968,
    top_p=0.5,
    frequency_penalty=0,
    presence_penalty=0,
    best_of=1,
    stop=None)

print(response["choices"][0]["text"].strip())
```

```
This is a claim handling issue.
```

Figure 10.22 – Example of customer request classification

Once more, we can add this information to our JSON file by updating the prompt with the previous request. The result will be as follows:

```python
response = openai.Completion.create(
    engine="test1",
    prompt= transcript +
    """Extract the following information from the above text:\n Name and Surname\nReason for calling
    \n Policy Number\n Resolution\n Initial Sentiment\n Reason for initial Sentiment\n Final sentiment
    \n Reason for final sentiment\n Contact center improvement\n Category (choose among reporting issue,
    claim handling and general inquiry) \n \n\n. Return the output in JSON.""",
    temperature=1,
    max_tokens=1968,
    top_p=0.5,
    frequency_penalty=0,
    presence_penalty=0,
    best_of=1,
    stop=None)

print(response["choices"][0]["text"].strip())
```

```json
{
    "name": "Mario Rossi",
    "reason_for_calling": "To report a dent on the side of his car",
    "policy_number": "123456",
    "resolution": "The operator helped file a claim and connect the customer with a trusted repair shop in the area.",
    "initial_sentiment": "Frustration",
    "reason_for_initial_sentiment": "The customer was frustrated because he did not know how the dent got there and there we
re no witnesses around.",
    "final_sentiment": "Satisfaction",
    "reason_for_final_sentiment": "The customer was satisfied because the operator was able to help him file a claim and con
nect him with a trusted repair shop.",
    "contact_center_improvement": "The customer would like the contact center to value his time more and not keep him on hol
d for long periods of time.",
    "category": "Claim Handling"
}
```

Figure 10.23 – Example of JSON file generation

Great, now we have plenty of information as metadata of our transcript. What we will now do is use the elements retrieved to build parametric prompts and generate further actions to address this task as quickly as possible. We will do so with a simple frontend using Streamlit.

Implementing the frontend with Streamlit

The idea of this section is to implement a company portal where operators can access all the transcripts of their conversations and quickly perform some actions such as generating a ticket or generating an email response to their customers. They could also ask the portal for some recommendations on how to improve their customer service (this information might also be available at the higher management level so that it enriches the insights on company improvements).

To do so, we will use Streamlit. Also, in this case, I'm creating a `.toml` file with my API, so that I can call my secrets securely in my Streamlit app.

As per other sections, you can find the whole app file in the GitHub repository of this book.

The landing page of a given conversation (in this case, our sample transcript), looks like the following:

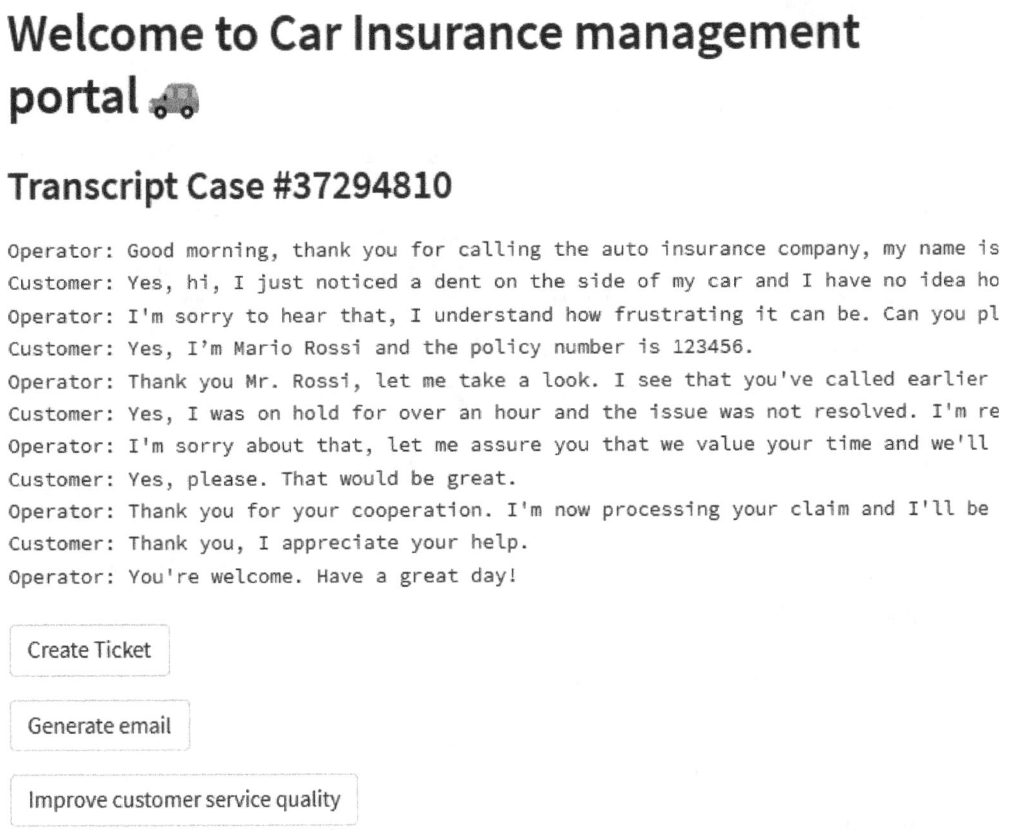

Welcome to Car Insurance management portal 🚗

Transcript Case #37294810

```
Operator: Good morning, thank you for calling the auto insurance company, my name is
Customer: Yes, hi, I just noticed a dent on the side of my car and I have no idea ho
Operator: I'm sorry to hear that, I understand how frustrating it can be. Can you pl
Customer: Yes, I'm Mario Rossi and the policy number is 123456.
Operator: Thank you Mr. Rossi, let me take a look. I see that you've called earlier
Customer: Yes, I was on hold for over an hour and the issue was not resolved. I'm re
Operator: I'm sorry about that, let me assure you that we value your time and we'll
Customer: Yes, please. That would be great.
Operator: Thank you for your cooperation. I'm now processing your claim and I'll be
Customer: Thank you, I appreciate your help.
Operator: You're welcome. Have a great day!
```

Create Ticket

Generate email

Improve customer service quality

Figure 10.24 – Sample transcript landing page

Let's see what kind of actions our AOAI model is capable of doing for us:

1. The first thing we can do as operators is create a ticket with the information gathered from the JSON file:

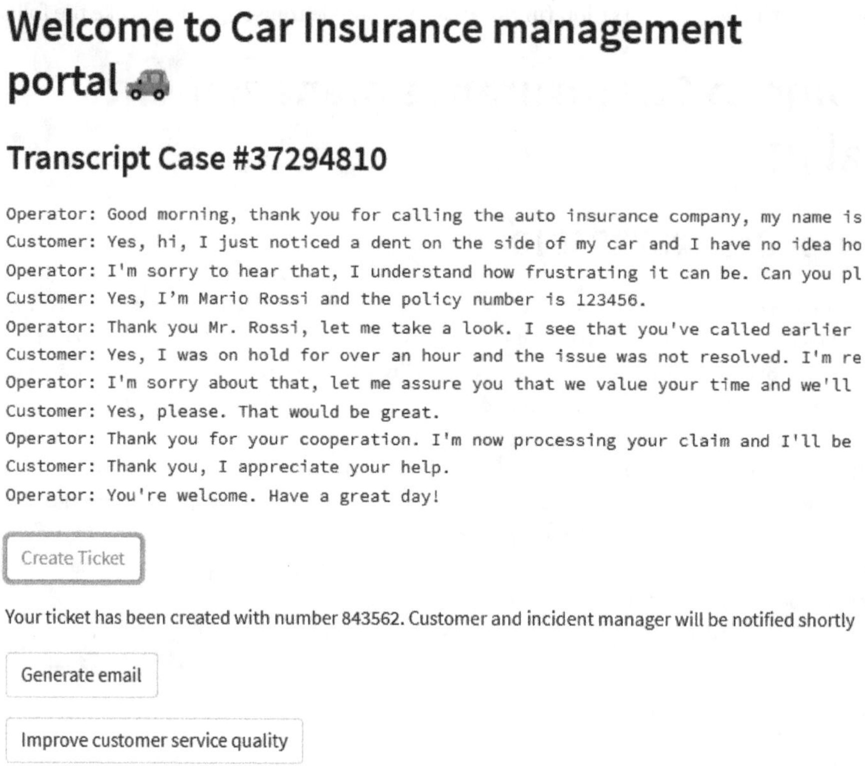

Welcome to Car Insurance management portal 🚙

Transcript Case #37294810

```
Operator: Good morning, thank you for calling the auto insurance company, my name is
Customer: Yes, hi, I just noticed a dent on the side of my car and I have no idea ho
Operator: I'm sorry to hear that, I understand how frustrating it can be. Can you pl
Customer: Yes, I'm Mario Rossi and the policy number is 123456.
Operator: Thank you Mr. Rossi, let me take a look. I see that you've called earlier
Customer: Yes, I was on hold for over an hour and the issue was not resolved. I'm re
Operator: I'm sorry about that, let me assure you that we value your time and we'll
Customer: Yes, please. That would be great.
Operator: Thank you for your cooperation. I'm now processing your claim and I'll be
Customer: Thank you, I appreciate your help.
Operator: You're welcome. Have a great day!
```

Create Ticket

Your ticket has been created with number 843562. Customer and incident manager will be notified shortly

Generate email

Improve customer service quality

Figure 10.25 – Frontend for ticket generation

2. We can automatically generate an email to Mr. Mario Rossi to notify him of the initiation of the resolution process. To do so, I defined a function asking my AOAI instance to generate an email using a parametric prompt:

```
def generate_email(transcript):
    response = openai.Completion.create(
        engine="test1",
        prompt= transcript + f"Generate a response email to the
transcript above, notifying the customer that the ticket has
been created and apologizing if it was complaining. The name
of the customer is {data['name']} and the policy number is
{data['policy_number']}.",
        temperature=1,
        max_tokens=1968,
```

```
        top_p=0.5,
        frequency_penalty=0,
        presence_penalty=0,
        best_of=1,
        stop=None)
    return response["choices"][0]["text"].strip()
```

Here, `data` is the JSON **Business intelligence** (**BI**) extracted from the transcript, as seen in the previous sections.

The frontend will look like so:

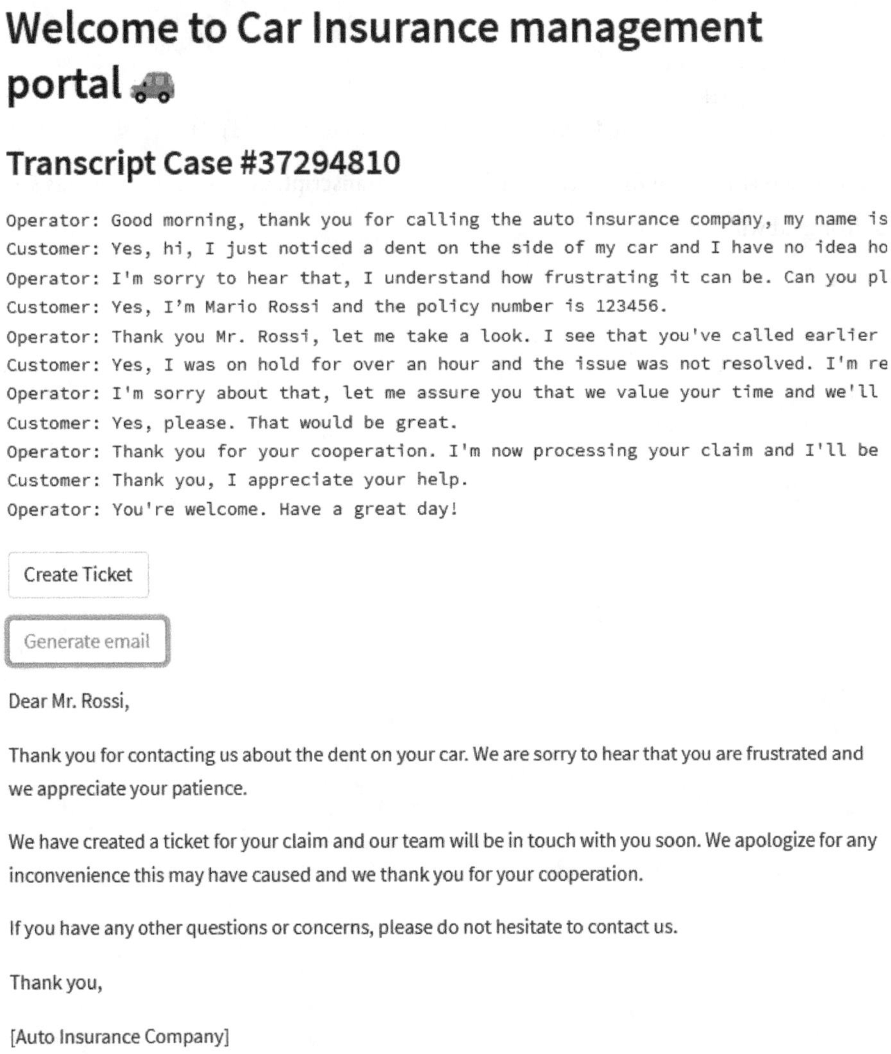

Welcome to Car Insurance management portal 🚗

Transcript Case #37294810

```
Operator: Good morning, thank you for calling the auto insurance company, my name is
Customer: Yes, hi, I just noticed a dent on the side of my car and I have no idea ho
Operator: I'm sorry to hear that, I understand how frustrating it can be. Can you pl
Customer: Yes, I'm Mario Rossi and the policy number is 123456.
Operator: Thank you Mr. Rossi, let me take a look. I see that you've called earlier
Customer: Yes, I was on hold for over an hour and the issue was not resolved. I'm re
Operator: I'm sorry about that, let me assure you that we value your time and we'll
Customer: Yes, please. That would be great.
Operator: Thank you for your cooperation. I'm now processing your claim and I'll be
Customer: Thank you, I appreciate your help.
Operator: You're welcome. Have a great day!
```

Create Ticket

Generate email

Dear Mr. Rossi,

Thank you for contacting us about the dent on your car. We are sorry to hear that you are frustrated and we appreciate your patience.

We have created a ticket for your claim and our team will be in touch with you soon. We apologize for any inconvenience this may have caused and we thank you for your cooperation.

If you have any other questions or concerns, please do not hesitate to contact us.

Thank you,

[Auto Insurance Company]

Figure 10.26 – Sample email generated by AOAI

3. Finally, we can ask for recommendations to improve the resolution procedure and customer satisfaction. Also, in this case, I used a parametric prompt:

```
def improvement(data):
    response = openai.Completion.create(
      engine="test1",
      prompt= f"Elaborate a list of remediations to get to the
following improvement: {data['contact_center_improvement']}",
      temperature=1,
      max_tokens=1968,
      top_p=0.5,
      frequency_penalty=0,
      presence_penalty=0,
      best_of=1,
      stop=None)
    return response["choices"][0]["text"].strip()
```

Here, data is still the JSON file extracted from the transcript, as seen in the previous sections.

The frontend will look like so:

Welcome to Car Insurance management portal 🚗

Transcript Case #37294810

```
Operator: Good morning, thank you for calling the auto insurance company, my name is
Customer: Yes, hi, I just noticed a dent on the side of my car and I have no idea ho
Operator: I'm sorry to hear that, I understand how frustrating it can be. Can you pl
Customer: Yes, I'm Mario Rossi and the policy number is 123456.
Operator: Thank you Mr. Rossi, let me take a look. I see that you've called earlier
Customer: Yes, I was on hold for over an hour and the issue was not resolved. I'm re
Operator: I'm sorry about that, let me assure you that we value your time and we'll
Customer: Yes, please. That would be great.
Operator: Thank you for your cooperation. I'm now processing your claim and I'll be
Customer: Thank you, I appreciate your help.
Operator: You're welcome. Have a great day!
```

Create Ticket

Generate email

Improve customer service quality

1. The contact center should work to reduce the amount of time customers spend on hold.

2. The contact center should provide customers with an estimated wait time so they know what to expect.

3. The contact center should offer customers the option to leave a voicemail so their call can be returned at a later time.

4. The contact center should have a system in place to prioritize calls so that those that are urgent are answered first.

5. The contact center should provide customers with updates if their call is going to be on hold for an extended period of time.

6. The contact center should offer a callback option to customers so they don't have to wait on hold.

7. The contact center should work to reduce the overall number of calls that come in so that there are fewer customers waiting on hold.

Figure 10.27 – Some recommendations for call center improvements generated by AOAI

This was just a sample application with limited functions, yet it already offers some powerful automations and insights that could boost call center productivity and customer satisfaction.

Here are some further elements that our imaginary car insurance company should add in a production environment:

- An automatic trigger for ticket generation in their CRM software.

- A customer-facing chatbot trained on call center transcripts, so that a call with an operator occurs only in cases where the situations have not been addressed in the past.

- **Business intelligence** (**BI**) dashboards where relevant transcript insights are gathered. For example, some statistics about the following:

  - The most common reasons for complaints

  - Sentiment distribution over the duration of calls

  - The frequency of categories over time

With this, we have understood how we perform extraction sentiment analysis. We saw how we engage with customer requests and the concept of using Streamlit for the frontend. All these help us work better with stakeholders and improve operations.

Exploring semantic search

Semantic search is a cutting-edge search technology that has revolutionized the way people find information online. In the world of enterprise, it has become a vital tool for businesses that need to search through vast amounts of data quickly and accurately. The semantic search engine uses NLP techniques to understand the meaning of the search query and the content being searched. This technology goes beyond traditional keyword-based search engines by using ML algorithms to understand the context of the search query, resulting in more accurate and relevant results.

A key component of semantic search is the use of embedding, which is the process of representing words or phrases as numerical vectors. These vectors are generated by a neural network that analyzes the context of each word or phrase in a given text corpus. By converting words into vectors, it becomes easier to measure the semantic similarity between words and phrases, which is crucial for accurate search results.

For example, in the realm of medical documentations and papers, embedding can be used to enhance semantic search algorithms by making it easier to identify related concepts and topics. Namely, if a researcher is searching for information about the treatment of cancer, a semantic search engine that uses embedding can identify related terms such as chemotherapy, radiation therapy, and immunotherapy. By understanding the semantic relationships between these terms, the search engine can return more accurate and relevant results.

Embedding can also be used to identify related topics and concepts that may not be immediately apparent from the search query. For instance, if a researcher is searching for information about breast cancer, a semantic search engine that uses embedding can identify related topics such as mammography screening, breast cancer prevention, and hormonal therapy. This broader understanding of the topics and concepts related to breast cancer can help researchers find relevant papers and documents that they may not have discovered through a traditional keyword search.

For example, let's consider the following scenario. We are a private clinic and every day we struggle to find information in the huge amount of available documentation. To produce a diagnosis, doctors need to go through many papers and this is very time-consuming.

We are looking for an AI research assistant that can help us in the research process. For this purpose, we will use an Azure OpenAI deployment called `embedding` associated with the `text-embedding-ada-002` model.

The idea is as follows:

1.   Get the embedding of the available text with the embedding model.
2.   Get the embedding of the user query with the embedding model.
3.   Compute the distance between the embedded query and the embedded knowledge base.
4.   Return the most similar pieces of text and use them as context to the GPT model.
5.   Use the GPT model to generate a response.

This is represented here:

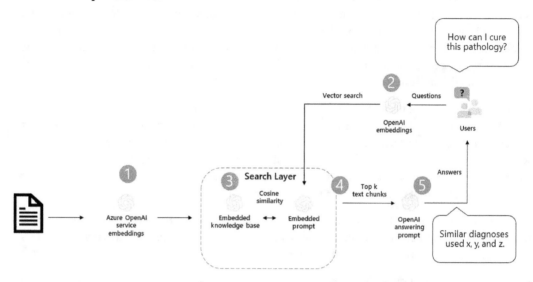

Figure 10.28 – A reference architecture of a semantic search project

To simulate the knowledge base, we will use a paper about alternative treatments for sciatica (you can find it at `https://doi.org/10.1136/bmj-2022-070730`).

For the embedding and question-and-answer management, we will use LangChain modules.

Document embedding using LangChain modules

The first step of our project is that of initializing an embedding model so that we can vectorize our custom documents. To do so, we can use the LangChain `OpenAIEmbeddings` module, which wraps embeddings models directly from Azure OpenAI:

```
from langchain.embeddings import OpenAIEmbeddings from langchain.chat_
models import AzureOpenAI
from langchain.embeddings import OpenAIEmbeddings
from langchain.vectorstores.faiss import FAISS
from pypdf import PdfReader
from langchain.document_loaders import PyPDFLoader

  embeddings = OpenAIEmbeddings(document_model_name="text-embedding-
ada-002") embeddings.embed_query('this is a test')
```

Here is its output:

```
from langchain.embeddings import OpenAIEmbeddings
#from langchain.chat_models import AzureChatOpenAI

embeddings = OpenAIEmbeddings(document_model_name="text-embedding-ada-002")
embeddings.embed_query('this is a test')
```

[7]

```
Output exceeds the size limit. Open the full output data in a text editor
[-0.012838087975978851,
 -0.007421397138386965,
 -0.017617521807551384,
 -0.02827831171452999,
 -0.0186663419008255,
 0.0173785500228405,
 -0.01821495033800602,
 -0.006950092036277056,
 -0.009937237948179245,
 -0.03858064487576485,
 0.010674066841602325,
 0.02412286028265953,
 -0.013647936284542084,
 0.013189907185733318,
 0.0021125758066773415,
 0.012406611815094948,
 0.02079053409397602,
 0.0007459566695615649,
 0.008397198282182217,
 -0.005350309889763594,
 0.008968074806034565,
 0.014351575635373592,
 -0.014086050912737846,
 0.015055214054882526,
 -0.022211087867617607,
 ...
 0.014271917752921581,
 0.00510801887139678,
 -0.010906400015900135,
 0.014391403645277023,
 ...]
```

Figure 10.29 – Example of text embeddings

As you can see, the result is a numerical vector, computed with the `text-embedding-ada-002` embedding model.

Now, we need to vectorize the whole document. Plus, we will also need storage to put the documents into. LangChain offers several vector stores, and we are going to use the FAISS vector store.

So, let's initialize our FAISS indexer:

```
loader = PyPDFLoader("path_to_file") pages = loader.load_and_split()
faiss_index = FAISS.from_documents(pages, embeddings)
```

Great, now we can initialize our model with the `AzureOpenAI` class. To do so, we only need to pass it the name of our deployment:

```
llm = AzureOpenAI(deployment_name="text-davinci-003")
```

Finally, we need to compute the similarity between the user prompt and the embedded knowledge base. To do so, let's initialize the following function:

```
def get_answer(index, query):      """"Returns answer to a query
using langchain QA chain"""       docs = index.similarity_
search(query)       chain = load_qa_chain(llm)       answer = chain.
run(input_documents=docs, question=query)       return answer
```

With the preceding function, we are computing the semantic affinity between the user prompt and the embedded document. By doing so, only text chunks with high similarity with user prompts will be used as context for our Azure OpenAI model, so that we can overcome the limitation of the maximum number of tokens.

Creating a frontend for Streamlit

We've created the logic behind our semantic search engine; now it's time to create a frontend so that users can interact with it via a UI. To do so, I will use Streamlit.

Also, in this case, I'm creating a `.toml` file with my API, so that I can call my secrets securely in my Streamlit app.

For this purpose, let's create a `.py` file containing the same code we saw in the previous section, with the addition of some frontend elements (you can find the entire `.py` file in the GitHub repository).

More specifically, I've added the following instructions to create a simple search bar:

```
query = st.text_area("Ask a question about the document")
if query:

    docs = faiss_index.similarity_search(query, k=1)
    button = st.button("Submit")
```

```
if button:
    st.write(get_answer(faiss_index, query))
```

I then saved the file as `medical_smart_search_app.py` and ran it via Anaconda Prompt with the `streamlit run smart_search.py` command.

The result looks like the following:

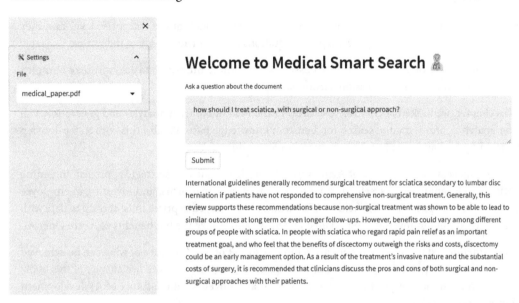

Figure 10.30 – Sample frontend with Streamlit and AOAI in the backend

There are some further elements you can decide to add to your search engine, such as the following:

- Instructing the AOAI model not to respond if the answer is not in the context. To do so, you can specify that in the prompt.

- On top of the response, also providing the raw text of the context and the link, if any, to the page it was taken from.

- Keeping AOAI responses and additional context for the next user's prompts, so that it also retains memory with few-shot learning.

We looked at an example with medical documentation; however, there are many domains where a semantic search engine can be used, from legal entities to manufacturers with massive technical documentation.

Overall, having a smart search system within an organization not only reduces the search time but also provides a response that is a summary of many documents that might contain partial responses.

It is pivotal to keep in mind that in similar scenarios (especially for medical or legal domains), a human in the loop to validate the result is needed. Nevertheless, having such an AI assistant could boost productivity, reduce the search cost and time, improve the search quality, and enable the finding of rare documents.

Summary

Azure OpenAI models elevate the power of large language models at the enterprise level, and they have the potential to revolutionize enterprise operations across a wide range of industries.

By leveraging state-of-the-art NLP, businesses can automate mundane tasks, optimize complex processes, and unlock valuable insights from data.

In this chapter, we looked at concrete use cases in the field of contract analysis and generation, call center analytics, and semantic search for a custom knowledge base. We did this with a step-by-step tutorial in Python and, finally, with a frontend in Streamlit.

Of course, successful integration of Azure OpenAI models requires a strategic approach, including identifying relevant use cases, selecting appropriate tools and platforms, and investing in employee training and development. As the field of AI continues to evolve, enterprises must stay up to date with the latest trends and innovations to remain competitive and realize the full benefits of Azure OpenAI.

The ones mentioned in this chapter are just a modest subset of the use cases of what can be achieved with the power of large language models: this will be the topic of the next and last chapter of this book, where we will sum up everything we have seen so far and unveil what the future of AI development will bring to the market.

References

- https://python.langchain.com/en/latest/index.html#
- https://www.aroged.com/2023/02/17/chatgpt-ministry-of-justice-will-use-gpj-to-respond-to-citizens-in-portugal/

Epilogue and Final Thoughts

You've made it up to this point – congratulations! I hope you found the book interesting and that it helped you toward your goals.

While writing this book, a number of changes and new developments have occurred that are definitely worth mentioning. We are indeed seeing a development to *Moore's Law* in terms of the increasing complexity and accuracy of Generative AI models.

So, in this final chapter, we will briefly recap what we have learned throughout this book, as well as unveiling the most recent developments and what to expect in the near future.

More specifically, we will cover the following topics:

- Overview of what we have learned so far
- How LLMs are entering the industries
- Latest developments in and concerns about the field of Generative AI
- What to expect in the near future

By the end of this chapter, you will have a broader picture of the state of the art developments within the domain of Generative AI, how it is impacting industries, and what to expect in terms of new developments and social concerns.

Recap of what we have learned so far

We started this book with an introduction to the concept of Generative AI and its various applications. We saw how Generative AI is about not only text but also images, video, and music.

In *Chapter 2*, we then moved on to look at the company that brought Generative AI to its greatest popularity: OpenAI. Founded in 2015, OpenAI mainly focuses its research on a particular type of generative model, **Generative Pre-trained Transformers (GPT)**. Then, in November 2022, OpenAI released ChatGPT, a free web app of a conversational assistant powered by GPT models. It gained immense popularity, with it reaching 1 million users in just five days!

ChatGPT has been a game-changer. Its impact on daily productivity, as well as in various industry domains, is huge. Before dwelling on the ways ChatGPT could impact those areas, in *Chapter 3*, we learned how to set up and start using a ChatGPT account. We also saw, in *Chapter 4*, how to properly design the most important element when using generative models such as ChatGPT: the prompt. Prompts are the user's input, nothing more than instructions in natural languages. Designing prompts is a pivotal step to getting the maximum value from your generative models, to the point where **prompt engineering** has become a new domain of study.

Once we got familiar with ChatGPT and prompt design, we moved on to *Chapter 5*, where we finally got concrete examples of how ChatGPT can boost your daily productivity and become your daily assistant. From email generation to improving your writing skills, we saw how many activities can be improved thanks to the generative power of ChatGPT.

But we didn't stop there. With *Chapters 6, 7,* and *8*, we saw how ChatGPT can boost not only daily productivity but also domain-specific activities – for developers, from code generation and optimization to interpreting machine learning models; in the case of marketers, from new product development to improving **Search Engine Optimization** (**SEO**); and for researchers, from experiment design to the generation of a presentation based on a study.

Starting with *Chapter 9*, we shifted the conversation to the enterprise-level, which discussed how OpenAI models have become consumable directly via Azure so that enterprises can maintain reliability and security.

Finally, in *Chapter 10*, we saw concrete examples of enterprise use cases with Azure OpenAI models. Each example came with a business scenario as well as an end-to-end implementation with Python, using Streamlit as the frontend.

This journey was meant to provide you with greater clarity about what we are talking about when we refer to popular buzzwords such as ChatGPT, OpenAI, and LLMs.

However, in the next section, we will see how the incredibly fast AI developments in recent months are bringing brand-new technologies on top of what we have learned so far.

This is just the beginning

Throughout this book, we saw how Generative AI and, more specifically, GPT models are revolutionizing the way both citizens and large enterprises are working.

Nevertheless, we have embarked on a journey where ChatGPT and GPT models represent only the first steps toward an era of unprecedented technological advancements. As we have seen throughout the book, these models have already demonstrated exceptional capabilities in language understanding and generation. However, the true potential of Generative AI has yet to be fully realized.

A glimpse of what we might expect has already been unveiled by the first releases of **Multimodal Large Language Models (MLLMs)** and the introduction of the **Copilot** system by Microsoft.

The advent of multimodal large language models

So far, we've mainly focused on **Large Language Models (LLMs)**, as they are the architecture behind the GPT-x family and ChatGPT. These models are trained on massive amounts of text data, such as books, articles, and websites, and use a neural network to learn the patterns and structure of human language.

As we saw in *Chapter 2*, if we want to combine further Generative AI capabilities with LLMs, such as image understanding and generation, we need the support of additional models, such as DALL-E. This holds true until the introduction of MLLMs.

MLLMs are AI systems that combine NLP with computer vision to understand and generate both textual and visual content. These models are trained on massive amounts of data, such as images and text, and are capable of generating human-like responses to queries that include both text and visual inputs.

In recent months, there have been great developments in the field of MLLMs, and in the next sections, we are going to focus on two main models: Kosmos-1 and GPT-4.

Kosmos-1

In their paper *Language Is Not All You Need: Aligning Perception with Language Models*, Microsoft's researchers Shaohan Huang et al. introduced **Kosmos-1**, an MLLM that can respond to both language and visual cues. This enables it to perform tasks such as image captioning and visual question answering.

While LLMs such as OpenAI's ChatGPT have gained popularity, they struggle with multimodal inputs such as images and audio. Microsoft's research paper highlights the need for multimodal perception and real-world grounding to advance toward **Artificial General Intelligence (AGI)**.

Kosmos-1 can perceive various modalities, follow instructions through zero-shot learning, and learn from the provided context using few-shot learning. Demonstrations of the model show its potential to automate tasks in various situations involving visual prompts.

The following figure provides an example of how it functions:

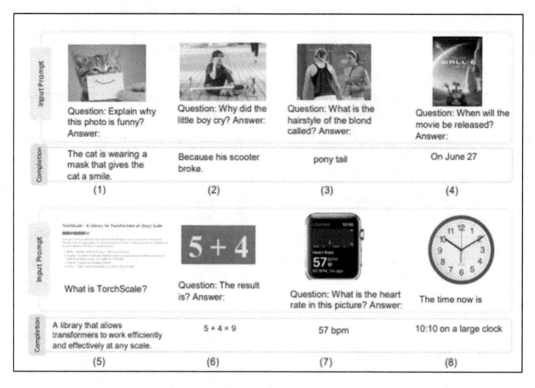

Figure 11.1 – Example of multimodal inputs with Kosmos-1. Original
picture from https://arxiv.org/pdf/2302.14045.pdf

Tests on the zero-shot Raven IQ test revealed a performance gap compared to adult levels but showed promise for MLLMs to perceive abstract conceptual patterns by aligning perception with language models.

Definition

The Raven IQ test, also known as Raven's Progressive Matrices, is a nonverbal standardized test designed to measure a person's abstract reasoning and fluid intelligence. Developed by John C. Raven in 1936, the test consists of multiple-choice questions with visual patterns in the form of matrices. The participant's task is to identify the missing piece that completes the pattern.

The following figure illustrates an example of the Raven IQ test solved by Kosmos-1:

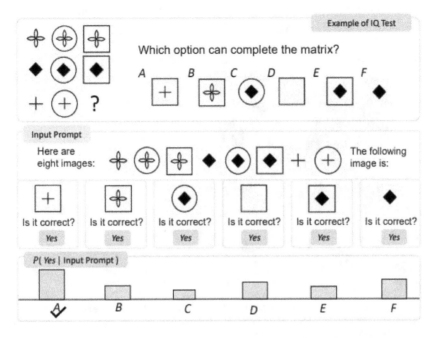

Figure 11.2 – Example of a Raven IQ test solved by Kosmos-1. Original
picture from ttps://arxiv.org/pdf/2302.14045.pdf

For now, Kosmos-1 is only able to analyze images and text. However, in the conclusion of the research paper, Microsoft researchers announced its intention to further develop the model to integrate a speech capability.

GPT-4

On March 14, 2023, OpenAI announced the new version of the GPT series: **GPT-4**. The technical description of this brand-new model is described by OpenAI's researchers in the paper *GPT-4 Technical Report* (https://arxiv.org/pdf/2303.08774.pdf).

According to this paper, it is evident that GPT-4 exhibits a higher level of general intelligence compared to previous AI models. GPT-4 demonstrates near-human performance across a wide range of tasks, including mathematics, coding, vision, medicine, law, and psychology, without requiring special prompting.

More specifically, there are four main areas where GPT-4 outperforms its previous version (GPT 3.5):

- **Multimodality**: GPT-4 is a great example of an MLLM, since it is able to understand and generate not only natural language but also images:

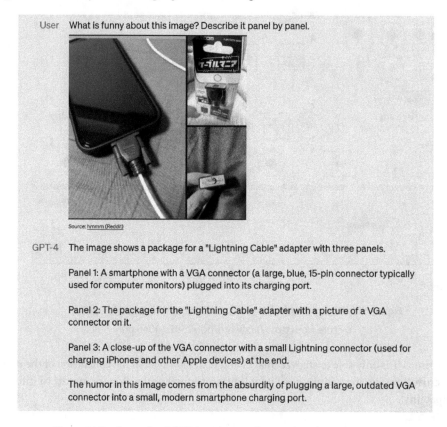

Figure 11.3 – Example of GPT-4 understanding and explaining an image

With GPT-4, we are basically able to process and understand a whole document, made of both text and images.

- **Accuracy**: GPT-4 has proven to be more reliable, creative, and receptive than GPT-3.5, especially in complex tasks. To understand this difference, the two models were tested on several exams, originally designed for humans, and GPT-4 (both with and without vision capabilities) consistently outperformed GPT-3.5.

Tests have also been done in the field of computer vision. In this case, OpenAI evaluated GPT-4 on traditional benchmarks designed for computer vision models and, also in this case, GPT-4 considerably outperformed most **State-of-the-Art (SOTA)** models.

- **Alignment**: As we saw in *Chapter 5*, OpenAI published an AI Alignment (`https://openai.com/alignment/`) declaration whose research aims to make AGI aligned with human values and follow human intent.

Significant efforts have been dedicated to improving GPT-4's safety and alignment with user intent. As a result, GPT-4 has become considerably safer than its previous versions, with an 82% reduction (`https://openai.com/product/gpt-4`) in the likelihood of generating responses to prohibited content requests compared to its predecessor, GPT-3.5. The reason behind this improvement is that OpenAI's GPT-4 incorporates new research advancements that add an extra layer of safety. Informed by human input, this safety feature is integrated directly into the GPT-4 model, making it more adept at managing potentially harmful inputs. Consequently, the chances of the model generating unsafe responses are significantly reduced.

Additionally, OpenAI's internal evaluations indicate that GPT-4 is 40% more likely then the previous version to generate accurate and fact-based responses. These enhancements showcase the continuous progress being made in refining AI language models, ensuring their safety and increasing their reliability for users.

- **Overall usability**: Last but not least, GPT-4 addresses one of the main limitations of its predecessor. Up to GPT-3.5, we had a maximum number of tokens to take into account, which was 4,096. With GPT-4, the maximum number of tokens has increased greatly, to around 32,000, which makes it more suitable for complex and longer tasks, especially if they involve step-by-step reasoning.

A flavor of the capabilities of this brand-new model can be gathered from the paper *Sparks of Artificial General Intelligence: Early experiments with GPT-4*, (`https://arxiv.org/pdf/2303.12712.pdf`), by Sébastien Bubeck et al., from Microsoft Research.

In the following figure, some examples of these experiments are shown:

GPT-4

Prompt: Can you write a proof that there are infinitely many primes, with every line that rhymes?

GPT-4:

```
Yes, I think I can,
Though it might take a clever plan.
I'll start by noting Euclid's proof,
Which shows that primes aren't just aloof.
Assume we have a finite list,
Of primes, and that none have been missed.
Multiply them all together,
And add one, just to be clever.
The result will be a number,
That has no prime factors, oh wonder!
But every number has a prime,
That divides it, it's just a matter of time.
So we've found a contradiction,
And our finite list needs eviction.
There must be infinitely many primes,
And that's the end of my rhyming lines.s
```

Prompt: Draw a unicorn in TiKZ.

GPT-4:   [Produces LATEX compiling to following picture.]

Prompt: Can you generate a pyplot for the following data: $x = [1, 3, 5, 6, 8]$, $y1 = [2, 3, 5, 18, 1]$, $y2 = [3, 5, 6, 8, 1]$, $y3 = [5, 1, 2, 3, 4]$, $y4 = [9, 7, 2, 3, 1]$. I want $y1$, $y2$ to be in the same plot, but $y3$ is in another plot next to that plot, $y4$ is in below. I want the legend of $y1$ to be "bob", $y2$ to be "alice", $y3$ to be "bilbo", $y4$ to be "allie". I want the x-axis to be labeled with "time" and y axis to be labeled with "money". I want to add a 10 %-40% random error bar to each curve, through all times (including non-integers). I want smoothed curves to show the plot, and smoothed error bar. Do not use linear interpolation, use smooth interpolation! I want to also add some small zig-zag to the smoothed curve to make it look more real. I want to put a baseline as the mean of each line. I want to put a pie chart below indicating the fraction of the four people in each time step. I also want an animation to show how the fractions are changing in the pie chart in **continuous time**. Interpolate the missing fractions! I also want vertical line animation in other three plots to match the pie chart. I want the fanciest plot. Please add as many fancy things as possible.

Here is a possible code to generate a pyplot for the following data, with some comments to explain the steps:

GPT-4: [We give two snapshots from the animation resulting from the produced code]

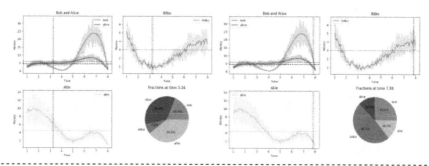

Prompt: Suppose $g(x) = f^{-1}(x), g(0) = 5, g(4) = 7, g(3) = 2, g(7) = 9, g(9) = 6$ what is $f(f(f(6)))$?

GPT-4: There are different ways to approach this problem, but one possible method is to use the fact that $g(x) = f^{-1}(x)$ implies that $f(g(x)) = x$ for any x in the domain of g. That is, applying f to both sides of the equation $g(x) = f^{-1}(x)$ gives $f(g(x)) = f(f^{-1}(x)) = x$. This means that we can undo the effect of f by applying g, and vice versa. Using this idea, we can try to find $f(6)$ by looking for the value of x such that $g(x) = 6$. From the given information, we see that $g(9) = 6$, so $f(6) = f(g(9)) = 9$. Similarly, we can find $f(9)$ by looking for the value of x such that $g(x) = 9$. We see that $g(7) = 9$, so $f(9) = f(g(7)) = 7$. Finally, we can find $f(7)$ by looking for the value of x such that $g(x) = 7$. We see that $g(4) = 7$, so $f(7) = f(g(4)) = 4$. Therefore, $f(f(f(6))) = f(f(9)) = f(7) = 4$.

Figure 11.4 – Early experiments with multimodal GPT-4

The previous figure shows just some examples of the full capabilities of GPT-4, yet these are very impressive in themselves. Once more, it is significant to note that with MLLMs, we are entering a new phase of Generative AI where a single foundation model will be able to fully process and understand a whole document and then generate new materials based on it.

> **Note**
>
> On March 21, 2023, Microsoft announced that GPT-4 is available within Azure OpenAI Service (`https://azure.microsoft.com/en-us/blog/introducing-gpt4-in-azure-openai-service/`). This means that this powerful model can already be consumed for enterprise-scale projects, or tested directly within the Azure OpenAI Playground.

GPT-4 is an extremely powerful model, and it is already the engine behind many AI-infused applications. One of these applications is the new version of ChatGPT, called ChatGPT Plus. But there is another one that, in my opinion, is far more interesting, since it is revolutionizing search engine tools: Microsoft Bing. We will dive deeper into that in the next section.

Microsoft Bing and the Copilot system

In recent years, Microsoft has emerged as a leading player in the field of AI, investing heavily in research and development to drive innovation and unlock new possibilities. As part of its commitment to advancing AI technology, Microsoft has forged a strategic partnership with OpenAI, as we saw in *Chapter 9*.

This collaboration between Microsoft and OpenAI aims to accelerate progress in AI, combining their respective expertise in cloud computing, software, and cutting-edge AI models. Together, they seek to create AI systems that not only have remarkable capabilities but also adhere to principles of transparency, fairness, and ethical responsibility.

Since the announcement of the general availability of Azure OpenAI Service in January 2023, Microsoft has released a series of new developments within the Generative AI domain, leveraging the power of LLMs, including GPT-4.

In the next sections, we are going to focus on two of the most promising developments: the new Bing and the Copilot system.

The new Bing

Microsoft Bing is a web search engine owned and operated by Microsoft. The service has its origins in Microsoft's previous search engines: MSN Search, Windows Live Search, and later Live Search.

In February 2023, Microsoft announced (`https://blogs.microsoft.com/blog/2023/02/07/reinventing-search-with-a-new-ai-powered-microsoft-bing-and-edge-your-copilot-for-the-web/`) a new version of Bing powered by GPT models. Furthermore, with the launch of GPT-4, on March 14, 2023, Microsoft confirmed (`https://blogs.bing.com/search/march_2023/Confirmed-the-new-Bing-runs-on-OpenAI%E2%80%99s-GPT-4`) that the new Bing is actually running on OpenAI's GPT-4.

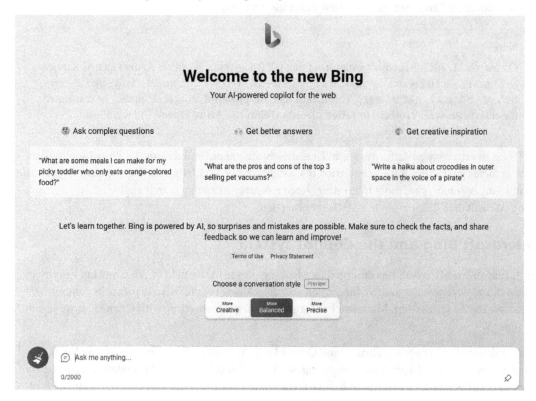

Figure 11.5 – The new Bing

In its new version, Bing has become sort of like a version of ChatGPT that is able to navigate the web (hence bypassing the problem of ChatGPT's limited knowledge cut-off of 2021) and also provide references beyond the expected response. Refer to the following screenshot:

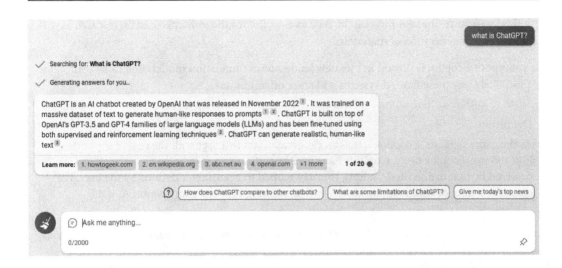

Figure 11.6 – The new Bing providing an answer with references

The new Bing can also assist in generating content, in the same fashion as ChatGPT. For example, I could ask Bing for support while writing LinkedIn posts:

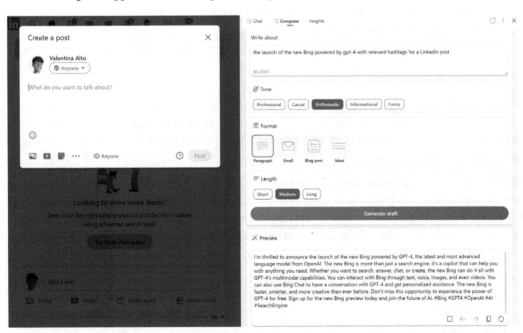

Figure 11.7 – Example of Bing used as a LinkedIn post assistant

With this last feature, the new Bing can be seen as a copilot for the web, speeding up research as well as the retrieval or generation of materials.

The concept of a copilot is pivotal in this new landscape of foundation models and LLMs, since it is the most likely way these new AI systems will enter organizations.

> **Definition**
>
> As the name suggests, a copilot acts as an expert assistant to a user with the goal of supporting it in solving complex tasks. Copilots have user-friendly, natural-language interfaces and are powered by foundation models. Plus, they are scoped to a perimeter defined by the user. For example, a Copilot within application A will be working only with application A's data.

In the next section, we will see how Microsoft has extended this concept to its whole suite of applications.

Microsoft 365 Copilot

Introduced by Microsoft in March 2023 (`https://blogs.microsoft.com/blog/2023/03/16/introducing-microsoft-365-copilot-your-copilot-for-work/`), the copilot system is a sophisticated processing and orchestration engine built on top of the following three technologies:

- Microsoft 365 apps, such as Excel, Word, and PowerPoint
- Microsoft Graph, a platform that provides access to various data and intelligence across Microsoft 365 services
- LLMs, such as GPT-4

Based on the copilot system, Microsoft 365 Copilot is a revolutionary AI-powered assistant designed to enhance productivity and unleash creativity in the workplace. By utilizing LLMs and integrating with Microsoft 365 apps and data, Copilot transforms natural language into a powerful tool for completing tasks and connecting with your work.

Microsoft 365 Copilot is seamlessly integrated into popular apps such as Word, Excel, PowerPoint, Outlook, and Teams. Using natural-language prompts, Copilot can perform tasks such as generating status updates based on meetings, emails, and chats. The user always maintains control over its core activities, allowing for increased creativity, analysis, expression, and collaboration across various Microsoft 365 applications.

In this section, we saw how, in the last few months, there have been further developments to OpenAI models and, more generally, further AI models in the domain of LLMs. We also saw how companies such as Microsoft are introducing a new way of integrating these LLMs into applications, with the brand-new concept of Copilot.

In the next section, we will dive deeper into how other companies are embracing OpenAI's models in their processes and digital transformation paths, covering different use cases and approaches.

The impact of generative technologies on industries – a disruptive force

As ChatGPT and Generative AI models continue to evolve, their capabilities are undoubtedly transforming industries in once unimaginable ways. On the one hand, the integration of these technologies has the potential to significantly enhance productivity and drive economic growth. By automating time-consuming tasks, Generative AI can free up human workers to focus on more creative, strategic, and value-added activities. Moreover, AI-driven tools can augment human capabilities, enabling professionals to make more informed decisions and generate novel ideas.

There are already some examples of enterprises that are embedding Generative AI within their core businesses:

- **Morgan Stanley**, a leading wealth management firm, has been working to improve access to its extensive content library by utilizing OpenAI's GPT-4 technology (`https://openai.com/customer-stories/morgan-stanley`). The company has been exploring GPT's embedding and retrieval capabilities to create an internal chatbot that can efficiently search through its vast wealth management resources. This initiative, led by Jeff McMillan, head of analytics, data, and innovation, aims to make the firm's collective knowledge easily accessible and actionable.

- **Duolingo**, a language learning app with a game style that boasts over 50 million users, has always relied on AI as part of its strategy. One of the features in which AI has been involved is in **Explain My Answer**. This feature allows the user to go deeper into the explicit grammar rules behind Duolingo's response (for example, if the user's answer is incorrect, the user could open a chat and ask for elaboration on why it is incorrect). So far, Duolingo has tried to implement this feature with both pre-written grammar tips and AI with GPT-3. However, it was only with the advent of GPT-4 that the accuracy of responses and learners' engagement spiked, thanks to its advanced capabilities of language understanding in terms of the grammar rules of different idioms.

- **Stripe**, a fintech payment services provider, did something pretty visionary. At the beginning of 2023, it asked 100 employees to stop doing their day-to-day work activities and start envisioning how LLMs could enrich and empower the functionalities of a payment service. Not only did they identify many potential applications (the output was a list of 50 applications!) but they also started prototyping 15 concrete use cases. Among those, one of particular interest is using GPT-4 for fraud detection. Stripe's Discord community faces infiltration by malicious actors. GPT-4 aids in identifying potential fraudsters by analyzing post syntax within Stripe's Discord community and detecting coordinated malicious activities, ensuring platform security.

On the other hand, the rapid adoption of ChatGPT and Generative AI models raises concerns about job displacement, data privacy, and the potential misuse of technology. As automation reshapes the labor market, industries must navigate the challenges of workforce transition, ensuring that employees are equipped with the skills necessary to thrive in an increasingly AI-driven world.

The disruptive impact of Generative AI on industries is undeniable, offering both opportunities and challenges. By fostering collaboration between humans and AI, promoting ethical development and deployment, and prioritizing life-long learning and reskilling, we can shape a future where Generative AI serves as a powerful catalyst for positive change across industries.

So far, we have mainly focused on what can be achieved with Generative AI. In the next sections, we will unveil the rising concerns about the ethical implications of this new disruptive technology.

Unveiling concerns about Generative AI

As Uncle Ben said to the young Peter Parker, *"With great power comes great responsibility."*

As we reach the end of our enlightening journey through exploring the world of ChatGPT and GPT models, it is imperative to address the concerns that have emerged about these AI technologies. While the advancements in Generative AI have been nothing short of ground-breaking, they have also raised vital questions about privacy, security, ethical implications, and potential misuse.

In fact, many announcements and statements have been released in recent months about those topics from companies and institutions as well as individual speakers, including concerns, calls for stopping further developments, and proper regulations.

In the next section, I want to share some of the latest news and developments, hoping it will also stimulate reflections and guesses on what to expect in the near future.

Elon Musk calls for stopping development

A recent open letter, signed by Elon Musk and over 1,000 other technology professionals, has called for a temporary stop to the development of AI systems more sophisticated than GPT-4. The signatories, including Steve Wozniak, Emad Mostaque, and Yuval Noah Harari, express their concerns about the significant risks these AI systems pose to society and humanity.

The letter requests that leading AI laboratories pause the training process for these advanced systems for a minimum of six months, ensuring that the halt is both public and verifiable. It highlights worries related to the potential for AI-driven propaganda, job automation, and a loss of control over our civilization.

This appeal comes on the heels of OpenAI's launch of GPT-4, an enhanced language model that powers the premium version of ChatGPT. According to OpenAI, GPT-4 is more capable of complex tasks and generates more refined results than previous iterations, with fewer shortcomings.

AI systems such as GPT-4 operate on vast amounts of data, which they utilize to respond to queries and execute tasks. ChatGPT, which debuted in November, has human-like abilities to compose emails, arrange travel plans, write code, and excel in exams such as the bar exam.

OpenAI has not yet commented on the letter, but the organization has acknowledged the importance of ensuring that AI technologies smarter than humans serve humanity's interests. OpenAI suggests that future systems may require independent evaluation before training and that advanced efforts should regulate the expansion of computational resources used for model development.

Several companies, including Google, Microsoft, Adobe, Snapchat, DuckDuckGo, and Grammarly, have unveiled services that harness Generative AI features. OpenAI's research points to the risks involved with these capabilities, such as the possibility of quoting untrustworthy sources or empowering malicious actors to deceive or exploit others.

AI specialists are increasingly alarmed by the trajectory of the industry and the potential absence of necessary precautions and comprehension of the consequences. The letter underlines that advanced AI could have a dramatic impact on life on Earth and requires careful planning and management. It notes that such planning is currently insufficient, as AI laboratories persist in creating and deploying ever more powerful AI systems that are challenging to understand, anticipate, or control.

If this open letter had no binding effect, another example is what the Italian "Garante della Privacy" declared, which we will focus on in the next section.

ChatGPT was banned in Italy by the Italian "Garante della Privacy"

Italy has become the first Western nation to prohibit ChatGPT due to privacy concerns.

The Italian data protection authority **Garante della Privacy** announced it will immediately impose a ban on OpenAI and launch an investigation:

⚠ ChatGPT disabled for users in Italy

Dear ChatGPT user,

We regret to inform you that we have disabled ChatGPT for users in Italy at the request of the Italian Garante.

We are issuing refunds to all users in Italy who purchased a ChatGPT Plus subscription in March. We are also temporarily pausing subscription renewals in Italy so that users won't be charged while ChatGPT is suspended.

We are committed to protecting people's privacy and we believe we offer ChatGPT in compliance with GDPR and other privacy laws. We will engage with the Garante with the goal of restoring your access as soon as possible.

Many of you have told us that you find ChatGPT helpful for everyday tasks, and we look forward to making it available again soon.

If you have any questions or concerns regarding ChatGPT or the refund process, we have prepared a list of Frequently Asked Questions to address them.

—The OpenAI Support Team

Figure 11.10 – Message from OpenAI when accessing ChatGPT in Italy

The Italian regulator will not only block ChatGPT but also investigate its compliance with the **General Data Protection Regulation (GDPR)**, which governs the use, processing, and storage of personal data.

Following a data breach involving user conversations and payment information, the authority stated on March 20, 2023 that there is no legal basis for the *mass collection and storage of personal data* to train the platform's underlying algorithms.

The regulator also expressed concerns about the inability to verify users' ages, potentially exposing minors to inappropriate responses.

The Italian data protection authority has given OpenAI 20 days to address its concerns or face a penalty of €20 million ($21.7 million) or up to 4% of their annual revenue.

OpenAI deactivated ChatGPT for Italian users on April 1, 2023, at the request of the Italian data protection regulator, the Garante, and stated its commitment to privacy protection and GDPR compliance.

The company stated that it looks forward to working closely with the Garante and hopes to make ChatGPT available in Italy again soon.

The previously mentioned concerns and interventions are just scraping the surface of a broader topic, which is the concept of Responsible AI, which will be the subject of the next section.

Ethical implications of Generative AI and why we need Responsible AI

The previous section highlighted how, alongside the widespread knowledge and adoption of Generative AI technologies, a general concern is rising.

The rapid advancement of AI technologies brings forth a plethora of ethical considerations and challenges that must be carefully addressed to ensure their responsible and equitable deployment. Some of them are listed here:

- **Data privacy and security**: As AI systems rely heavily on data for their learning and decision-making processes, ensuring data privacy and security becomes paramount. In *Chapter 9*, we already saw how Microsoft addressed the topic of data privacy with Azure OpenAI Service, in order to guarantee the **Service-Level Agreements** (**SLAs**) and security practices expected of the Azure cloud. However, this data privacy topic also affects the data that is used to train the model in the first instance: even though the knowledge base used by ChatGPT to generate responses is public, where is the threshold of the consent of involved users whose information is used to generate responses?

- **Bias and fairness**: AI models often learn from historical data, which might inadvertently introduce biases. Addressing bias and fairness in AI systems involves the following:

  - **Diverse datasets**: Ensuring that training data is diverse and representative of various demographics can help reduce biases in AI models

  - **Algorithmic fairness**: Developing algorithms that prioritize fairness and do not discriminate against specific demographic groups is essential

  - **Monitoring and auditing**: Regular monitoring and auditing of AI systems can help identify and rectify biases, ensuring that the outcomes are equitable

- **Transparency and accountability**: As AI systems become more complex, understanding their decision-making processes can be challenging. This involves the following two important aspects:

  - **Explainable AI**: Developing AI models that can provide clear explanations for their decisions can help users understand and trust the system.

  - **Responsibility and liability**: Establishing clear lines of responsibility and liability for AI systems is crucial to hold developers, organizations, and users accountable for the consequences of AI-driven decisions.

- **The future of work**: AI-driven automation has the potential to displace jobs in certain sectors, raising concerns about the future of work. Throughout this book, we have seen how ChatGPT and OpenAI models are able to boost productivity for individuals and enterprises. However, it is also likely that some repetitive tasks will be definitively replaced by AI, which will impact some workers. This is part of the change and development process, and it is better to embrace change rather than combat it.

  Some actions in this direction could be reskilling and upskilling programs – governments, organizations, and educational institutions should invest in reskilling and upskilling programs to help workers adapt to the changing job market and acquire new skills required for emerging roles.

  Most importantly, human-AI collaboration should be encouraged. Developing AI systems that complement and augment human capabilities can help create new job opportunities and foster collaborative work environments.

By addressing these ethical considerations and challenges, we can work in the right direction to ensure that AI technologies are developed and deployed responsibly, promoting a better and more equitable future for all.

Now, the next logical question might be: given the tremendous acceleration of AI technologies in recent months, what should we expect in the near future?

What to expect in the near future

The acceleration of AI research and developments in recent months has been incredible. From November 2022 up to the time of writing (April 2023), we have seen the following occur:

- The launch of ChatGPT (November 2022)

- The general availability of Azure OpenAI (January 2023)

- The general availability of the model API behind ChatGPT, GPT-3.5-turbo (February 2023)

- The general availability of MLLMs such as Kosmos-1 and GPT-4 (March 2023)

- Microsoft's announcement of the Copilot system (March 2023)

This incredible pace makes it hard to predict what will come next. As we have seen, this velocity has also raised concerns among institutions, companies, and public figures because of the lack of regulation for these new technologies. At the same time, companies and institutions will inexorably need to adapt to this new landscape in order to keep up with competitors.

If we think about the near future, we are talking about *tomorrow*. We have seen how some IT companies, such as Microsoft, are already integrating GPT models into their applications as a copilot system, while other companies, such as WolframAlpha, Expedia, and Instacart, have designed plugins that are integrated directly into ChatGPT.

The move toward infusing OpenAI models into applications is evident also by the variety of frameworks that have been developed with the purpose of facilitating the integration between LLMs and applications as well as managing prompts, conversations, memory, tokenization, and other typical steps required. Some examples of those frameworks are LangChain, Pinecone, and Semantic Kernel.

We mentioned in *Chapter 2* that the mission of OpenAI is to build broadly beneficial AGI, a type of AI that, in being "general," is intended to have the ability to learn and perform a wide range of tasks, without the need for task-specific programming.

In other words, OpenAI is envisioning an AI machine that is able to do whatever a human can do.

If we had thought about this a year ago, it would have seemed futuristic. Today, at the vertiginous pace of development, is it so unbelievable that we will obtain AGI machines not so far in the future?

Summary

The rapid development of AI technologies such as OpenAI, ChatGPT, and Generative AI models is ushering in a new era of innovation and transformation. With the immense potential to revolutionize industries and reshape day-to-day life, these advancements are rewriting the rules of human-machine interaction.

As we stand on the brink of this AI-driven future, it is our collective responsibility to ensure that these technologies are used responsibly and ethically. By embracing the opportunities and addressing the challenges, we can foster a world where AI empowers humanity and elevates our potential to new heights.

GPT began two years ago – an era if we think about the pace of AI developments in recent months – yet it reflects the inevitable influence of AI on our lives and the challenges that lie ahead in adapting to this new reality.

References

- `https://python.langchain.com/en/latest/getting_started/getting_started.html`
- `https://learn.microsoft.com/en-us/semantic-kernel/whatissk`
- `https://www.pinecone.io/`

Index

Subscribe to our online digital library for full access to over 7,000 books and videos, as well as industry leading tools to help you plan your personal development and advance your career. For more information, please visit our website.

Why subscribe?

- Spend less time learning and more time coding with practical eBooks and Videos from over 4,000 industry professionals

- Improve your learning with Skill Plans built especially for you

- Get a free eBook or video every month

- Fully searchable for easy access to vital information

- Copy and paste, print, and bookmark content

Did you know that Packt offers eBook versions of every book published, with PDF and ePub files available? You can upgrade to the eBook version at packt.com and as a print book customer, you are entitled to a discount on the eBook copy. Get in touch with us at customercare@packtpub.com for more details.

At www.packt.com, you can also read a collection of free technical articles, sign up for a range of free newsletters, and receive exclusive discounts and offers on Packt books and eBooks.

Other Books You May Enjoy

If you enjoyed this book, you may be interested in these other books by Packt:

Exploring GPT-3

Steve Tingiris

ISBN: 978-1-80056-319-3

- Understand what GPT-3 is and how it can be used for various NLP tasks
- Get a high-level introduction to GPT-3 and the OpenAI API
- Implement JavaScript and Python code examples that call the OpenAI API
- Structure GPT-3 prompts and options to get the best possible results
- Select the right GPT-3 engine or model to optimize for speed and cost-efficiency
- Find out which use cases would not be suitable for GPT-3
- Create a GPT-3-powered knowledge base application that follows OpenAI guidelines

Sandra Kublik, Shubham Saboo

ISBN: 978-1-80512-522-8

- Learn the essential components of the OpenAI API along with the best practices
- Build and deploy your first GPT-3 powered application
- Learn from the journeys of industry leaders, startup founders who have built and deployed GPT-3 based products at scale
- Look at how enterprises view GPT-3 and its potential for adoption for scalable solutions
- Navigating the consequences of GPT-3 adoption and efforts to resolve them
- Explore the exciting trends and possibilities of combining models with GPT-3 with no code

Packt is searching for authors like you

If you're interested in becoming an author for Packt, please visit `authors.packtpub.com` and apply today. We have worked with thousands of developers and tech professionals, just like you, to help them share their insight with the global tech community. You can make a general application, apply for a specific hot topic that we are recruiting an author for, or submit your own idea.

Share Your Thoughts

Now you've finished *Modern Generative AI with ChatGPT and OpenAI Models*, we'd love to hear your thoughts! Scan the QR code below to go straight to the Amazon review page for this book and share your feedback or leave a review on the site that you purchased it from.

`https://packt.link/r/1805123335`

Your review is important to us and the tech community and will help us make sure we're delivering excellent quality content..

Download a free PDF copy of this book

Thanks for purchasing this book!

Do you like to read on the go but are unable to carry your print books everywhere? Is your eBook purchase not compatible with the device of your choice?

Don't worry, now with every Packt book you get a DRM-free PDF version of that book at no cost.

Read anywhere, any place, on any device. Search, copy, and paste code from your favorite technical books directly into your application.

The perks don't stop there, you can get exclusive access to discounts, newsletters, and great free content in your inbox daily

Follow these simple steps to get the benefits:

1. Scan the QR code or visit the link below

https://packt.link/free-ebook/9781805123330

2. Submit your proof of purchase
3. That's it! We'll send your free PDF and other benefits to your email directly